GW00731428

SOME LIVES

First published in 2020 by
The Dedalus Press
13 Moyclare Road
Baldoyle
Dublin D13 K1C2
Ireland

www.**dedaluspress**.com

ISBN 978 1 910251 73 7 (paperback)
ISBN 978 1 910251 74 4 (hardback)

Dedalus Press titles are available in Ireland
from Argosy Books (www.argosybooks.ie) and in the UK
from Inpress Books (www.inpressbooks.co.uk)

Cover image: detail of *Still Life with Egg and Twine* (1932)
by Horacio Coppola © Galería Jorge Mara-La Ruche 2019/
The Estate of Horacio Coppola. By kind permission.

Printed in Ireland by Print Dynamics.

The Dedalus Press receives financial assistance from
The Arts Council / An Chomhairle Ealaíon.

SOME LIVES

LEEANNE QUINN

DEDALUS PRESS

ACKNOWLEDGEMENTS

Thanks are due to the editors of the following magazines where versions of a number of these poems first appeared: *Cyphers, The Irish Times, Long Poem Magazine, The Moth, Poetry Ireland Review, PN Review, The Stinging Fly*. Thanks to Maeve O'Sullivan and Breda Wall Ryan for their careful reading of this collection in manuscript form: your feedback was invaluable, thank you. Sincere thanks also to Kathleen Rabl and Stephen Stacey. I wish to acknowledge with gratitude the assistance of The Arts Council of Ireland for a Bursary in Literature, awarded in 2018. This financial assistance was integral to the completion of this project. Thanks also to the Heinrich Böll Foundation for awarding me a two-week residency in the Heinrich Böll Cottage in August 2018 where some of these poems were written.

My sincere gratitude to Pat Boran for his trust in the manuscript, his insightful editing of the collection, and his patience in allowing me the time I needed to write these poems.

Contents

for Georgina Nugent-Folan

Don't dictate to me, I can hear it myself:
A warm shower presses on the roof,
I hear the ivy whispering.
Someone small has decided to live,
Has turned green, has fluffed out, and will try,
Tomorrow, to shine in his new cloak.

— Anna Akhmatova, 'Poem Without a Hero'
(tr. Judith Hemschemeyer)

September

Wasps, then rain. Below, streets clear
to a silent siren. Some citizens scatter,
others stand looking upwards.

Wasps nestle into the neck
of abandoned sugar canisters, the wood
of balconies sways.

In parks, the remnants of summer
still — dug-up earth, a brittle mound
of clay, some small animal's refuge.

The leaves here are beginning to fall.
Sun bleached, they swirl like shadows
in the *Föhn*, like shadows adjusting.

The Distant Past

But miracles, as we know, are not repeated.
— Nadezhda Mandelstam

This all happened in the distant past
when, in my borrowed coat, I buried
a book.

It was a time of miracles.
I don't know if bad things come
in twos and threes, or if luck

bears its own pattern,
but miracles cannot be repeated.

I learned this quickly, if not easily,
as I patted down my coat
on the snowy street, like someone

being searched. Of course I've been
complicit too. So many people
want only to make others happy,

but why should I expect to be happy?
Why do I go on
misreading the signs at every turn?

A man walks out in a dead man's
clothes, still holding the shape
of the dead man's body.

There's many deaths
I don't wish for, one in particular
taunts me. I've dreamt it

so many times it's as good
as done, but somehow, like this
stubborn snow, I am still here.

I once saw a man threaten
to toss a live mouse onto a hot pan.
I know what the idea was,

can still see the mouse
dangling by its tail from his fat
fingers. And that could probably

sum it up. But as the snow sticks
to the cuff of my coat, I glimpse
from the corner of my eye the shade

of a future where, warmed
and absolved, we'll spend our time
living this down.

Precedence

The trams still run on time
people still lie in the sun
on our backs in a room
a stack of books is a home

we can still walk in and out
of galleries look at the sky
and think it is a paint shade
of blue we have waited to see

in the city where the trams still
run and we greet each other
with smiles and greet each other
with smiles while the trams still

run our hands are not too tight
in each other's and what precedence
has this day over any other
we have lived in the cold

where the cold kept us pacing
and our lips moving and your lips
moving your hand at your ear
where your blood echoes the blue

could be winter blue where
the ice grows grounding
the town the river beneath
still seething where nothing

appears to move it is moving
as we are moving in the coarse
light of the tram in the coarse
moving light of the tram

Not At All Like The Sea

The sea — is here, and — not here.
— Marina Tsvetaeva

And what kind of silence is the silence
of seeing the sea behind glass as white
waves crash without sound, without.

The ridge of the waves is a ridge of ice
covering the ridge of a mountain,
the waves are tankers, or roads

revealed by tankers. Is that the sea?
*That's not the sea at all, not at all
like the sea.* And, of course, how could it be?

The sea holds you horizontal,
what can I do with that? Waves
cannot be walked, the sea

can only bring me under,
like love. I want to be high
in the blue mountain,

I want to be the mountain, high
in the blue, above this soft,
above this silent sea.

Magnesium, or Akhmatova's Dream

But a dream — is also something real.
— Anna Akhmatova

Winter shadows
the last frost of spring.
Soon it will be bright
early.

A flash of square light
from a window,
no one is sleeping.

A knock on the door,
wood shapes
your name.

I fetch you
from behind a curtain
where you are only
a child.

I am happy
to give you up.
Magnesium pulses
behind my eyes,
an empty room

the only exhibit.
No need for acquittals.

I am tired of dreaming
only of the dead.

Besides,
I will have plenty
more nights
to save you.

Interference

Try not to listen, avoid admission.
Electrical currents emit perceptible sounds.
Don't power down appliances, let sound carry.

Try not to think in terms of the body, the racket
of the blood is not your concern. Learn the habit
of distraction, above all don't personify,

don't permit, this is not a human voice.
Electrical currents do emit perceptible sounds.
The trick is not to listen.

Avoid admission. The racket of the blood
is not your concern. Don't power down.
Learn the habit of distraction.

Don't think in terms of the body. Electrical
currents do emit. The racket of the blood.
Above all, try not to listen.

Don't personify, learn the habit.
Let them carry perceptible sounds.
This is not a human voice.

The Good Going Up to Heaven
and the Wicked Going Down to Hell

In the citizenry of the dead
the soul still holds the shape of the body
still weighs a human care as a body
bent low.

The good ascend with no sign
of remorse, still bearing the marks
of skin, of bone.

Hell is local. Heaven is the landscape
of home. Christ stands among the ruins
where there is no water flowing

in a valley of stone.

Shells

I never knew the world as something
to be in, until it pushed me out.

Then I was in and behind it, in
and behind me.

I knew I was weak.

People say I carry a kind of whispering
inside me, that is and isn't me.

I cannot reassure.

My mother tries to listen but hears only
the sea of her own hands.

She is right. I am a listening thing.

I lift a shell to my ear, take
what cannot be returned.

On Time

Then the sound wakes me
on time, again.

The street sweeper's machine
follows the grid.

A scatter of dead leaves
disappears with the slush

of night. And though
it is light, the dead eye

of sleep still slumbers
on the arc of tomorrow.

The machine hums
its frayed tune

as it follows the grid
into morning,

which is neither
ahead nor behind.

The Same Sea

The same sea rings in my ears.
Though they say it is the wind
making its way through the valley,

I can tell it is the same sea.
The wind doesn't ring, the wind
goes right through me, leaves

the hair of my skin standing high.
We are miles from sea! they hiss,
as though I have suggested

we roam on a flat earth.
When I lie down it is all
I can hear. The lap and pulse,

even when I hold my breath
the sound never ceases. I sleep
with arms outstretched,

head steady, a dead man's float
all I have
to shore me to morning.

Chloroform

The wind squalls through the tree. Resistance
isn't feasible. Shear the leaves, sever the limbs
until only a stump remains.
But what would that say?

Murder in the body. Cells bellow their crime
in another language. I opt again for the ear, sough
of disease through my door. A few small drops

to untether the wave from its high decibel.
And here it is, my chloroform dream — leaves
flap about my room like inflown birds, branches

plead into a burst of colour. Better to withhold
alms, best to be gone
before the silent stump gathers its limbs,
breaks me back into wood.

On a Flat Earth

What colour is the sky? Why does a ship's hull disappear
before the mast? What is the true distance of the Sun
from the Earth? Explain the cause of tides.
What is the dip sector? What causes the Sun to rise?
Explain lunar and solar eclipses. Account for daylight.
Explain winter and summer. Account for loss
of time when sailing. Explain the deflection
of falling bodies. Elaborate on experiment three.
Account for the moon's phases. Discuss the planet
Neptune. Elaborate on experiment six.
Explain the stages of the Earth. Give Earth's true position
in the Universe. Account for formation.
Account for destruction by fire.

Cave of the Firbolg

Not even a trespass of sky to compromise the dark
where blood beats in the body of the heart.
Nobody thinks, Why do we do this?

The nervous system ferries its thin shards of glass
down among the clay, where the blunt flint
of the soul remains.

Pollen embedded in the riverbed, a prehistory
of refuse in the lower layers, every end
is a chance to start over, but the river

cannot start again, or the voice in the cave
speak in a righteous tongue. The body too
gives way as the blood deposits its memory

in the tributaries of the cave, the sky
pushed out, the heart yet to know
it can go without.

Elegy

Nobody died nobody mourned
we love a kill we love a kill
we love a kill and we love nothing more
than to mourn but nobody died
nobody mourned the dead
are walking they've left
their allotted plots and are back
in the arms of the living
we never reached such heights
O nobody nobody nobody mourned
nobody died nobody killed
we love a kill we love a kill
we love a kill
the dead are walking back
to the living under
a mute
and granite sky

Glass

Not possible this fibre could travel,
yet here it is, small and precise
as a chip of tooth in your mouth.

Step on broken glass, the body
will find a way to push out
the broken.

The body is equipped, is wiser.

Here is where you stood on glass,
the ground unharmed.
You can see the scar

on the fleshiest part of the sole,
the ground unharmed,
wiser.

A sliver of glass
nips at the cells, floats
like a floe of ice towards the heart.

Not possible. Yet here it is,
journeyed through blood,
wiser.

Rings

Ring of ice around the moon, winter's halo
turning the mud of autumn to brittle bark.

Houses turn inside out. Bare hands cover
bare heads. Women rob me, know by the cut

of my hair my former self, that I don't know
by sight the weight of pounds from ounces,

can't measure eight yards from ten.
Dye seeps from my hands to theirs.

The train stops, a man whistles, a gold ring
falls to the floor. Look, look away. I have paid

in silk for my fare but have brought you gifts
from the sea — fine shells to shape into hearts

or bones, rough salt carried on my skin,
rings of sand to wear as amulets.

Look how far I have travelled to see you,
how sand falls like gold from my sleeves.

Scenes from a Life

Hanging by a hook on the wall,
mirroring the mirror,

she has stitched leaves
for wings, a remedy for boredom.

Riven by the absence of stone, she burns
down a suburb made of wood,

slumps her body under a tree,
as good a place as any to lie down

forever. On the brittle foliage
she thinks, If the soul has texture

it will feel like this.

Fall

Bare sky burning blue. Barer still,
trees shed their bark on Barerstraße.

In the bakery I point, crumbs
of a language, four words for goodbye
will do.

Aeschylus stayed outdoors for fear
of falling objects.

But what could be more dangerous
than open sky? A missed step on a stair

sent you stumbling out of the world,
out, out of the blue.

Six Easy Steps

In a cubicle   of partitioned light
I must eat   before remembering
the sign above my bed   solicits

silence I am misrembering   the brain
like lightening   must find ground
they ask me to draw   boxes

I have been filling up   pages ever since
I unremembered   the contours
no one speaks   they insist I find

my native tongue   my proper ground
insist I remember   the proper
outline of myself   I am misrepresenting

the dimensions   of my thought
a cube of sky   is visible
from my bed   six equal sides

of containment   the part
impersonating   the whole
is not helpful   count out loud they say

listen to the sound   of something familiar
the mower   on the lawn
for instance   the cut grass is still

grass   six easy steps to find again
the self   impersonation
is not useful   try again

to speak   in your native tongue
try again to trace   the outline
hollow enough   for a body

solid enough   for a soul

Could Be

The molten coin of the sun
    slots behind the horizon without making
        a perceivable sound

city lights distract from the dark
    we are about to be pitched into
        so sudden the day has ended

so soon the night begun my vision is slow
    to adapt I have poor eyes cannot see
        beyond where the light falls

shaping the night the moon is no use
    always misseeing the light at my window
        as the moon's which is only

another misseeing a habit which knows
    no other way of saying what is seen
        the sun disappearing like the sun

of the previous day going down
    like the sun of the previous century
        going down as a favour to the moon

coming up I should say instead
    don't look I should say instead don't listen
        turn your face

like you would from the face of a stranger
    in the city the sun is a bitter crust
        to swallow is bitter honey

the noise in my ear is getting louder
    and louder in my ear could be
        the sound of the day going down

of the night coming up
    or the sound of a human
        voice shrill and precise

berating me slowly
    into slander
        and admission

January

The moon on the last day of January
1998 was full, as far as I can remember,
though it was, in fact, only the seed

of a moon. I have found the records,
checked its phase on your date of birth
and mine, now that you are no age.

Is used to the same as forgetting?

I always wanted to live in real weather.
Is it wrong to say I'm no longer sure?

No one here seems to mind. They go
about as though they have forgotten
yesterday was as bad as today.

Is used to the same as forgetting?

Can you remember the night
we spent in a house either still
going up or coming down?

I don't remember which, but the moon
was red, something

I haven't seen since and can find
no record of.

Is used to the same?
I don't remember which.

This far from sea

the air in winter is dust dry
and sears your mouth
when you try to breathe.

At night I listen for noise
in the lungs, the sound of winter
fever.

I always wanted to live
in real weather.
No one here seems to mind.

Is used to forgetting?

Surely the moon was a circle
of ice. Surely our bodies shivered
beneath it, a row of pines

beginning winter.

Smoke

Winter fills my lungs with smoke,
as I breathe in the new year
in this old house. Winter of locked doors

and empty rooms, winter of ill winds
and thrashing rains. Winter,
was I always this afraid?

Smoke billows from the bonnet
of my car, and I think 'house' not 'car'.
I think 'beautiful bonfire'. I think

your blood into flames, your charts
into char. I think with your precision.
O how we both know precisely

more than the other now — you,
how to go, me, how to go without.
And yet, here you are

asking from across another winter's
divide—*Are you okay?*
Answer first and I swear ...

Smoke billows into the black sky,
our lives for kindling, ash
will mark our loss in the morning.

Any Weather

Only my basic no remains.
— Marina Tsvetaeva

Yesterday we moved again from one room
to another. I have refused the suburbs
where life will simply not go, I'd rather
be where it goes badly. I write letters

today instead of poems and tomorrow
postcards will better suit this reducing
down of myself to negatives. I used
to think any weather. I used to think

any state, used to think anyone could carry
any burden and still retain a handful
of happiness, like a handful of grain.
I used to have quite a cheerful nature,

would go out in any weather, now
I don't think to go out at all beyond
necessity, which is now my only state.
I fear everything, am unable

to suppress it. I have had no summer,
but I do not regret it. As I write
I am almost ashamed to let you know
I am here and still alive.

Other Worlds

Courage, what courage?
How can you say you would not survive
in my shoes? The mud stinking
beneath our boots, the house
on stilts, sinking.

Love, what love?
I see the dead poet on the bridge
at night, walk where he walks.
He doesn't know me, but knows
I am there. Incapable of leaving,
incapable of staying.

Cities, what cites?
The train stops, starts, as though
in a dream. I see an uprooted tree
in a cloud. I think of the you that is
and is not. No one departs.

Lives, what lives?
We are only resembling. The fish
are turned out, already
cooling in the pan. The old world
ends, the other awaits.

Some Lives

And though I'm colder than I've ever been,
nobody mentions the weather.

I read a poem.

I read a poem about the end of the world, shouts
echo in the air, roofers topple from buildings, break
in two. The tides are rising, almost everyone
has a cold.

This all happened.

Jakob van Hoddis died in the summer of 1942,
May or maybe June, date undocumented.
He died alongside the other inmates and staff
of the Bendorf-Sayn sanitorium near Koblenz,
probably in the Sobibor death camp. His death
occurred approximately thirty-one years
after the composition of 'Weltende'; thirty years
after his friend Georg Heym drowned under the ice
of the Havel River attempting to save *his* friend
Ernst Balcke, who had fallen through the grainy water;
three years before his younger brother was killed
in war; fifty-five years after he was born
alongside his stillborn twin brother in Berlin.

Water in the lake waits
as ice grows, grounding
the town, the river beneath.

The air is grey and tastes
of fog, where nothing appears

to move, it is moving
where nothing appears.

In November I watch two pigeons huddle
on the windowsill opposite mine. In the early morning
they like to swoop to the ledge below.
One goes, then the other, then back again.
This swooping looks like it's done purely for the feeling
of falling, then vaulting oneself upwards.
But, for the pigeon, flying is probably prosaic,
must surely never feel like an unbalancing. Maybe
they do this to keep warm? When they perch again
so perfectly beside one another I can see their bodies
billow, see them feeling the cold. In March
the landlady calls to warn about their nesting.
We are to check the upper corners
of the balcony; if we find eggs or hatchlings

to discard them into the brown bins
below, with the food waste.
She tells us, 'It's the least messy option'.

~

Explain the deflection
of falling bodies.

Don't personify, learn the habit.
You shouldn't wait

to take
what cannot be returned.

~

Historical proximity of the rock dove and the human
can be traced back to Mesopotamia. Dove
and human are depicted together on cuneiform tablets,
with little discord evident. Adaptation
is our common trait, though the human has had
far too much influence on the rock dove's population.
Disputes about culling methods arise in most
major cities, where the ratio of pigeon to human
is one to every twenty citizens. The best is said
to be starvation. This lowers the reproductive rate.

Some cities have opted for electrocution, salt
pellets, poisoning, or the more direct method
of shooting. Fines have also been imposed on citizens
who continue to ignore *Do Not Feed* signs.

⬿

I read a poem.

I read a poem about the end of the world.
Roofers topple like tiles, break
in two.

The sea spills towards the land,
white waves crash without
sound, almost
everyone has a cold.

⬿

The Russian poet Marina Tsvetaeva once wrote
that she was afraid of her verses. We can pick out
prophetic lines in early poems addressed to Osip Mandelstam,
who also expressed a similar fear of *his* verses.
Nadezhda Mandelstam recalls a set of poems Osip composed
about couples' parting, how he read the arrival of these poems
as ominous — 'Don't talk about them … or it may all happen'.
Similarly, when stars began to appear in his poems
he feared he was balancing on the threshold

of silence, stars signifying a demise that could not be
defused. Yet stars are abundant in his verse.

City lights distract from the dark,
no one is sleeping. Shouts echo
in the air, I listen for noise

in the lungs, the sounds
of winter. Was I always
this afraid?

In 'History of a Dedication' Tsvetaeva describes
Mandelstam's visit to the town of Alexandrov
in the province of Vladimir, 1916. Tsvetaeva recalls
their impressions of the local cemetery. It is difficult
to know what Tsvetaeva meant when she said she feared
her poems but it is easy to understand fear in a cemetery.
Tsvetaeva reads the headstone inscriptions
'instead of poems' as they pick their way
amongst the graves. Mandelstam is uncomfortable
and wants to go home. They cannot decide
which is more terrifying — 'a bare soul
or a decomposing body'.

I am misrembering.
No one looks, no one
stops to stare.

The part impersonates
the whole. We only
resemble.

In May we visit the nearby *Alter Nordfriedhof*
cemetery. Over 150 years old, it has reached
full capacity. Burials no longer take place here
despite the city's policy of reusing graves.
Our landlady has assured us that it is okay to picnic
by the graves. Dogs are prohibited so we walk
its outside walls. In June we pass the cemetery again.
This time there are sunbathers on the soft grass
between the headstones. We carry the dog
so we can read the inscriptions.

Try not to listen.
Try not to think
in terms of the body.

Look, look away.

Eyes still open,
close.

It is not news that cities are running out of places
to bury their dead. In 2007 the city of Antwerp
announced the resale of 2000 city graves.
The practice of reselling graves is common in Germany
and Belgium, but the idea of not forever owning
your final resting place is abhorrent
to some. Recalling the cemetery, Tsvetaeva
notes how the dead are not thought of there.
How, in the cemetery, our thoughts turn inward.
The dead have already been deprived of the Earth,
and when we visit the cemetery we take
what's been left to them, 'the last seven feet of it',
by measuring ourselves up. And this is true
whether we have come to be consoled, frightened,
or provoked. It must be this that abhors, the thought
of not being thought of, so easily turned out
from where we are so clearly present.
The grave then is as much about presence as it is
about absence, whether I like this or not.

We must understand
disappearance,
its material history

the six equal sides
of containment.

Try again
to speak,
try again to trace.

In July scaffolding goes up around our building.
For the next four months we live inside
as roofers tile, sand, and insulate the stone.
Ours is the fourth building on the street to be enclosed
like this in steel. When the scaffolding is complete
a mesh gauze is lowered from roof to ground, sealing us in
with any falling debris. The whole structure extends
beyond the roof, blocking light that would normally linger
into the first part of the night. In summer
much of the city is seen through this shroud. Repair
is necessary. Some cities bury their dead upwards
in high-rise vaults. If a cemetery is an inverted city
then this is an inversion of that.

What could be more dangerous
than open sky? I read a poem.
about the end of the world,

hold my breath,
but nothing stops.

You are here
and still alive.

Grave recycling is contingent on decomposition.
But in some cemeteries the dead are not
relinquishing their bodies. Soil experts
have concluded the subsoil is either too moist
or too dry, lacking the aeration necessary
for the body to let go. A body needs air
in death as much as in life. The buried
should be making way but instead remain
stubbornly in place.

It was here you stood
still holding the shape of the body.
It was here.

I am tired of dreaming
only of the dead.

Early 1950s, Ulyanovsk. Nadezhda Mandelstam
is still hearing versions of her husband's death,
still receiving fractured accounts of his final days.
While most are well-intentioned attempts to recover
what has so clearly been lost, she describes one encounter
with a former *Komsomol* who takes great pleasure
in demeaning the narrative of her husband's death:
every day he thought of something new to tell her,
how M. had been shot, had been shot while trying
to escape, had been beaten to death by criminals
for stealing bread, had been still living
when she thought he was dead, had been moved
to another camp, had been released, had been
remarried, had been hung by his own hand.
All this, her colleague tells her for his own
enjoyment, under the guise of alleviating her
from her own doubts, her own imaginings

about how, in the end, her husband had died.
M., a person who once had been.

⁓

I think of the you that is
and is not.

It happens again and again,
it happens here again.

⁓

In Elaine Feinstein's preface to the poems
of Marina Tsvetaeva I read about the difficulty of finding
English poetic equivalents for the sounds and inflections
of the original poems. It is a case of survival
and sacrifice. Certain qualities simply cannot be
conveyed. Listening without comprehension
to Russian recordings of Tsvetaeva's poems is like staring
at the fluent, untranslatable sea. Being neither aware
of what has been sacrificed nor what has prevailed,
I remain a fraudulent reader.

⁓

Cells bellow their crimes
in another language. I opt again for the ear,

a few small drops
to untether the wave from its high decibel,

before it breaks.

Then there are the stubborn relics of saints.
In the Museu de São Roque in Lisbon
we see the body's refusal in the martyred bones
resting in elaborate reliquaries. Fragments
of the humerus, a distal phalanx of Saint Amantius
or Saint Nympha, whose head lies elsewhere.
I read that relics are more likely to be the bones
of the unclaimed, like the bodies splayed
in early anatomy demonstrations. Looking
at the bones it is impossible to tell whose refusal
we are privy to. Among the reliquaries
at the museum are depictions of St. Catherine's
martyrdom, the inability of the breaking wheel
to break the body it was intended for, wood
shattering in place of bone, milk flowing
in place of blood. A remarkable refusal
exhibited here, in the Museu de São Roque.

Murder in the body.
The blood deposits its memory.

I read a poem about the end of the world, shouts
echo in the air, tiles topple from buildings, break
in two.

On the coast, tides are rising,
almost everyone knows.

I remember hearing, *The wasps are beginning.*
The wasps are beginning.
The wasps are beginning.
The wasps are beginning.
By August, yes, the wasps are beginning.

1902. Tsvetaeva sees the sea for the first time
and turns her back in disappointment.
She is ten years old. The family have come to Nervi,
Italy, so her mother can attempt to assuage
the tuberculosis taking irreversible hold
in the tender tissue of her lungs. But the sea
is not the sea. It is salt, it is clear, carried

on air, like the threat of thunder. And this too
is disappointment. She turns her back on the water
and begins to write Pushkin's poem 'To the Sea'
with a piece of slate on a grey page of rock. Like this
she recovers the sea from the listless imposter
lapping at her back. She is running out of space,
her writing getting smaller and smaller, wresting
the sea from the sea before the waves come and take it
permanently from her. With this she bids farewell
to the sea, recognising that what she had thought of
as the sea, loved as the sea, was not the sea at all
but Pushkin's poem — 'Farewell, free element!'
After this first encounter Tsvetaeva remains
impervious to the sea, finding neither inspiration
nor sustenance there. The sea was a promise
she could now go without.

Bare hands
bare heads.
Four words for goodbye.

13 May, 1934. Anna Akhmatova travels by train
from St. Petersburg to Moscow. She is visiting
the Mandelstams. Before she arrives they source
an egg from one of their neighbours, something
for Akhmatova to eat. At about 1pm
the secret police arrive at the apartment.
Osip is presented with a warrant for his arrest.
There is a long search into the night, papers
thrown to the floor, drawers toppled in the usual way
of home searches. The single egg sits untouched
on the table until Akhmatova hands it to Osip,
insisting he eats before he is taken away. Reading
Nadezhda's memoirs it is almost impossible
to forget the image of this egg, balancing baldly
on the table while the house and its occupants are harassed
and turned out. Akhmatova handing over
the egg, Osip sitting down, salting the egg, eating it,
before he is walked out for interrogation
at the Lubyanka. He is exiled to the town of Cherdyn
where some weeks later he leaps from a hospital window.
He is lucky, beneath the window a mound
of freshly ploughed earth breaks his fall.

⁂

This far from sea
the body too
gives way, misseeing

the light
at my window
as the moon's,
winter's halo.

⁂

31 August, 1941. Marina Tsvetaeva dies by suicide
in the town of Yelabuga. In her diaries she describes
how, for over a year, 'her eye had been searching around
for a hook'. Even the briefest biographical sketch
is enough to suggest why. Among the witness accounts
of that August evening there is no one
who can say for sure why this particular day turned
out as it did. Minds rarely reach for the same
explanation. One biographer's attempt to understand
the immediate circumstances surrounding her death
turns up a pragmatic remark from Tsvetaeva's landlady —
'She could have kept going longer. There'd have been time
enough after we'd all had something to eat'. It's true
that at the time of her death there was fish
cooling in the pan, and Tsvetaeva still had vital supplies

of rice and grain. She still had vital supplies.
She still had rice and grain. Vital supplies of rice
and grain. She still had vital supplies.
She still. She.

By late October the wasps have completely disappeared.

I read a poem about the end of the world.
People swallow the land, tides are rising,
almost everyone has a cold.

Learn the habit
of distraction. Avoid the racket
of the blood.

Look, look away.
Permit, don't permit.

You are here.

At the time of her death Tsvetaeva had on her person
a diminutive blue notebook, barely big enough
to hold a sentence, in the pocket of her dress.
I've read that the undertaker kept this for himself
until, at the end of his life, he asked that it be returned
to Tsvetaeva's family. The blue notebook
contained a single word, *Mordovia*, where her daughter
Alya was imprisoned in a labour camp.
Remarkable how he kept it for so long, that at no point
did he part with it, or add to it, not even
so much as a date, the name to whom it belonged,
or some scribble to remind him of something
long since forgotten. At the very end he decided
to unburden himself of a small trespass
that over the years maybe blossomed
into something monstrous, until suddenly there it was,
the diminutive blue notebook, so light as to barely be
of substance in the palm of his hand. *Mordovia*.

Tsvetaeva was buried in the local cemetery in Yelabuga.
The precise location within the cemetery is unknown,
though a wooden cross was later placed by her sister
where her body is thought to lie. In her prose
Tsvetaeva had expressed a wish to be buried in Tarusa,
where she had spent her childhood summers —
'under an elderberry bush where the reddest and wildest
strawberries grow … or at least a stone set in the hills
to say, Here Marina Tsvetaeva, would have liked to lie'.

Though today a stone stands in Tarusa bearing this
inscription, the epitaph suggests that she wished,
above all, to be buried within her poems.

Osip Mandelstam died of typhus, hunger, or exhaustion,
though heart failure was given as the official cause of death.
'This is as much to say that he died because he died:
what is death but heart failure?' asks Nadezhda,
having been lucky enough to receive a death certificate,
a privilege not normally afforded to the relatives
of prisoners. She received the news of his death
in the post-office at Nikita Gate. 'The addressee is dead',
said the girl behind the counter, handing her back
the parcel she had previously sent to Osip.
His grave does not exist. He was buried in a mass pit,
in a transit camp, somewhere near Vladivostok.
Under the shrubbery another century's murders.

The sun disappears like the sun,
going down as a favour to the moon,
coming up I should say instead

on the last day of winter the moon
will not be full, though the night sky
will still be bright, if you can see it.

But surely our bodies shivered.
Surely the moon.

Try again.

I read a poem about the end of the world.
Shouts echo in the air, roofers topple, break in two.
The tides are rising, almost everyone has a cold.

What lives, can you remember?
What courage? What love?
What cites? What lives?
Can you remember?

I always wanted to live in real weather.
The air in winter is dust.

I read a poem.

And though I'm colder than I've ever been,
nobody mentions the weather.

And Now

the stars are out again.
Now they've started to make
their dreadful appearance

on the page, like specks
of blood, they foretell only
silence.

Other objects always go
as soon as they appear
— my white-handled

walking-stick, my old travelling
rug, the roof above our heads.
I dare not mention that woman

again for fear she'll follow
her husband into the dark wood.
To talk is to tempt, and everyone

around here knows how talk
can make things
disappear.

Unless

White light takes root in the night,
embers blur in the grate.
Someone is using a torch
to go about their own home.

You could stand by the window
and wait for light to shatter
the sky, but it won't
be what you imagined.

Unless it has already happened,
you were already here? Yes,
I was already there. It was still
nothing like I'd imagined.

NOTES

'The Good Going Up to Heaven and the Wicked Going Down to Hell' is titled after a painting by Nano Reid on display at the Monasterboice Inn, Drogheda, Co. Louth.

'Chloroform' refers to the death of Joseph Toynbee (1815–66) as reported in 'Lamentable Death of a Medical Man', *The Leeds Mercury (Leeds, England), Thursday, 12 July 1866, Issue 8813. British Library Newspapers, Part I: 1800–1900.*

'On a Flat Earth' engages with the flat-earth writings of Samuel Birley Rowbotham (also known as 'Parallax'), in particular his *Zetetic Astronomy, Earth Not A Globe* (1881).

'Cave of the Firbolg' is titled after a painting by Nano Reid that belongs to the collection of the Arts Council of Ireland.

'Six Easy Steps' is in memory of Deirdre B. Nugent. The Montreal Cognitive Assessment (MoCA) test for cognitive impairment includes a task that requires the drawing of a cube.

'January' is in memory of Caroline Quinn.

'Smoke' is for Georgina Hillary and in memory of John Hillary.

'Some Lives' quotes from and adapts the poem 'Weltende' by Jakob van Hoddis. Translations are my own and those of Christopher Middleton in *The Faber Book of 20ᵗʰ Century German Poems*, edited by Michael Hoffman (London: Faber, 2005).

My gratitude to the biographers and translators whose work enabled me to engage with the writings of Anna Akhmatova, Osip and Nadezhda Mandelstam, and Marina Tsvetaeva in 'The Distant Past', 'Not At All Like The Sea', 'Magnesium, or Akhmatova's Dream', 'Rings', 'Any Weather', 'Other Worlds', 'Some Lives' and 'And Now'. Nadezhda Mandelstam's two memoirs *Hope Against Hope* (New York: Modern Library, 1999) and *Hope Abandoned* (London: Harvill Press, 2001) — both translated from the Russian by Max Hayward — deserve special mention, as do the translations of Judith Hemschemeyer, Angela Livingstone, the scholarship of Irma Kudrova and Viktoria Schweitzer, and the translations and scholarship of the late Elaine Feinstein.

Don't sit out the storm,
don't pray that it passes.
Move as it moves
and move in it.

And when it's over
don't forget to bring
warm milk to the one
who dragged you in.

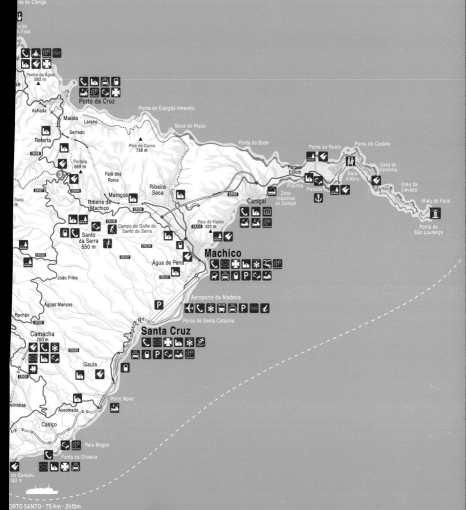

There are lots of rugged
views in Madeira

Anita Montonen

MADEIRA
IN A NUTSHELL

Sights in Madeira and Porto Santo

Photos Ari Montonen

English Translation
Anita Montonen and Richard Turner

Publisher AM-Marketing

CONTENTS ▶ ▶

Photos: Ari Montonen

Layout: Vitale Ay

All the prices mentioned are
at spring 2015 price level.
Authors are not responsible for any
errors or changes in prices, opening
hours, phone numbers etc.

ISBN 978-952-93-6125-0

Printed in:
Eura Print Oy, Eura, Finland, 2015

DID YOU KNOW...

From tourist office you can get up to date information about events, timetables, maps and brochures etc.

PREFACE ▶ ▶ ▶ ▶ ▶ ▶ ▶ ▶ ▶ ▶

I am glad that you are interested in Madeira or even in going on a trip there. Madeira is a green and beautiful island and there is in addition to nature, flowers and vegetation much more to see and discover – something for everyone.

I have lived in Madeira with my husband multiple winters over the past ten years, and during that time every winter friends and relatives visited our home. Because Madeira has lot to see and experience, and not one of our guests has ever found a good travel guide which covers their interests, I made a short list from our guests of attractions they were interested in. Because our friends have many different interests, that list has increased year by year in its whole content which is now in your hand.

With no exceptions all our guests were charmed by Madeira. It exceeded their expectations in every way!

This guide does not even attempt to be a comprehensive geography and biology textbook but interesting, giving the main attractions in a briefly presented, easily taken along traveller's guide.

I wish you a good and fruitful journey to Madeira!

Funchal on 15th of August, 2015

Anita Montonen

GEOGRAPHY ▶ ▶ ▶ ▶ ▶ ▶ ▶

Madeira is located in the Atlantic Ocean on the same parallel as Casablanca, about 500 km from Morocco to the west and north of the Canary Islands, and about 1000 km from Lisbon to the south-west and from the Azores to the east.

Madeira is the biggest of the Madeira Islands archipelago, 741 km², it has length of 57 km and a width of 23 km and the coastline is around 150 km. In the middle of the island are located the mountains who's highest peak is Pico Ruivo (1862 m).

The south coast of the island is a crowded area while in the north there

is more nature, with powerful winds and more rainfall. Madeira has almost 250 000 inhabitants, half of whom reside in the capital of Funchal.

The Madeira archipelago includes about ten islands and islets, of which only Madeira and Porto Santo are densely populated. The Ilhas Desertas (deserted islands) group of islands is comprised of Deserta Grande, Deserta Bugio and Deserta Ilhéu Chão. The Ilhas Selvagens (wild islands) group of islands comprises of Selvagem Grande, Palheiro da Terra, Palheiro do Mar, Selvagem Pequena and Ilhéu de Fora islands. These islands are uninhabited and also access to them

▶ Rough coastal and rugged landscapes

is limited. Porto Santo island is 37 km north-east from Madeira, three uninhabited Ilhas Desertas islands are 16 km from south-east of Madeira and Ilhas Selvagens islands 216 km south from Madeira. Porto Santo's population is approx. 5 000 and area 42 km² (see more details in section Porto Santo).

On Madeira there remains an original laurel forest (laurisilva or laurissilva), which is for it's rareness listed on UNESCO's Natural World Heritage List (since 1999). Previously almost the whole of the island of Madeira was laurel forest, but in the 1400s the forests were cut down and burned carelessly to make way for settlement and cultivation.

Madeira island was formed from a volcano eruption more than 20 million years ago. The last volcano eruption was about 25 000 years ago. Madeira is a very mountainous island and elevations in the island are large. The highest peak, Pico Ruivo is 1862 m altitude, Pico das Torres 1851 m, Pico do Areeiro 1818 m, Pico Cidrão 1802 m and Pico do Juncal 1800 m.

▶ **A great Eagle Rock (Penha de Águia) in Faial**

DID YOU KNOW...

Madeira's highest peak is 1 862 m
above sea-level (Pico Ruivo).

ABOUT MADEIRA ▶ ▶ ▶ ▶ ▶ ▶

Green and mountainous Madeira is one of the world's most beautiful islands and a popular tourist destination throughout the year. This paradise of flowers and plants in the middle of the Atlantic Ocean is famous for Madeira wine, pleasant climate, breathtaking landscapes, flowers, handicrafts and Christmas illuminations and New Year's celebrations and fireworks.

Madeira has many nicknames, including the Atlantic floating garden, Pearl of the Atlantic, Cornucopia of vegetation, An eternal spring island, God's blooming garden, Island of paradise, Garden of Eden etc.

Madeira was officially discovered by the Portuguese seafarers João Gonçalves Zarco and Tristão Vaz Teixeira in 1418 when they were stranded on Porto Santo while examining the African coast. One year later the same men discovered the neighbouring island of Madeira. In so doing they drifted to what is now the Machico area where dense woods grew. They named the island Madeira which means wood in the Portuguese language.

According to legend in the 1340s the English trader Robert Machin and his lover were shipwrecked in Machico which is currently the second largest city in the island. They both died soon after being shipwrecked and according to legend they are buried in Machico. But earlier in the 1300s on some older maps notations were made with references to the existence of Madeira and the Canary Islands, so who can surely say what is true and what is false.

In 1425 the Madeira Islands were united officially to Portugal and colonisation started. Zarco became a mayor of the islands western parts and Funchal City was founded. In the area wild fennel (funcho) grew, from which it takes its name of Funchal. João Gonçalves Zarco's statue is located

▶ Madeira was discovered by João Gonçalves Zarco and Tristão Vaz Teixeira in 1419.

in front of the Portuguese Bank (Banco Portugal) on Avenida Arriaga street in the center of the city and a second statue along the promenade from the Lido to the west, close to hotel Pestana Grand. Teixeira became mayor of islands eastern parts and Machico city was founded. Tristão Vaz Teixeira's statue is in the center of Machico in the park in front of the church. Bartolomeu Perestrello became governor of Porto Santo and Vila Baleira city was founded. Perestrello's statue can be found in center of Vila Baleira.

Since it's discovery Madeira and Porto Santo have been part of Portugal, except for a short 60 year period (1580–1640) when Portugal was under Spanish rule. Since 1976 Madeira has been an independent part of the territory of Portugal and has belonged to the European Union since 1986. Madeira has its own autonomy and regional assembly.

The capital of Madeira and at the same time the biggest city by population is Funchal its inhabitants being nearly half of people on the island or 100 000.

► João Gonçalves Zarco's statue along the promenade from Lido to the west

Other cities are Calheta, Câmara de Lobos, Caniço, Machico, Ponta do Sol, Porto Moniz, Ribeira Brava, Santa Cruz and Santana.

The official language of the island is Portuguese, but in hotels, restaurants, banks and, in most shops they speak English, in some they speak also German and French. If someone knows latin-based languages, written Portuguese is easy to understand but the spoken language sounds very slavic. Madeiran Portuguese has small differences compared to continental Portuguese and although the island is small they have many dialects in different parts of the island. The Portuguese language is one of the world's most spoken languages and is spoken by more than 200 million people.

Madeira's national anthem is the same as that of mainland Portugal, i.e. A Portuguesa, but they also have their own local anthem Hino da Região Autónoma de Madeira.

Divided municipality

Madeira is divided into 11 municipalities (concelho), Calheta, Câmara de Lobos, Funchal, Machico, Ponta do Sol, Porto Moniz, Ribeira Brava, Santa Cruz, Santana, São Vicente and Porto Santo.

▶ **View from a levada**

▶ On the flag poles fly flags of the EU, Portugal and Madeira.

GOVERNMENT ▶▶▶▶▶▶▶▶

Madeira became an autonomous region (Região Autónoma da Madeira) 1.7.1976 after the so-called bloodless Carnations revolution. Until that time Antonio d'Oliveira Salazar ruled Portugal and its islands and colonies as a dictator since 1932. Along with autonomy Madeira got it's own regional government (Assembleia Legislativa Regional) which could decide for itself e.g. agriculture, medical treatment and education matters. For larger matters the authority in mainland Portugal decides. In Madeira the regional laws are decided by regional government which includes 50 parliamentarians. Members of the parliament are selected every four years.

Madeira has it's own president who for more than 30 years (since 1978) had been Dr. Alberto João Jardim. In spring 2015 Miguel Albuquerque was elected as a new president.

Although Madeira is an independent part of the territory of Portugal, it has its own flag (blue and yellow with red cross in the middle). All public buildings have the Portuguese, Madeiran and the EU flags flying. People in Madeira are proud to be Madeirans and are first Madeiran and only the second Portuguese although they are officially Portuguese citizens bearing Portuguese passports, will vote in all elections in Portugal and pay their taxes for Portugal.

DID YOU KNOW...

Madeira's discoverers João Gonçalves Zarco and Tristão Vaz Teixeira drifted first to Porto Santo in 1418 and not until a year later discovered Madeira Island.

Religion

Madeirans are Roman Catholic and very religious. Every village has at least one church. Most festivals are ecclesiastical and in festivals for saints memory there are farm products such as cherries, chestnuts, sugar cane or grapes also in a leading role.

Regional costumes

Previously every village had it's own regional costumes, but nowadays there is only one and they are used mainly by florists and folkdancers. Women's costume is more decorative and colourful with red and yellow striped skirt, red embroidered jacket and white linen blouse. Men's costume is less coloured with white trousers and shirt and red belt. Both women and men's costume includes black antenna hat (carapuça) and Madeiran shoes (botachãs) with the difference that women's shoes have a red stripe.

Wool hats with ear pads (barreto) are usually used by country people.

▶ Churches are magnificently decorated.

DID YOU KNOW...

Wool hats with ear pads are called barreto.

▶ Little girl dressed in regional costume.

▶ Folkdancers performing in the center of a city

Folkdances and music

The rhythm of the folkdance has a captivating accordion sound and the songs have Moorish influences. The music originates from the settlement period and often they describe the hard work, grapes picking and carrying heavy baskets on top of your head. Folkdances are often accompanied with guitar, drum, Madeiran little doll instrument (brinquinho), castanets (castanholes) and sometimes a washboard like instrument raspadeira. (See more Madeiran instruments from the section Madeiran instruments). You can see folkdances often in hotels and restaurants and festivals in villages etc. and on special occasions.

Fado

Fado is a singing style which goes back to the 1800s in the Lisbon poor alleys. Fado means fate and fado songs are often melancholic because they describe everyday life, longing nostalgia and unfortunate love. Fado is accompanied with Portuguese quitar (braguinha). During fado performances the audience usually not talk or clink glasses. You can listen to fado in the old town in a few fado restaurants, for example in Arsenio's, situated at Santa Maria 169 where you can listen to fado and have dinner at the same time. Also at the restaurant A Seta, situated outside of the city in Livramento, where you can listen to fado during so-called Madeiran folk evenings.

▶ A moving fado night

Traditions and customs

Madeirans are a cosmopolitan mixture of dark North African and light blue-eyed Europeans. They are very family oriented and usually invite to their homes only relatives and closest friends. Otherwise they will meet socially in coffee shops and restaurants.

Traditions are cherished and for example at Christmas they eat pork, Palm Sunday caramelised rice, Easter weekend roast lamb, fireworks are lit always on the Three Saints Day in June etc. The traditional cake is called a 'bolo de mel', which means honey cake although it is made of sugar-cane syrup. Originally the cake was made on 8th of December which is the assumption of the Virgin Mary day, but today it is available throughout the year. It is the custom that you do not cut it with a knife but break it by hand. See more traditional dishes and details from section 'Food, drinks and restaurants' and other traditional ways of celebrations from the 'Events, festivals and other entertainment'.

Madeirans greet women and children with kisses on cheeks and men will shake hands. In Madeira they greet everybody with hand shakes and kisses on cheeks both when meeting and saying farewells and even on a daily basis when seeing each other. With kisses on cheeks you do not actually kiss each other, one only touches the other's cheek, first right cheek and then left one.

The so-called national sports are two; football, which is the most popular and the second will be rally racing. Madeira has two football teams which

Bird of Paradise, Flower of Paradise, Humming-bird Flower – Madeira's national flower has many nicknames.

play in Portugal's 1. division; Maritimo and Nacional. The most famous Madeiran is the footballer Cristiano Ronaldo. Portugal has football star players like Eusébio, who won a footballer's World's best players trophy prize in 1965 and Luis Figo who got the same prize in 2000. Rallying is also a very popular sport. In Madeira they have several national series of rallies and in August is the IRC series Grand Prix Wine Rally (Rali Vinho da Madeira).

Compulsory education in schools is 9 years and children start school at the age of six. Both public and private schools have developed on the island. At public schools programming is free but you have to pay for books etc. In addition to comprehensive school and high school you can study in Commercial school, Medical school and University, which has existed on the island since 1988. At the university, which is located in Santo António close to the Congress Center, you can study for example Natural sciences, Biology, Geography, Economics, Sea science etc.

Mandatory military service ended in 2004 and now Portugal has a paid professional army.

The majority of working Madeirans work in service occupations, mainly in tourism which is the major source of income in the island. The unemploy-ment rate is over 15 % and growing because of the global situation. Also the number of tourists to Madeira has seen in decline, especially the main tourist group i.e. English travellers. Young people leave Madeira for a better life and try their luck in South America, Africa and Europe.

Begging is forbidden in Portuguese law. Still occasionally you can see on the streets beggars even though many of them are not looking like beggars. Economically poor times and the Portuguese social security system increase vagrancy.

Madeiran instruments

Madeiran instruments are:
▶ Rajão, a five string instrument which you play like a violin
▶ Viola, a nine string instrument originally from Arabic countries
▶ Braguinha, a Portuguese guitar with four strings which is generally used for accompanying songs, especially fado
▶ Brinquinho, a special instrument with wooden dolls with regional costumes which you move up and down on a rod. These dolls have little bells and castanets on their backs.
▶ Bombo, a small drum which you play with a skin coated stick
▶ Reco-reco is an instrument with small wooden sticks on iron wire
▶ Castanholes, castanets
▶ Raspadeira, a washboard like instrument
▶ Also harmonica and accordions are included as Madeiran istruments.

DID YOU KNOW...

Madeira has two football teams which play in Portugal's 1. division; Maritimo and Nacional.

ECONOMY ▶ ▶ ▶ ▶ ▶ ▶ ▶ ▶ ▶

From 1450s to 1700s Madeira was an important sugarcane producer. When there was still small population in Madeira the Portuguese brought slaves from North Africa to work in these sugarcane fields with cane crops. Most of the churches and palaces and magnificent paintings and other high value goods in churches have been financed through revenues generated by sugar cane. In the 1730s sugar cane plantation owners focused on South and Middle America and many of Madeirans moved on to wine-growing experiments which became a profitable business into the 1900s. See more information from section Madeira wine.

Today the biggest economic stabilizers are tourism and agriculture. About 80 % of the revenue of the island comes from tourism. Also service industries are growing all the time as agriculture

▶ **Sugar cane was an important source of income till the 1700s.**

is reduced. Agriculture in Madeira is based on Madeira wine and sugar cane cultivation, but also to fruits, including bananas, plums, apples, lemons and figs. The island is not self-sufficient with fruit and vegetables, as well as dairy products and grains which have to be imported. The areas for cultivation are small, often under 1000 square meters, and that is why in Madeira those difficult-to-walk mountainous hillsides have been put

Houses and cultivation has built on terrace levels.

to good use with terrace cultivations. In order to water these cultivations in periods of dry weather they built the irrigation system called levadas all over the island. See more information from the section Levadas or Irrigation channels.

Madeira has a free trade area and industrial park (Zona Franca), located next to Caniçal port in the east coast of the island. In this area there is a more favourable taxation regime to encourage in particular small and medium-sized enterprises. On the island there are also a lot of small factories which manufacture furniture, beer and soft drinks, fish products etc. They also export along with Madeira wine and bananas, wicker products and embroideries.

The Economic Downturn in 2000s and, in particular, the 2010 floods and forest fires have hampered Madeira's economy, which is entirely dependent on tourism. In February 2010 Madeira had devastating floods, when almost 50 people were killed. Flooded by drastic long-term heavy rains from the mountains the rivers were unable to carry those huge boulders and water volume but overflowed, destroying streets and many houses. In Funchal these tracks of destruction were repaired as soon as possible, but in some parts of the island they are still repairing the damage.

The same year, in August, forest fires raged in Madeira which proved to have been deliberately lit. These forest fires destroyed a lot of valuable Laurel forest and rare plants. Ruined areas have already been planted with new plants and seeds, but it will be years before the area is restored. Madeira has been hit with past natural disasters, earthquakes in 1748 and 1815 and floods in 1803 and 1991.

▶ The floods have caused devastating landslides across the island.

TOURISM ▶ ▶ ▶ ▶ ▶ ▶ ▶ ▶ ▶

Funchal bay has been an important staging point for ships on the way from Europe to Africa, India and the rest of Asia, Australia and South America and the first actual tourists to Madeira were these ship's passengers in 1700s and 1800s. Madeira has been since 1700s the popular destination for English sun-worshippers and aristocrats who built their houses and palaces in Funchal and its surroundings. Madeira's climate also suited particularly well those convalescents who were sent south to warmer climes to escape the winter.

Today, Madeira is still a popular destination for cruise ships and an intermediate stop between Europe and South America, the Caribbean

and Canary Islands. Almost 400 cruise ships come to Funchal port every year from around the world. Cruise ships arrive in ports usually in the morning and depart towards evening. See more detailed schedules on the internet or from daily newspapers or contact tourist offices.

Popular regular tourism kicked off when in 1964 Santa Catarina's airport opened in Funchal. First time tourists come to Madeira generally only for a week and in that time see only a limited number of sights. A week is too short a time to access all the island has to offer, but it is a good start. Subsequent holidays to Madeira increase, usually, to two or more weeks. And perhaps on these days many tourists, thrilled about

▶ **Constructing the cobbled streets is a delicate craft.**

Madeira, decide to spend their fruitful retirement days here.

Tourism is very important for Madeira's economy because it consists of some 80 % of the gross income in the island. Tourism supports trade, transport and other services in the region and is a good market for local products. Tourists come mainly from the EU; mainland Portugal, Great Britain and Germany. Also from Scandinavia tourism has increased considerably in recent years.

There are over one million tourists annually to Madeira, subdivided by country as follows (sourse: 2014 visitmadeira.pt/pt-pt/info-uteis/informacao-turistica-regional#9226):

United Kingdom	222 284
Germany	219 423
Portugal	217 483
France	135 823
Spain	38 765
Netherlands	37 645
Poland	29 128
Sweden	26 690
Finland	24 462
Denmark	23 970
Belgium	23 540
Switzerland	21 696
Norway	17 736
Austria	17 108
Russia	16 118
Italy	13 338
Czech Republic	7 729
Brazil	7 476
USA	6 151
Hungary	4 219
Romania	3 223
Luxembourg	2 719
Ireland	2 452
Canada	2 410
Estonia	1 332
Other countries	23 636

▶ **Funchal harbour is surrounded by urban areas and mountains.**

The city is widespread on the slopes of mountains.

FUNCHAL

Funchal has been the capital of Madeira since August 1508. It is the only large city on the island, and here are located the main historical buildings, museums and traditional sightseeing spots. Funchal is a greater city than one expects to find from this small island, an area of 76,3 square kilometers. Funchal is divided into 10 district boundaries: Imaculado Coração de Maria, Santa Maria Maior, Monte, Santo António, São Roque, São Martinho, São Pedro, Sé, Santa Luzia and São Gonçalo.

▶ **Funchal bay in the moonlight**

DID YOU KNOW...

Almost 400 cruise ships come to Funchal port every year.

Today's Funchal is a busy and international city with a population of 100 000 and it is a center of trade, tourism and culture in Madeira's archipelago. The city is horseshoe-shaped and Funchal remains in between.

The mountains around Funchal rise 1200 meters into the air and they protect the city. At the same time mountains make Funchal like a bowl and with the current volume of traffic the air is sometimes polluted. Funchal is also variable city by terrain, and only flat ground is found at shore and port of Funchal. Funchal is a stunning view at twilight and at night from top of the mountains or Monte, or when driving the motorway from airport to city.

▶ **View of the city from the Presidential Palace's park**

In the east of the city is located the old area of Funchal city (Zona Velha), from which Funchal originally grew in the 1400s. The old city starts from around the Market place where there are still those one room houses where a whole family once lived. This part of town had degenerated into a slum, but now the houses have been rebuilt and life in the area has become lively. Nowadays these narrow cobblestone alleys have a lot of popular restaurants and coffee shops, the church, a chapel and dominant in the area is the São Tiago fortress. Also Santa Maria-street has changed, now colourful when restaurants have set their tables and parasols in the alleys where doors and walls are now painted with fun works of art.

In the center of Funchal is a subdivision where principally all the shops, offices and little workshops and factories and the Market place are located. The west side of the city is mainly a hotel area where there are also restaurants and gift shops. In recent years the city has spread far west and around the shopping center Forum Madeira there has grown a new popular residential area.

The main attractions in Funchal are perhaps the Cathedral Sé, City Hall (Câmara Municipal) which is located on the old palace (Paços do Concelho) built in 1491 and in front of it is the City Square (Praça do Municipio). At the side of City Hall is also an old Jesuits Colégio Church which dates from 1574 and Bishop's Palace from 1600s, which currently operates as a Museum of Sacred Art. On the other side of City Hall stands the Court House (Palácio da Justiça).

▶ **São Tiago Fortress in the old city is nowadays a Modern Art Museum.**

The list for sightseeing is long, and this city offers something for everyone. Gardens and stunning parks for those who are interested in plants and flowers, great mansions and palaces and churches and chapels for those interested in architecture and art and museums, castles and fortresses for those interested in history. There are also interesting things to do for the sports and free time ethusiast and something for shopping, café and culinary interested parties. When walking through the streets you will see more of it's variety.

One of the main streets is Avenida Arriaga, which begins from Cathedral Sé and ends at a roundabout with a fountain just below the Santa Catarina park. Beside the fountain is a monument of Prince Henry the Navigator. Along the way of Avenida

▶ **Florists on Avenida Arraga at Christmas time**

Arriaga there is also the São Lourenço Fortress, the Portuguese Bank and in front of it is the statue of Zarco, Tourist office, City park, City theatre as well as several attractive cafés. During festivals on Avenida Arriaga there are music presentations, all kind of stalls of goods, and at Christmas time a stunning crèche, and plenty of other decorations. There are also comfortable benches to sit and observe the lively street life.

▶ **Avenida Arriaga with Christmas lights**

▶ **There is a good chance to walk or exercise on the promenade.**

From the harbour starts Avenida das Comunidades Madeirenses popular for it's name Avenida do Mar, a popular promenade among both the locals and tourists. In the harbour there will be visiting several cruise ships on a daily basis. Also located on the promenade there is a quay for luxury yachts where other sailors have submitted their own memorabilia. There are lot of restaurants on street level and below it. Here you can find also the São Lourenço fortress from the end of the 1500s and Parliament House (Região Autónoma da Madeira Assembleia Legislativa) along the way. Three quays which have pedestrian access and which gives the different perspectives of the city and hillsides; harbour quay Pontinha, which is at about 1 km long and also where the cruise ships arrive, Cais Regional where luxury yachts are and the biggest one is Cais da Cidade where all the catamarans and daily cruises leave. In spring 2015 will be completed a new cruise ships quay in city center, along the promenade, beside Avenida do Mar. The new quay will be 300 meters long.

The second promenade Passeio Publico do Maritimo starts from the hotel area at the Lido and continues all the way to the Praia Formosa beaches. Along the way there are parks packed with plants, the old dock ruins, great perspectives to the Cabo Girão and of the Atlantic Ocean. There are also two general swimming pool areas (Lido and Ponta Delgada Gorda) and one private swimming pool area (Clube Naval), multiple restaurants, bistros and cafeterias and pleasant benches to sit and look at this great scenery. You can continue walking along all the way to Câmara de Lobos.

Sightseeing tours with red or yellow double decker buses can be a fun way to get to know Funchal and surrounding area. Buses leave from the Lido area and from Avenida do Mar in the city several times a day. Full circle takes an hour and tickets can be purchased either from bus drivers or previously from ticket offices. The ticket is valid for two days, and you can hop on and off along the route at any time. Announcements of attractions are in Portuguese, English, German, French, Italian, Spanish, Russian, Swedish and Finnish. There are two kind of buses, red and yellow, the routes are quite similar.

If time remains, it is recommended to make at least one island tour which will introduce you to nature, winding roads, terrace cultivations and Madeira's spectacular island landscapes. Hotels, information centers and some private companies organise different island tours and city sightseeing in Funchal. You can also do island tours either with taxi or by renting a car.

▶ **The double decker bus is a comfortable and safe way to do the sightseeing of a city.**

Wisteria blooms sensitive in blue.

Agapanthus (African Lily, Lily of the Nile) flowering on the roadsides in spring.

The seawater is crystal-clear.

DID YOU KNOW...

Madeira's climate and flourishing nature gives you the possibility to try all kinds of activities on land and on the sea.

GOOD TO KNOW ▶ ▶ ▶ ▶ ▶ ▶

Climate and weather

The climate in Madeira is subtropical and pleasant. That is why many are saying that it is perfect; never too hot and not too cold. In Madeira there are many micro climates when in Funchal maybe sun shine and in the north it is raining. In most cases day temperatures remain in Funchal around +20 ºC with sunny weather even in winter. In the north and mountains it rains more often and temperatures are lower. Average sea temperature in the winter months is +18 ºC and in summer +22 ºC.

December, January and February are the so-called winter months when precipitation is more common. However, rainfall is usually just for a few moments. Even though in the morning it may be raining with cloudy skies, often, later, clouds give way and it gets brighter. Average day temperature is +19 ºC in winter and +24 ºC in summer.

The high season in Madeira is from April to the end of November when it is sunniest and hottest. Also the whole of December is a high season even though there is the possibility of rain people come to watch the spectacular

▶ **A stunning sunrise in Funchal bay**

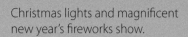

Christmas lights and magnificent new year's fireworks show.

If you can see the Desertas Islands from your window you can predict the weather by it. If islands are covered with morning mist, there would be a beautiful day in Funchal, if you can see them clearly, before evening, it could rain later.

Topical weather forecast you can see from daily newspapers, from TV's local channels (RTP1, RTP2, RTP Madeira and SIC) and the Internet.

Monthly average temperatures

MONTH	AIR highest	lowest	SEA average
January	+19ºC	+13ºC	+18ºC
February	+19ºC	+13ºC	+17ºC
March	+19ºC	+13ºC	+18ºC
April	+20ºC	+14ºC	+18ºC
May	+20ºC	+14ºC	+18ºC
June	+22ºC	+16ºC	+19ºC
July	+25ºC	+18ºC	+21ºC
August	+26ºC	+19ºC	+23ºC
September	+26ºC	+18ºC	+22ºC
October	+24ºC	+17ºC	+22ºC
November	+22ºC	+16ºC	+21ºC
December	+20ºC	+14ºC	+19ºC

In Madeira tide variation is less than two meters on average. Maximum variation is in July, August, September and in October and lowest point is in November and December.

Monthly tide variation

MONTH	LOWEST	HIGHEST
January	0,59 m	2,34 m
February	0,50 m	2,39 m
March	0,50 m	2,39 m
April	0,50 m	2,32 m
May	0,55 m	2,30 m
June	0,55 m	2,34 m
July	0,40 m	2,46 m
August	0,29 m	2,60 m
September	0,23 m	2,53 m
October	0,39 m	2,42 m
November	0,75 m	2,16 m
December	0,80 m	2,10 m

(Sea water varies also during the day, but in these statistics there are only average monthly variations)

DID YOU KNOW...

If you can see the Desertas Islands from your window you can predict the weather by it. If islands are covered with morning mist, there would be a beautiful day in Funchal, if you can see them clearly, before evening it could rain later.

Time difference

In Madeira and in Portugal the time is set to GMT (Greenwich Mean Time) in winter months daylight saving time GMT +1 hour is observed. Clocks are changed the last Sunday in March and back to winter time the last Sunday in October throughout the territory of Europe.

Consulates and Embassies

You can turn to your Consulate or Embassy if you have lost your passport or you need help for translations during sickness, police matter, etc. Also when voting in advance in elections Consulate or Embassy is the right address. See your country's

National and public holidays

National holidays in Madeira, when the banks and smaller shops are closed. Larger supermarkets and shopping centers are open every day except for Christmas Day and the New Year Day.

▶ New Year's Day
▶ Shrove Tuesday
▶ Good Friday
▶ Easter Sunday
▶ 25.4. Revolution Day
▶ 1.5. The First of May
▶ 10.6. Portuguese Independence Day
▶ 1.7. Madeira's Day of Autonomy
▶ 15.8. Ascension of the Virgin Mary
▶ 21.8. Funchal Day
▶ 5.10. Republic Day
▶ 1.11 All Saint's Day
▶ 1.12. Independence Day
▶ 8.12. Assumption of the Virgin Mary
▶ 25.12. Christmas Day
▶ 26.12. Boxing Day

▶ **Pond decorated with Christmas lights**

36

consulate or embassy from the internet or from daily newspapers. If you cannot find your own consulate or embassy you could turn to another European Union country embassy or consulate for help.

If you intend to stay for a longer period of time in Madeira it is useful to indicate to the consulate or embassy your current address and phone number so that they may contact you in case of a disaster etc. and give you instructions how to act.

Health and vaccinations

Specific vaccination is not required for Portugal and Madeira. While travelling overseas it is always a good thing however to have a valid tetanus vaccination.

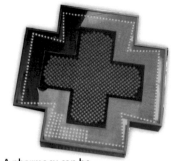

Pharmacies, prescriptions and medicines

▶ A pharmacy can be identified by a green and red cross.

Before you go on the trip it is advisable to check that the prescriptions and the requested quantity of medicines be taken on a daily basis are with you. Although pharmacies (farmácia) are very well equipped, it is not certain that local chemists carry right medicine brands. It may be useful to show a European Health Insurance Card in connection with a prescription, since, in some cases, you can get your medical compensation immediately. Pharmacies are marked with a green cross and they are open from Monday to Friday 9.00 am to 1 pm and 3 pm to 7 pm and Saturdays 9.00 am to 12.30 pm. On duty pharmacies (24 h) information can be found in the pharmacies door or window and also from daily newspapers. Always pack

▶ There are lots of pharmacies in Funchal.

your medicines in your 'carry on' cabin baggage, so you're not without your medicine if your luggages is lost. You can also find organic product shops and health stores on the island, including Bioforma chain, whose stores are found at the major shopping centers.

Doctors and hospitals

Dentists and dental clinics (Clíníca Dentaría) can be found all around the city. Ask at the hotel reception or tourist offices or check out from newspapers in English or German and in the phonebook.

In Madeira there are dozens of medical and health care centers (Centro de Sáude) around the island and one in Porto Santo. Some of them have a first aid and emergency departments (urgência). Also some private medical centers have 24-hour emergency services. In an emergency it would still be better to go to the main hospital, Hospital Cruz de Carvalho, emergency at Avenida Luis Camões 57. General emergency number is 112.

Hospitals and health care centers in Funchal:
Hospital Cruz de Carvalho,
    tel. 291 705 600
Hospital Dr. Nélio Mendonça,
    tel. 291 705 666 or 291 705 641
Hospital S. João de Deus,
    tel. 291 741 036 or 291 741 037
Hospital dos Marmeleiros, Monte,
    tel. 291 705 730
Hospital Dr. João de Almada, Monte,
    tel. 291 780 300

Clinica da Sé, tel. 291 207 678,
    address Rua dos Murças 42
Clinica de Santa Catarina,
    tel. 291 741 127,
    address Rua 5 de Outubro 115
Clinica Santa Luzia, tel. 291 200 000,
    address Rua da Torrinha 5
Madeira Medical Center,
    tel. 291 003 300,
    address Rua do Hospital Velho 23

Health care centers in other cities:
Calheta: Centro Clinico da Calheta,
    tel. 291 822 244
Camacha: Centro de Sáude,
    tel. 291 922 316
Câmara de Lobos: Centro de Sáude,
    tel. 291 910 380
Caniço: Policlinica do Caniço,
    tel. 291 934 504
Machico: Policlinica de Machico,
    tel. 291 969 130
Madalena do Mar: Centro de Sáude,
    tel. 291 972 271
Ponta Delgada: Centro de Sáude,
    tel. 291 860 000
Ponta do Pargo: Centro de Sáude,
    tel. 291 880 000
Ponta do Sol: Cento Clinico da Ponta
    do Sol, tel. 291 972 297
Porto da Cruz, Centro de Sáude,
    tel. 291 563 258
Porto Moniz: Centro de Sáude,
    tel. 291 850 170
Ribeira Brava: Cento Medico da Ribeira
    Brava, tel. 291 950 200
Santa Cruz: Policlinica de Santa Cruz,
    tel. 291 524 103
Santana: Policlinica de Santana,
    tel. 291 570 300
Seixal: Centro de Sáude,
    tel. 291 850 240
Porto Santo: Centro de Sáude, tel. 291
    980 060

Emergency numbers

In urgent cases, general emergency number is 112, otherwise 291 700 112, which is manned by an English language skilled person. To emergency numbers you can call free of charge, as well as landline and mobile phones.

Other important phone numbers:
- ▶ Hospital (hospital) 291 705 600
- ▶ Police (polícia) 291 208 400
- ▶ Fire brigade (bombeiros) 291 222 122
- ▶ Airport (Aeroporto) 291520 700
- ▶ Highway assistance (assistência) 800 290 290
- ▶ Rescue services at sea (socorro no mar) 291 230 112
- ▶ Red Cross (Cruz Vermelha) 291 741 115
- ▶ Phone operator (local) 118
- ▶ Phone operator (international) 177

▶ **Oleanders (Rose Bay) along the way in Avenida do Mar**

Sun and sun protection

The sun shines strongly throughout the year in Madeira and light skin burns easily. It is recommended to use sun protection which protects for both UVB and UVA radiation. The sun lotion's number indicates what protection the lotion gives against UVB radiation. In Madeira it is wise to use lotion which has protection number 15 or preferably 30 and over. The European Environment Agency's Web site you can get up-to-date information on ozone layers in Europe (www.EEA.Europa.eu/maps/means/map).

Insect bites

Mosquitoes and other insects which bite are generally only in mid-summer. In Madeira there are no snakes or other poisonous animals.

Insurances

EU citizens will not necessarily need a separate health insurance, because the European Health Insurance Card in most cases is sufficient for normal injury and disease care. But it only covers medical care from a local doctor or hospital, but not, for example, private doctors, flight returns to home or hotel expenses when continuing stay in case of illness. Travel insurance is a good thing when travelling abroad, because it, in most cases, covers above mentioned additional costs and ambulances etc. The European Health Insurance Card is free of charge to all European citizens and you can order it from your local health care authority. All European Union citizens have the right to the same health care services as citizens of that country. Nevertheless, every country has its own rules for public health-care level. It's a good idea to clarify in advance the terms of European Health Insurance Card and Travel Insurance when spending more time abroad.

For more information about health care and travel insurance abroad contact your own country's authorities in mentioned areas.

Drinking water and tap water

You can drink tap water although often local people buy their water from a store. The tap water is fresh and clean, but the pipes and tubes in old houses are not necessarily so. Water is available to buy all over and the prices vary considerably. Water is cheapest in supermarkets and grocery stores and most expensive in the so-called tourist shops, wine stores and restaurants. Effervescent (sparkling) water with gas is 'agua com gas' and spring water 'agua sem gas'. For preparation of food and coffee the tap water is safe.

DID YOU KNOW...

In Madeira there are no snakes or other poisonous animals.

▶ **Beautifully tile decorated water source**

Telephone

When you make a call from Madeira and Portugal via landline abroad, e.g. a call from hotel room to Finland, foreign area code is 00 + country code (e.g. Finland 358) and phone number, including the area code. When you make a call with a cell phone it is sufficient to mark + country code and phone number, including the area code. When you make a call to Portugal or Madeira from abroad Portugal's foreign area code is 351.

If you call on your mobile phone in Madeira to local numbers you do not need the area code. It is sufficient that you select Madeira's and Porto Santo's area code 291 or mobile phone's area code, for example 91 or 96 etc. and then telephone number. If you call from telephone booth or from a hotel this is so-called a local call, only a phone number without the area code is enough.

Phone operator/directory enquiries: local phone numbers 118 and international numbers 177.

Most answering machines on phones work so that you call to your own phone answering number and when you hear your own message you stop it by pressing #. Then you hear a request to dial your password and when you enter it, it works like the answering machine in your country. Best answering machine works when already at home you check out answering machine's phone number and save it your mobile phone memory. Automatic call forwarding to voicemail does not usually work abroad.

Madeira still has telephone booths in towns and cities and more often than not they are operated with phone cards (credifone), which can be purchased from some news stands and cafés. Also post offices lets you make calls for a fee.

▶ **Madeira still has some telephone booths.**

If you are staying for a longer period of time in Portugal or Madeira, it is advisable to purchase a local pre-paid phone number, then making a call to local numbers is cheaper than for example from other European phones. These pre-paid numbers you can purchase from any phone operator, e.g. Vodafone, Meo etc. Pre-paid numbers does not cost anything, but you have to charge it from time to time with the operator's actual fees. Pre-paid number will expire in six months unless it is not kept active. If you want to keep the same phone number every time you visit Madeira, it is worth calling within half a year to this Portuguese number from another number so the number remains active again the following half year period.

Internet cafés and at internet kiosks you can also make internet phone calls (Skype etc.) with rental computers. The computer rental is about 2 €/hour. In Funchal most shopping malls and centers as well as in some coffee shops and restaurants you can use free wireless (WIFI) connections with your own laptop or smart phone.

A few foreign country dialing codes: Finland 358, Sweden 46, Denmark 45, Norway 47, Belgium 32, Spain 34, Netherlands 31, Ireland 353, UK 44, Italy 39, Austria 43, Canada 1, Greece 30, Portugal 351, France 33, Germany 49, Switzerland 41, Hungary 36, Russia 7, USA 1.

From a phonebook's yellow pages (páginas amarelas) or their net pages (www.pai.pt) you can find information on companies and services that are available to you.

▶ **If staying for a longer period of time in Madeira, it is advisable to purchase a pre-paid phone number.**

Internet connections

Most hotels have both wireless and wired internet connections for their customers. Many hotel lobbies also have wireless connections for your own laptop and you get your password from the reception. Some hotels charge per hour for using internet but the fee is dependent on the hotel.

In Funchal most shopping malls and centers as well as in some coffee shops and restaurants you can use free wireless (WIFI) connections with your

▶ **In the city center there is a free internet (WIFI)**

own laptop or smart phone. Internet cafés and at internet kiosks you can rent computers for a small fee, usually about two Euros per hour. Often there you can also make prints and photocopies. In these internet cafés and kiosks you can also make internet phone calls (Skype etc.).

Photocopies and prints

Most internet cafes and kiosks makes prints and photocopies and also from Copia Universal, Centro de Copias store, address R. Netos 64. This store prints very well, from small slips to big posters. But also, in some hotels you can make prints and photocopies.

Post offices and stamps

There are post offices (CCT or correios) in every large city or town. In Funchal there are several; the head post office on Avenida do Zarco, next to Bank of Portugal, the second one behind of the Market place and the third one on Avenida Calouste Gulbenkian 3, just opposite the La Vie shopping mall. In the hotel area in the Lido there is also a post office, address Estrada Monumental 318. Post offices are open from Monday to Friday from 8.30 am to 8 pm and Saturdays from 9 am to 12.30 pm. Lido's post office is closed on Saturdays.

Poste restante services are in all mentioned post office counter services. If you want mail to be sent to you, there must be in addition your name also mentioned 'Poste restante'

▶ There are three post offices in Funchal city and one in Lido area.

▶ Red mailboxes are easily identified.

▶ You can also buy stamps from machines.

and a post office address, for example, the EC Calouste Gulbekian, 9000-998 Funchal or EC Zarco, 9000-999 Funchal or EC Mercado (Funchal), 9060-999 Funchal.

Stamps (selo) you can buy from most cards merchants, newspaper stands, post offices, stamp machines and from most supermarkets. Postal charges, e.g. , postcards (postal) and the letters (carta) to Europe are 0,72 € (spring 2015). Mailboxes are usually red and it says 'correio' or 'correio normal' on it. Sometimes side-by-side there are two mailboxes, one of which is blue, displays with 'correio azul'. It is for

express and letters to abroad. Sometimes side-by-side is also two red mailboxes, and the other displays 'correio international'. It is for mail abroad and the second 'correio local', which is for mail sent to Madeira.

In 1868 Portugal published Madeira's own postage stamp, i.e. Portuguese postage stamp which was printed over word 'Madeira'. This was a practice that continued until 1928 when Madeira's very own postage stamp series was released. Since 1980 postage stamps reads both Portugal and Madeira and they are also valid in continent Portugal.

Banks and money

Madeira and the Portuguese currency is the Euro (100 cents) as in many European countries. Previous currency, the escudo (100 centavos) changed to euros at 1.1.2002.

Banks are open from Monday to Friday from 8.30 am to 3 pm, and closed at weekends and on public holidays. Foreign exchange offices are open from Monday to Friday from 9 am to 1 pm and again from 2 pm to 7 pm and on Saturdays from 9 am to 7 pm. Western Union's small office is located next to the Sé Cathedral. From there you can exchange, send and receive remittances if you do not have a local bank account.

MB Multibanco bank cash machines are plentiful, and they provide cash on general credit and debit cards. When you enter foreign cards in the machine, it usually goes directly into language selection menu. Select your language, e.g. English and confirm your language selection pressing the green continuar-button. Next the machine asks you to enter your password. Although space is for six digits password, it is enough to you enter for example four, which is most common in Europe. Do not add zeros if your password is shorter than most. Press again the green continuar-button to confirm your password. If you selected English, then press the withdrawal button, enter the amount, and press again continuar-button. Wait until the machine pushes your card out, remove the card, and the money with your receipt. Receipt does not show your account balance when money taken out abroad.

If your credit card is lost, report it immediately to your card holder company or to your own bank. With this in mind, it is recommended that you keep a bank or card holder company's phone number and the card's pin number other than in your wallet.

If you live in Madeira a longer period of time and you need to pay for local electricity, water, gas, etc. bills, you can pay them all in one place at 'Loja do Cicadão' in La Vie shopping center or at Avenida Arriaga 42 A. If you have an account in a Portuguese bank, you can pay your bills from your account at the bank or through the internet. For example, Banif is a Madeiran bank which has branches also in continental Portugal. Also you can pay your bills through Multibanco bank cash machines when there is a sign 'Caixa automatico'.

▶ **There are many bank cash machines around the island.**

▶ Madeira produces electricity by using water from mountains.

Electricity

Voltage is 220V and plug similar to a double-pole like most countries in Europe.

Madeira produces electricity for their own use by utilizing the mountain water for power plants. There are also many wind-energy mills mainly in the Pául da Serra area. In addition, solar panels have increased both for private and public use. Caniçal has one of the biggest solar panel power plants on the island.

Opening hours

Stores are open from Monday to Friday from 9 am to 7 pm and often small stores in the centrum closes their door also for lunchtime from 1 pm to 3 pm. On Saturdays stores are open from 9 am to 1 pm, and are closed on Sundays.

Shopping centers and larger grocery stores are open from 10 am to 10 pm or 11 pm seven days a week. By Christmastime in November and December, stores are open until midnight.

Market hall is open weekdays from 7 am to 7 pm and on Saturdays from 7 am to 2 pm.

Banks are open from Monday to Friday from 8.30 am to 3 pm, and money exchange offices daily at 9 am to 1 pm and again from 2 pm to 7 pm.

Post offices are open from Monday to Friday from 8.30 am to 8 pm and Saturdays from 9 am to 12.30 p.m.

Pharmacies are open from Monday to Friday from 9 am to 1 pm and again from 3 pm to 7 pm and on Saturdays from 9 am to 12.30 pm. Pharmacies on duty or open 24 h, information can be found on pharmacies doors or windows or from daily newspapers.

Museums and other sights opening hours vary and for example, many museums are closed at lunchtime from 1 pm to 3 pm. Check opening hours from tourist offices or see more information from section 'Museums'.

▶ Small Proteas and Petunias in flowerbed

Discounts

Students and pensioners receive discounts for entry fees by showing students or pensioners card. Children often have access to in for half price or free of charge.

Tips and service charges

Tips are recommended but not mandatory. In restaurants service and taxes are included in the invoice, but if service has been good, it is usual to round the sum upwards, if excellent, you can add 5 to 10 % or more. In bars and pubs it is sufficient to round it upwards. In some restaurants they will charge the so-called ready-laid fee covering e.g. bread and other starters they bring to the table.

For taxi drivers, hairdressers, barbers etc. add about 5 to 10 %. Carriers, porters, bus drivers (on organised trips) and guides 1 €, cleaning ladies 3 to 5 € /week.

Handicapped

It is not easy to move in Madeira's bumpy and steep streets and slopes. In addition locals park their cars carelessly on pavements making walking even without a handicap difficult. In some shopping malls and museums and at some sights they have recognized the handicapped by installing ramps and lifts. Handicaps have been taken into account in most good planned hotels by installing ramps in lobbies and entrances, but most hotel rooms have been ignored.

Laundry and repairs

Hotels have usually their own laundry service which may be expensive. You can find laundries (lavandaria) in almost every shopping center and they wash items either individually (shirts, trousers, jackets, etc.) or by the kilo which is more affordable. Delivery is quick and the prices are reasonable. There is only one laundromat in Nazare part of the town.

Sewing service and minor repairs for clothing is carried out in most laundries. In addition, in some shopping centers, including La Vie, you may find small kiosks (Amarca costuramos), which makes small and larger repairs either while you wait or in a few hours.

Toilets

Lavatories (toilete, lavabo) are marked with signs 'senhoras' or 'damas' (women) and 'senhores' or 'homens' (men). Each other very similar names, so watch carefully not to mix them up. Some lavatories are only marked with simple letters and symbols. In coffee shops and restaurants toilet doors often do not have locks, so Madeirans leave the door in the half-open position when the booth is vacant and if the door is closed it means it is occupied. Usually wash-basins are common for men and women.

▶ **The Stiff Bottlebrush blooms from February to July**

▶ A great Kapok Tree (Floss Silk Tree) in Santa Catarina Park

Safety and police

Madeira is a very safe destination and it is extremely rare that tourists are involved with crime. However it is a good idea to be careful and leave your valuable goods at the hotel's safe. Also, do not leave your belongings unattended in cafés or swimming pool areas and beware of pickpockets in crowded streets, during festivals etc. events. At night when walking alone you should avoid the old city's dark and narrow alleyways. Do not leave anything on display in your rental vehicle or any important papers in the glove box.

If you are involved in a crime, call 112, or 291 700 112, where there is also English spoken. The general alarm number is 112 and it is only intended for emergencies as police, fire brigade and ambulance. Contact the main police station (Polícia) on Rua Dr. João de Deus 6, tel. 291 222 022, file a report and ask for written proof for your insurance company. If your passport is stolen or goes missing contact your consulate or embassy and then also police. Lost or stolen credit card you should void immediately with your bank.

On Funchal streets there are many police officers and they are friendly and helpful. Some of them wear a red armband using a T-sign. This means that the policeman speaks at least English, possibly also French or German.

Lost and found

If you lose or mislay your valuables, Lost property office's address is Polícia de Perdidas & Achados, Rua da Infáncia 28, tel. 291 222 022.

▶ **Podranea (Ricasol Podranea) is blooming in Santa Cruz**

Tourist offices

Madeira's tourist offices (www.visitmadeira.pt), can be found in major cities of the island and they are happy to provide information about attractions, topical events, bus time tables, maps, and brochures etc. Tourist offices publish monthly forthcoming events calendar (Cultural Agenda) about exhibitions, theatres and other events. Furthermore, there are separate programs for Carnivals, Flower festivals etc. and Christmas season events. There you can also buy tickets in advance for some of cultural events. Also from hotel receptions you can get information and brochures, maps and in some hotels they can order tickets also for different events.

▶ **The tourist office is clearly indicated with i-sign.**

Funchal's tourist office, Avenida Arriaga 16, tel. 291 211 902. Open from Monday to Friday from 9 am to 8 pm and on the weekends from 9 am to 3.30 pm.

Monumental Lido's tourist office, Shopping Center Monumental Lido, Estrada Monumental 284, tel. 291 775 254. Open from Monday to Friday from 9 am to 3.30 pm.

Pontinha's tourist office, Molhe da Pontinha, Funchal port, tel. 291 281 743. Open only when cruise ships are in port, between 8 am to 11 am.

Airport's tourist office, tel. 291 524 933. Open every day from 9 am to 9.30 pm.

Porto Moniz' tourist office, Porto Moniz Village, tel. 291 853 075. Open from Monday to Friday from 10 am to 4 pm, Saturdays from 10 am to 12.30 pm.

Ribeira Brava's tourist office, Forte de São Bento, tel. 291 951 675. Open from Monday to Friday from 9 am to 4 pm, Saturdays from 10 am to 12.30 pm.

Santana's tourist office, Sítio do Serrado, tel. 291 575 162. Open Mondays from 2 pm to 4.30 pm, from Tuesday to Friday from 9.30 am to 4 pm and Saturdays from 9 am to 1 pm.

Porto Santo's tourist office, Avenida Dr. Manue Gregório Pestana Junior, tel. 291 985 244. Open from Monday to Friday from 9 am to 5.30 pm, Saturdays from 10 am to 12.30 pm.

▶ From Madeira you can also find exotic places such as this in the Monte Palace Tropical Garden

▶ Tourist office on Avenida Arriaga

Animals

In Madeira there are no snakes or other poisonous animals. In addition to the domestic animals and birds there are wild animals like rabbits and lizards. As much you can see lizards on walls or stone fences, they are timid and are fleeing quickly after even the slightest movement. Variation in size of lizards from tiny to approximately 20 centimetres long and colour green brown or grey to black. Farmers feelings about lizards are varying; on the one hand, it is good that they keep pests in control, but, on the other hand, they can eat all soft fruits.

There are approx. 200 different kind of species of bird in Madeira and some of them nesting here are very rare, e.g. Madeiran Petrel and Long Toed Pigeon. On the Desertas islands there is a rare and endangered monk seal of which there were only eight individuals when protection program started, but now population has grown to 40. There are about 100 different species of fish in the sea which are edible. Dolphins and whales there are about 30 species in Madeira waters. There are also some bats. And the frog's croak can be heard especially in the spring.

Few years ago there were many stray dogs and cats. Now at least in Funchal the number of them has declined. Most dogs who are loose in cities are not actually strays. They usually are healthy-looking and most of them wear collars. They are somebody's pets whose owners will let them wander at daytime and at nights they go back to

▶ **Lizards are rapid and timid.**

▶ There are lots of stray cats in Jardim Panoramico Park in Lido-Ajuda area.

▶ All loose dogs are not strays.

their homes. While driving it is wise to keep a watch out for them even though they quite well can ignore cars and traffic.

You can see lots of loose cats and not everyone of them are strays. But in Jardim Panoramico Park in Lido-Ajuda area there are dozens of stray cats which are timid but friendly. Most of these cats are neutered. Staff of near restaurants and many tourists are feeding them and they are fairly healthy-looking.

There are no actual zoos in Madeira, but you can see animals for example; Birds in the park of Presidencial Palace and in Botanical Gardens (Jardim Botanico da Madeira) Bird park (Jardim dos Loiros), where there are lots of colourful birds. In Santo da Serra, outside of Funchal, there is a park where you can find red deer, birds etc. and in Prazeres there is the Quinta

Pedagógica where you can find lamas, emus, pigs, turtles etc. Also in Porto Moniz there is Madeira Aquarium (Aquário da Madeira), with 11 water tanks showing the whole of Madeira's underwater species.

When bringing pet animals to Madeira, see more information from section 'Travelling with pets'.

Ticket office

An actual ticket office does not exist on this island, but from the Tourist office you can purchase tickets in advance to a number of cultural events. City theatre (Teatro Municipal Baltazar Dias) cashiers sell tickets for a variety of events and in some hotels they serve their customers by organising tickets for various events. Otherwise tickets can be purchased at the event doors.

▶ **Wine and spirits are sold in wine stores, but also in all supermarkets.**

Alcohol policy, alcoholic beverages and liquer stores

In Madeira alcohol policy is open and spirits, wine and beer can be bought from wine stores, but also from ordinary supermarkets. Supply is plentiful and all ordinary international brands, but in addition also they have their own alcohol products such as wines, brandies and all kind of liqueurs. During various festivals there are lots of booths and kiosks selling alcoholic beverages, beer and home-made wines.

Madeiran liqueur drinks are for example; Poncha, which is sugarcane spirit flavoured with lemon and honey. Local sugarcane spirit (aquardente)

made of sugar cane. Liqueurs lovers can find many local specialities including produced from passion fruit (maracúja), bananas (banana), annona (anona), chestnut (castanha) and cherry (ginja) liqueurs.

In addition to Madeira wine (see more information from section Madeira wine) they produce also local red wine (vinho tinto), white wine (vinho branco) and rosé wine (vinho rosado). Beers (cerveja) from Madeira are the bands Coral and Super Bock. Also beverages (brisa or sumo) are manufactured on the island for example Brisa-drinks are Madeiran.

Although alcohol policy is open you rarely see public drunkenness in Madeira.

Sales taxes and VAT

VAT or sales tax is 23% in Portugal and Madeira. VAT for food is 6 %.

Timeshare and club memberships

The biggest hotel chains such as Pestana offer for tourists the possibility of buying timeshare or club memberships during presentations. If you want to spend few hours of your holiday by having this presentation, you are rewarded by lower-cost or completely free tickets for island tours, boat cruise or a dinnershow at the Casino. This timeshare selling in Madeira is safe and the companies behind it are big and highly successful.

Buying timeshare is completely voluntary and does not require sales to get a gift. Trading observes EU legislation.

▶ Information centers are not official Tourist offices.

Information centers

Are not to be confused with the official Tourist offices these information centers which most hotels' timeshare and club membership sellers have in hotel areas or in the harbour. They are not tourist offices but selling low-cost island tours and boat cruises which usually are associated with a few hours presentation in a near-by hotel or resort.

▶ River-bed covered with Bougainvillea (Paper Flower)

Recycling and ecology

Madeira recycles effectively. The island has it's own waste incineration plant and what cannot be burned or recycled will be transported to continental Portugal to be destroyed.

Nearly in all hotels you can find bins which will specify glass, plastic, paper and carton and mixed household waste. Also shopping centers and fastfood restaurants recycle effectively and recycle bins can be found also in plenty of side streets. Symbols on the side of containers are easy, but glass is vidro, plastic is plástico and paper is papel.

▶ **Chalice Vine, Cup of Gold, Trumpet Flower, this plant has many names**

Here are few tips which show the way a traveller can also save energy and reduce emissions:

▶ Europe's eco-label 'flower' will guide you through to find more eco-friendly non-durable goods.

▶ Flower can be used to find environmentally friendly hotel. Flower indicates that accommodation provider has reduced energy and water consumption and quantity and volume of the waste and uses renewable energy sources.

▶ Use bottled water sparingly. Bottled water production and marketing takes energy, and plastic bottles do not always end up in recycling.

▶ Always take a shower rather than a bath – a bath can consume many times more energy compared to shower.

▶ Do not switch on lights when they are not required.

▶ Turn off the TV and other electrical equipments when not in use.

▶ Remove the mobile phone charger once you have charged your phone because the charger uses electricity even if your phone is not connected to it.

▶ Do not leave the tap running when you are cleaning your teeth.

▶ Before you go on your travels remove plugs on your TV and other electrical equipments even at home.

▶ If your home remains empty turn thermostats down to spare energy.

▶ Pride of Madeira is blooming from January to July.

GETTING AROUND
ON MADEIRA ▶ ▶ ▶ ▶ ▶ ▶ ▶

Airport

Madeira has two airports, the first one in Funchal on Madeira island and the second one on Porto Santo island in Vila Baleira. Funchal international airport (Aeroporto da Madeira) is famous for it's special runway which extends out over the sea. In the beginning it was a short runway, only 1600 m, but in the year 2000 runway was extended to 2800 m, so now large big jumbo jets can also land easily. The extension of this runway was built on top of huge concrete pillars and a motorway passes below. At the same time a new airport terminal was built and from the roof terrace you can watch planes arriving and departing. Madeira international airport is very vulnerable to winds and when heavy storms occur arriving flights sometimes are diverted to nearby Porto Santo Airport. Outgoing flights accordingly are delayed until the weather improves. Madeira airport is very safe and fulfils all international safety criteria.

Scheduled flights to Funchal are mainly coming from Lisbon, but charter flights are coming from all the biggest European cities and from Brazil and Venezuela. About 10 flights per day are departing from Funchal to Lisbon; morning, afternoon and evening (flight duration approx. 1,5 hours) and to Porto in continent Portugal one flight per day. Few flights a day are departing to London and few flights per week across all over Europe. Few flights also to Azores (duration 2 hours) and to the Canary Islands (duration about 1 hour) in a week. To Porto Santo there are three flights a day; morning, afternoon and evening (duration 15 minutes).

Tap Air Portugal is the national airline, address Avenida das Comunidades Madeirenses 10, Funchal, tel. 291 239 210 or 291 239 232. Other Portuguese airlines are Portugal and Sata. Funchal airport phone number 291 520 700 and Porto Santo 291 980 120. Also timetable inquiries from net www.anam.pt.

Distance from airport to Funchal is approx. 22 km and takes by coach or bus approx. 50 min. and by taxi or a car about 30 min. Taxis have fixed prices from airport to hotels which in spring 2015 it was about 30 € on weekdays.

Buses (Aerobus) from airport to Funchal center leaves at 9.15 am, 9.45 am, 10.30 am, 11.30 am, 12.00 am, 1 pm, 2.30 pm, 3.30 pm, 4 pm, 5.15 pm, 6.15 pm, 8 pm and 9.30 pm. From Funchal to airport buses leave at 8.00 am, 9.00 am, 9.45 am, 10.30 am, 11.15 am, 12.15 am, 12.45 pm, 1.45 pm, 3.15 pm, 4.15 pm, 5 pm, 7 pm and 8.45 pm. Schedules are subject to change, so be sure to check out times from timetables at the bus stops. A oneway ticket is 5 € per person and a return ticket 7,50 €.

▶ **Funchal international airport is famous for it's runway.**

▶ Cruise ships come to Funchal port every day.

Cruising and boat trips

Transportation and travel between the two islands, Madeira and Porto Santo, is by air or by the ferry. From Funchal port Porto Santo Line's ferry (MS Lobo Marinho) departs to Porto Santo every morning at 8.00 am and returns at around 8 pm. The ferry does not operate on Tuesdays, but on Fridays it makes night cruises to Porto Santo. Duration of the trip is approx. 2 hours 40 minutes. It holds 1153 passengers and there are restaurant, bar, shops etc. onboard the ferry. Tickets can be bought in advance either from travel agency or Porto Santo Line's office located in cruising terminal in Funchal port or the other office on Avenida do Mar, tel. 291 210 300.

There is no connecting ferry from Madeira to the Azores other than cruise ships which sometimes take passengers on board from Funchal. These cruise ships sometimes call at the Azores, although, generally they sail in the direction of the Canary Islands.

Madeira is a popular destination for cruise ships. Almost 400 cruise ships come to Funchal port every year from the Mediterranean, the Caribbean and north of Europe. Cruise ships usually arrive in port in the mornings and depart towards the evening. Sometimes at the port you can pick up several cruise ships at same time.

Many companies organize day trips every day from Funchal's luxury yacht marina to cruise the coast line of Madeira in either catamarans, motor boats or sailing boats. Exceptionally the Santa Maria boat leaves from the cruise ship marina. There are cruise trips from a few hours to all day cruises. Also all fishing trips leave from the luxury yacht marina. Tickets can be purchased from ticket offices at the luxury yacht marina, hotels or from tourist offices.

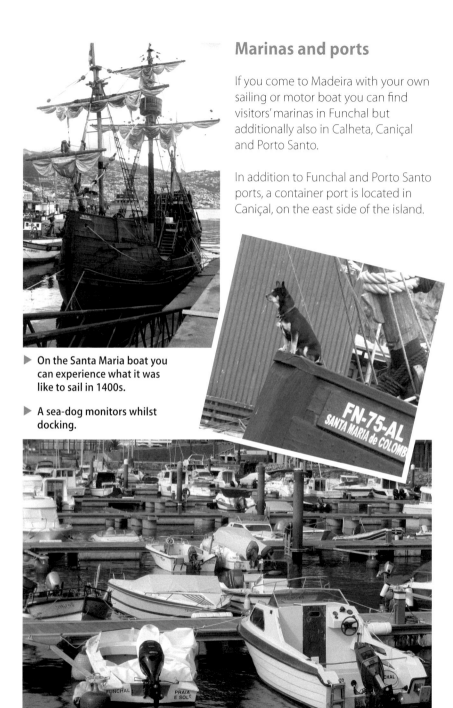

Marinas and ports

If you come to Madeira with your own sailing or motor boat you can find visitors' marinas in Funchal but additionally also in Calheta, Caniçal and Porto Santo.

In addition to Funchal and Porto Santo ports, a container port is located in Caniçal, on the east side of the island.

▶ On the Santa Maria boat you can experience what it was like to sail in 1400s.

▶ A sea-dog monitors whilst docking.

▶ You can find other visitors' marinas outside of Funchal.

Bus transportation

Along with joining the European Union, driving in these islands has nowadays become easy due to motorways and tunnels which have been constructed also public transport is extremely comprehensive. The first motorway was completed in 1997 and now between almost every larger city or town motorways and tunnels have been built through mountains. Madeirans say that Madeira is like a Swiss cheese, because there are so many tunnels.

These local public buses in Funchal are orange yellow, bus stops are clearly marked with a yellow Giro-sign and on

▶ **Bus stops are clearly labelled.**

the other side of most of those Giro-signs there is an electric timetable which shows the waiting times of buses. One-way ticket price is 1,95 € (spring 2015) and it can be bought

▶ **Local buses in Funchal are a bright yellow.**

▶ Tickets can be purchased from the bus driver, kiosks or from automats.

▶ You can get on and off free of charge by electric minibus in city centrum.

from the bus driver. That same ticket you can download the next day at post offices, in most news-stands with red 'P'-sign and from automats on Avenida do Mar. With this downloaded tickets the fare is only 1,25 € and all the tickets are personal, i.e. with one ticket you can pay only for one person's journey. You can buy these downloaded tickets also in advance and then the price of the ticket is 0,50 € + the price of journeys.

Almost all the buses stop on Avenida do Mar (the main promenade). For tourists there is the possibility to buy a one day, two day or 7 day ticket which during this time you can use buses as often as you like. Bus timetables and road maps you can get either from Horários do Funchal's (bus company) office or from timetables in bus stops.

In Funchal center there runs a yellow Horários do Funchal's electric minibus, which operates between Avenida do Infante, Anadia Shopping Center as well as other parts in the city area. You can stop the bus by waving and get on and off at any time during the

route. There is also a wheelchair ramp on the bus. At the moment use of this bus is free of charge.

Rural buses have other colours depending on where they go to on the island. As a general rule, red-white Rodoeste buses pass through Central and Western parts of the island and the green-white SAM's buses Eastern parts of the island. Almost all these rural buses stop at Avenida do Mar i.e. the promenade. This bus traffic to the countryside is very well organized and covers all the smallest villages and towns in the island. Rural bus stops (paragem) are in Funchal often side by side with Giro-bus stops and in rural areas these are marked by white paragem-signs. Prepare for the fact that the buses are slow and on the map short distance can take a long time because roads are mountainous and winding and buses will stop at almost all bus stops. Tickets can be purchased directly from bus driver. If your party consists of three or more than three passengers, it would be cheaper to drive by taxi than to take a bus.

Cars and car rental

There are several car rental firms, including international companies, and locals like Atlantic rent a car etc. You can rent car either directly from the company or order it through a hotel reception or your travel agency. Remember you need a valid driving licence. The driver must be at least 21 years old (and less than 75 years old) and must have held a driving license valid at least for one year. In addition you need to be a confident driver because many roads in Madeira can be twisty and narrow and Madeirans drive quite fast.

If the idea of driving a car in these steep mountain roads feels too much, then it's worth it to take a taxi or go with pre-organized bus trips. However, if you are a confident driver you will see many places which the tourist buses cannot reach.

It is worth it to buy a detailed map where the smallest roads are marked. Madeira seems bigger than it is, because roads are complex and steep, so we recommend you allow more time for these trips.

Depending on the size of the car rentals are about 30 euros and upwards. In most cases insurance is included in daily rent, but you may want to check it because it varies with the company. If you need the car for an extended period of time, rental companies will be happy to negotiate for weekly or monthly rentals. Motorcycles, scooters, and mountain bicycles are also for rent. However, most rental companies require you to pay by credit card, otherwise you must pay deposit (approximately 100 €), which you get back when returning the car. If you want to rent the car during public holidays (including

▶ In addition to big international car rentals there are also many local rental companies.

▶ **The road network is in good condition and it covers all four corners of the island.**

Christmas, New Year, Carnival, Easter, Flower festival etc.) it is well worth making a reservation well in advance.

There are no real limousines in Madeira, but the so-called black coloured taxis are newer and perhaps in better shape than some of the older yellow taxis. These black taxis can be rented for island tours and airport transfers etc. They are also more unnoticeable than the general yellow taxis.

Electric cars are on the increase in Madeira and will shortly also be rented. Electric outlets for these electric cars can be found for example at the bus station in marina and also at some parking buildings.

If you bring your own vehicle to the island don't forget to take registration papers and valid motor insurance for the vehicle! The so-called green card is proof of this road insurance and if the green card is not the case, there is every reason to take with you the insurance certificate itself. You may use a vehicle with foreign plates up to a maximum of 6 months without special permit.

It is wise not to leave anything to be seen inside the vehicle, not on rear seats or on the dashboard etc. Also it is not wise to leave wallets, passports and cameras in the glove box. Although it is still safe in Madeira, a small precaution is never a bad thing.

DID YOU KNOW...

Madeirans are polite and allow room for pedestrians.

▶ Mist can surprise you on mountain roads.

About traffic regulations

If you rent a vehicle or are travelling in Madeira in you own car, please note:

▶ speed limit on motorways (rápida, via rápida) is 100 km/h, on main roads 80 km/h and in urban areas 40 or 60 km/h

▶ seat belts are mandatory for both the front and rear seat occupants (including buses and minibuses)

▶ children less than 12 years of age must not be transported in front seat

▶ children must use proper safety seats

▶ mobile phones cannot be used while driving (fine approximately 120 €)

▶ the limit of intoxication is 0,2 promilles (since January 2012)

▶ Madeirans are polite and allow room for pedestrians, so you should too

▶ Madeirans sound their horn before steep turns, so that any oncoming traffic knows there is another vehicle coming

▶ on a narrow road or in a tunnel flashing your headlights means that 'here I come, give way'

▶ while driving it is wise to keep a look out for stray dogs even though they ignore cars and traffic

▶ otherwise traffic regulations are the same as elsewhere in Europe

There are two types of fuel (gasolina), lead-free (sem chumbo) and super and also diesel (gasoleo). In most cities and towns they have gas/petrol stations which are generally open from 8 am to 8 pm. Avenida do Infante's GALP station is open 24 hours a day. Most petrol stations accept credit cards.

▶ Avenida do Infante's gas station is open 24 h.

Parking spaces are marked with either white or blue lines. When parking in blue space you have to pay a parking fee to the nearby machine from Monday to Friday from 8 am to 8 pm and Saturdays between 8 am to 2 pm, at other times ticket is not required. White spaces are free of charge and white spaces marked with 'M' are intended for local residents. Absence of parking spaces or just for laziness Madeirans park their cars carelessly on pavements and at bus stops. It is not recommended for tourists to try this with their rental car, because sometimes vehicles are towed away and the penalty can be large.

There are two types of parking fines: given out by the parking attendant a small fine (approx. 3–4 €) which should be paid immediately. If it is not paid, the fine is raised to about 30 €. A parking fine issued by police will be higher (approx. 30 €) and should be paid to a police station. Police officers also have the right to collect fees on the spot if they catch you red-handed.

In recent times, the police forces in Madeira have introduced speed radars and in particular use them in Ajuda and Piornais areas. The limit of intoxication is 0,2 promilles, and although the police rarely test you in Madeira, it is no good to drive under the influence of alcohol because the fine it is large (i.e. a minimum of 500 €).

DID YOU KNOW...

Police officers who wear a red arm-band using a T-sign, speak at least English, possibly also French or German.

General road assistance (Assistância) phone number is 0800 290 290. If your rental vehicle breaks down, however, first contact your rental company. The phone number is usually mentioned in the rental documents.

Taxi

There are many taxis in Madeira (approx. 1000), of which about 500 are in Funchal. Taxi stands are in many places around the city and you can also stop the taxi by waving. Taxi driving is very cheap compared to many capitals in Europe. The taximeter must be on always when driving in an urban area, but for longer island tours etc. you can negotiate the fee either per hours or per day. To and from airport taxis have fixed prices. In spring 2015 it was to central hotels approx. 30 €. At weekends and at night (at 10 pm to 7 am) the fee is about 20 % higher. You can also call taxi in advance from phone number 291 764 476. Official taxis are yellow.

Madeira has also a few black taxis, which are official even if they are missing taxi signs on the roof. These taxis are low profile and the appropriate for limousine or private transportation. They also make island tours and transfers to the airport.

▶ **Taxi minivan takes 2–8 passenger.**

▶ **Taxis are a bright yellow and there are many of them.**

BEFORE TRAVELLING ▶ ▶ ▶ ▶

Good to know before travelling:

▶ Check if you need a visa to Portugal (EU citizens do not need a visa to Portugal or Madeira).

▶ Check the validity of your passport.

▶ Check validity dates of your credit cards.

▶ Take with you a photocopy of your passport, credit cards and other important documents (just in case a passport or credit cards gets lost or stolen).

▶ Also take with you the phone numbers of credit card companies or your bank in case these cards are lost, so that you can contact them.

▶ Take Travel insurance coverage.

▶ Keep your papers and other valuable assets in a safe place.

▶ Check what vaccinations you need (Portugal do not require special vaccination, but it's good to have in effect a tetanus vaccination when travelling).

▶ Take with you all the medicines and prescriptions you need during your travels and place them in your cabin baggage, so you are not left without if your luggages will be lost.

▶ If your journey will be for a long time, cancel your newspapers and turn off your mail.

▶ If you are away for a long time, ask someone to empty your mailbox so that it does not come to the attention of thieves.

▶ If you live in a house make sure in summer that someone cuts your grass and in the winter, shovels the snow, so that the house does not look empty.

▶ Arrange your pet care and flowers irrigation.

▶ Lock all doors and windows carefully before travelling.

▶ Do not leave on your phone any message that you are travelling.

▶ Remove plugs from your TV and other electrical equipment.

▶ Do not leave bicycles etc. out to attract thieves.

▶ If your home remains empty, turn the thermostats down to spare energy.

▶ Take your garbage out.

It is recommended that you weigh your luggages before you go to the airport, so that there are no surprises, since most of the airlines and charters flights only allow you to take baggage of 20 to 24 kg/person. On most charter flights you can take only one piece of luggage per passenger and the passenger baggage weight, size and number is limited. Check with your travel agency or airline how much luggage you can take to your flight.

Important checklist of items to take with you

▶ Passport
▶ Tickets
▶ Debit and credit cards
▶ Insurance certificate
▶ Medicines and prescriptions
▶ Spectacles
▶ Sunglasses and sun lotions
▶ Maps and guide books
▶ Address Book
▶ Dictionary
▶ Camera and binoculars
▶ Sewing kit
▶ Shoe polish etc.
▶ Personal supplies and clothing

It is worth taking with you to Madeira, a good pair of shoes which you will need when you are walking along levadas or rough streets and alleys of Funchal. You need for protection from the sun, a hat or scarves, sunscreen lotion, and if it rains, an umbrella. It is also a good idea to take some warm

▶ Check with your travel agency or airline how much luggage you can take on your flight.

clothing, because the weather varies, especially on mountains or, in particular, winter time. In some of the best hotels and restaurants a dress code is still applied but more often just clean and neat clothing is enough. In the Casino's cabaret and dinner restaurant, shorts or jeans are often not permitted.

▶ Kapok Tree (Floss Silk Tree) with sensitive red flowers.

ARRIVING IN PORTUGAL AND MADEIRA ▶ ▶ ▶ ▶ ▶ ▶ ▶

European Union Citizens

EU citizens do not need a visa for Portugal and Madeira. From Schengen countries new arrivals will not necessarily need a passport, your official national identity card with a photo is sufficient. Note: a driving licence is not valid as an identity card! While travelling abroad it is always a good idea to have a valid passport. Transactions with banks, hotels, offices etc. are considerably easier. All under age children must have their own a passport or identity card.

EU citizens do not need a visa when they come to Portugal or to Madeira from countries outside the EU, although citizens of that country may need a visa. Passports are usually not checked when arriving in Portugal or Madeira from Schengen countries. Fights from non Schengen countries, for example, Great Britain, USA, Brazil, etc. passports will be checked at all times.

EU citizens do not require residence, learning or work permits when staying for a longer period of time in Portugal or in Madeira. Notice, however, must be given to the authorities if staying

EU citizens do not need a visa for Portugal and Madeira.

for longer than 6 months. If staying for a longer period of time abroad, it is advisable to declare your stay to your own Ministry of Foreign Affairs or your Consulate or Embassy in Portugal. This is because, for example, in the event of a catastrophe or other events, State department etc. can check on their citizens' safety.

If you are going to work in Madeira or Portugal, you have to obtain a tax card from local tax office. The tax office, to which all notifications should be made, is DRAF (Direcção Regional dos Assuntos Fiscais) and it is located on Avenida Calouste Gulbenkian 3 (opposite the La Vie shopping center). A moving form also must be obtained from the tax office in Madeira, if you are staying more permanently, i.e. for more than 6 months (187 days) at a time.

Non European Citizens

Non-EU citizens need a valid passport when travelling in Europe.

Non-EU nationals who hold a valid Schengen visa, do not need additional visas, when moving inside the Schengen area. Non-EU citizens who wish to extended their residence, study or work in Portugal or Madeira, however, need a residence permit and/or a visa.

If coming to Madeira or Portugal from other than EU countries, in certain cases, there is a need of a visa. Also your passport should be valid for at least 6 months from the day of your arrival in Portugal. Verify with your travel agency or Portuguese Embassy or Consulate in your country exactly what documents are required for your trip before you leave home.

Blue Ginger (Blue-Flowered Bamboo) in bloom.

Customs and excise import and export

EU citizens can shop freely in all the countries of the EU while travelling between EU countries and there are no purchase or import restrictions when goods are for personal use (with the exception of tobacco and alcoholic products).

For personal use from one EU country to another while travelling you may export or import: 800 cigarettes, 200 cigars, 400 small cigars, 1 kg pipe tobacco, 10 litres of concentrated alcohol (more than 22 % volume), 20 litres of liqueurs, 90 litres wines (including a maximum of 60 litres which can be sparkling wine) and 110 litres of beer.

For personal use from a non EU country you may import: 200 cigarettes or 50 cigars, 100 small cigars or 250 g pipe tobacco, 1 litre of concentrated alcohol (more than 22 % volume), 2 litres liqueurs or sparkling wines, 4 litres wines and 16 litres of beer.

Persons under 17 years old may not import or export alcoholic beverages and tobacco products.

Portugal and Madeira do not permit the importation of drugs, firearms, ammunition and threatened species of flora or unregistered domestic animals.

Travelling with pets

While travelling with a dog or cat the EU pet pass is needed with the details of the current rabies vaccination. You can get the pet pass from your veterinarian. Your pet must have also the electronic microchip for identification purposes. For more information about travelling with your pet in the EU (www.EC.Europa.eu/food/animal/liveanimals/pets) and www.gov.uk/take-pet-abroad).

▶ Pets need their own passport when travelling abroad.

▶ Dogs that cats both need a microchip.

Fuchsia with lavish flowers

Colourful Bougainvillea (Paper Flower) blooms almost throughout the year.

LIVING ▶ ▶ ▶ ▶ ▶ ▶ ▶ ▶ ▶ ▶ ▶

Hotels and staying overnight

You can find hotels that suit every wallet, from Reid's Palace to tent accommodation and from your own house to rental homes. In most cases, however, tourists come to Madeira with pre booked organized tours or on cruises which means they do not need to search for accommodation. If you want to spent a all winter here, or extend your holiday for longer periods of time or you come to Madeira by yourself, you should check accommodation prices and possibilities e.g. from the internet, through a travel agency or make direct contact with an accommodation provider for assistance.

▶ **Nolina (Pony-Tail, Bottle Palm, Elephant's Foot) is blooming with splendid flowers.**

Hotel prices will vary from the 35 € a day to over 350 € with breakfast, depending on the standard of the hotel. On average, however, good standard hotel room is approx. 70 € per day. Some hotels also have apartments with mini kitchens and the possibility to cook for yourself. There are also so-called apartment hotels (apartamentos), in which all apartments have their own mini kitchen, living room and often also a separate bedroom. In addition to hotels, you can also stay in manor houses (quinta or estalagem), wine yards or family accommodation. The more affordable hotels and accommodation are generally further from the center or outside Funchal.

Accommodation rates will vary depending on the seasons, July and August are the most expensive, because there will be many holiday makers coming from the continent to Madeira. Also the last weeks of the year are costly, because of the Christmas illuminations and the spectacular New Years fireworks display, one of the most popular in Europe.

Almost every large town has a hotel, Quinta or some type of cottage accommodation. In Calheta for example there is now the brand new luxury Saccharum Hotel close to Calheta beach, in Santana, Quinta do Furão and in Camacha the charming Casas Valleparaizo.

Reid's Palace Hotel

Reid's Palace five star hotel was founded over a century ago by a Scotsman, William Reid. He did not live to see his dream realised, because he died three years before opening in 1888. His two sons, Willy and Alfred welcomed the luxury hotel's first guests in November 1891. The hotel was designed by the architects George Somers Clarke and John Thomas Micklethwaite.

This beautiful palace is set over-looking the Atlantic Ocean, on the terraced hillside above the bay of Funchal. Its subtropical gardens with old trees and blossoming plants is the ultimate place to sun bathe and relax.

The hotel itself has 128 elegantly decorated rooms and 35 magnificent suites, many restaurants and terraces, swimming pools, spa, sauna, steam room, beauty saloon, tennis courts, fitness room etc. It is an example of a sense of luxury, prosperity, fine dining and a romantic aristocratic style of golden times. While the dress code has been relaxed a bit, Reid's is still something from another era. And Reid's Palace is particularly known for its tradition of serving afternoon tea on the terrace.

Everyone who was anyone has spent time there; kings and queens of the ruling houses of the world, many international celebrities, the rich and the famous, statesmen, filmstars, writers, business tycoons etc.

Reid's Palace has had only a few owners since the beginning, after the Reid's family there was the Blandy family, and then Orient Express Hotels Ltd which changed its name to Belmond Ltd. The hotel's name is now Belmond Reid's Palace.

▶ Reid's Palace is known for its tradition of serving afternoon tea on the terrace.

▶ Quinta do Arco's magnificent rose garden in São Jorge

Manor house (Quinta) accommodation

If you want a little special feature or luxury to your hotel accommodation, it's a good idea to try a Madeiran quinta. These palace like mansions are often centuries old and were often lived in by wealthy Madeirans or English families. Part of that luxury still remain as they contain great antique furniture, paintings etc. These quinta's are refurbished for hotel use. They are usually surrounded by stunning gardens and most also have a high-quality restaurant.

In Funchal you can find for example Quinta da Casa Branca, Quinta da Bela Vista, Quinta Jardins do Lago, Quinta das Vistas, Quintinha de São João, Quinta Perestrello and many more.

From outside the city of Funchal you can find for example Casa Velha do Palheiro just above Funchal, Quinta do Estreito in Câmara de Lobos, Quinta do Monte in Monte, Quinta da Rochinha in Ponta do Sol, Quinta do Lordes in Machico, Quinta do Furão in Santana, Quinta do Arco in São Jorge, Quinta do Vale in São Vicente and Serra Golfe in Santo da Serra just to mention of few.

See more about manor house accommodation at www.quintasdemaidera.com or www.madeira-rural.com.

Inns – Pousadas

In continental Portugal you can find almost fifty inns (pousada). All of these pousadas are partly state owned, old historic buildings which were transferred to accommodation. They are high quality and more expensive than inns and motels in general, but well worth the cost because of their uniqueness. In Madeira there are only two pousadas which are, exceptionally, privately owned. These two offer hospitality and local food. Pousada dos Vinháticos is located in Encumeada and Pousada do Pico do Areeiro is located on a mountain of the same name.

Meetings and conferences

Madeira is also a popular meeting and conference destination and in most large hotels they have well-equipped meeting rooms and halls with office services. Madeira's actual business conference center is located close to university in Santo António. The old business conference center, which also carries events from time to time is located next to the Casino on Avenida do Infante.

Camping areas

In Madeira there are also two camp-sites located in Ribeira da Janela close to Porto Moniz and in Montando do Pereiro just above Funchal. These camping sites are controlled by Madeira's Regional Government and only for Montando do Pereiro you need separate authorisation as it is located in a nature reserve area. Camping is allowed outside the region's camping sites, but it is not encouraged. For more information about camping sites ask from the tourist offices. Porto Santo has also a camping site.

▶ **Golden Shower (Oranje Trumpet Vine) bordering the wall**

Rentals and ownerships

If you decide to stay for an extended period in Madeira, an alternative to staying in a hotel could be to rent an apartment or a house or even buy your own. Madeira has many houses and apartments available to rent, Madeirans who have moved elsewhere often rent their furnished property and this way they will get part of the maintenance costs of their investments back. Housing can be found in different price range categories, they vary in quality and size. It is not recommended that you rent any property without seeing it, because the standards and, in particular, equipment and furniture quality varies greatly. You cannot rely on images or photos because they may have been taken years ago.

Rent price level in spring 2015 was as follows: furnished studios from 350 € to 1 200 €/month, furnished one bedroom apartments from 500 € to 1 500 €/month and furnished two bedroom apartments from 600 € to 1 500 €/month. Prices vary by location, sea view, age of building etc. In addition to the rent usually you need to add the costs of water, gas, electricity and cable-TV & internet which depending on use and how many people are resident from approx. 30 € to 120 €/month. However, it is possible and advisable to negotiate a price, which includes all mentioned costs because, for example, the price of electricity in Madeira is expensive, and your bill could be high, in particular during the winter period when homes may need to be heated.

Only few houses in Madeira have central heating and because of that heating with radiators is costly.

Available apartments are advertised in local newspapers, and can also be found from the internet. Most real estate agents also offer rental homes. You can rent furnished accommodation for short or extended periods. You can hunt housing by yourself in the areas you prefer, because renters place signs in windows or on balconies with phone numbers. VENDE-SE means available to buy and ALUGA-SE for rent.

▶ Aluga-se (rent) and Vende-se (for sale) signs in windows and balconies.

At the moment in Madeira there are many homes and properties for sale and the price level is affordable. Please note, however, that under normal conditions prices are almost the same as housing prices around Europe.

Apartment prices in spring 2015, e.g. T1's from 80 000 € to 300 000 € depending on the age of the building, equipments and location. T2's from 100 000 € to 400 000 €. House prices will vary from house and land size and depending on the location from 100 000 € to 1 000 000 €. In adverts a T0 means a studio, T1 a one bedroom, T2 a two bedrooms etc. The number after the 'T' means the number of sleeping rooms.

▶ **In Funchal there are many rental and owned apartments available.**

When you buy homes or properties, consult a reliable lawyer and real estate agent and sign all documents at a bank.

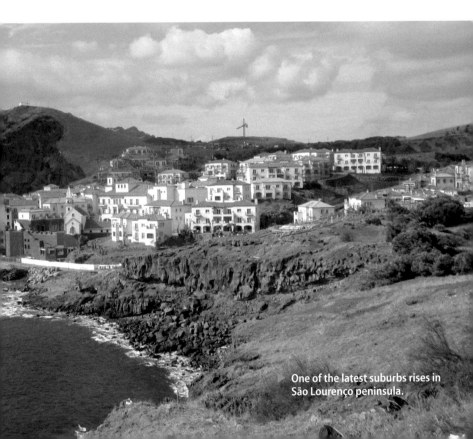

One of the latest suburbs rises in São Lourenço peninsula.

The small size of the island encourages building on terraced levels.

Promenade surrounded with Pride of Madeira.

Flowers in all their glory

CULTURE ▶ ▶ ▶ ▶ ▶ ▶ ▶ ▶ ▶ ▶

Architecture

In Madeira there is a tremendous variety of interesting architecture, centuries-old museums, churches, palaces, castles and mansions, statues and monuments. The architecture of the island comes in two styles; Gothic and Baroque. Typical Gothic style buildings of the island are mainly the old churches and the baroque found in public buildings and the old mansions. Madeiran and Portuguese architecture is presented by churches and houses with blue and white tile decorations (azulejos) and black and white cobblestone streets. If you are interested in architecture you should favour a walk in Funchal old city, around the Cathedral Sé and the area

around the City Hall also along the oldest street in town Rua da Carreira, where you can see Madeiran architecture from 1500s to the present day.

A more contemporary version of Portuguese and Madeiran architecture is represented in the new hotels, shopping malls and around the Forum Madeira's shopping center and new residential areas.

▶ **In the architecture of Madeira you will find both ancient buildings and ultra modern styles mixed together.**

Funchal's slopes are densely housed.

► Avenida Arriaga is decorated with flower carpets during the annual Flower festival.

Books and literature

Books in different languages can be borrowed from many of the hotels own libraries, travel agencies book shelves and from the Quinta Magnolia's foreign cultures library located in the Quinta Magnolia park. At these places you can also donate books, which you do not wish to take back home.

In some book stores and souvenir shops they sell books about local flora and levada guides in different languages. The documentation is usually in English, German, French and Portuguese. The best supplied book stores carry fiction books in English and sometimes in other languages too. One of these book stores is Livraria Esperança at Rua dos Ferreiros 156 in Funchal. This book store was established in 1886. It is one of the oldest and biggest book shops in Portugal, and has more than 100 000 different titles in stock.

Madeira does not have its own national author, but Portugal has Luís Vaz de Camões alias Luís de Camões, who wrote the Portuguese national epic Os Lusíadas (1572). He was born probably in the year 1524 in Chaves and died in Lisbon in 10.6.1580. During his travels to India, the Far East and South Africa, he garnered material for his works. In addition to this national epic, he wrote hundreds of poems and a few plays.

The second Portuguese national author is Fernando António Nogueira de Seabra Pessoa, i.e. Fernando Pessoa, who was a famous poet, author, translator and critic. He was born in 13.6.1888 and died at the age of 47 in Lisbon in 30.11.1935. Pessoa also wrote under the alias Alberto Caeiro, Álvaro de Campos, Ricardo Reis and Bernardo Soares.

The Portuguese national epic, Os Lusíadas, came out in 1572. It is an epic telling of the Portuguese Kingdom's crusades to the Far East, and Vasco da Gama's exploration to India in the years 1497 or 1498. This epic poem consists of 10 songs, which are at the same time history, fantasy, myths and symbolism.

Portuguese present-day author José Saramago received the Nobel Prize for Literature in 1998.

Books about Madeira include a romantic novel A Corte do Norte, written by Cristina Beça Luís and Winston Churchill's short story Mr. Keegan's Elopement which story relates to Madeira.

▶ **Many different species of Succulent Plants can be found on Madeira.**

Libraries (biblioteca)

You can borrow books from some hotels own libraries and some travel agencies, where there are books in different languages. Also from public libraries where there are mostly books in Portuguese but you may find some books in your own language. Quinta Magnolia's foreign cultures library located in Quinta Magnolia park has books in many languages. The above-mentioned places you can also donate your old read books, which you do not wish to take back home.

European Affairs Library CERNE
(Biblioteca de Assuntos Europeus CERNE – Casa da Europa na Madeira) is located on Rua Latino Coelho 57, #3. Open from Monday to Friday 10 am to 12 am and in the afternoon from 2 pm to 5.30 pm.

Funchal's Municipal Library
(Biblioteca Municipal do Funchal) is located on Avenida Calouste Gulbenkian 9. Open from Monday to Friday 10 am to 7 pm. This library is for the preservation of collections of documentation, especially useful for historians and researchers of different areas of knowledge.

Information and Documentation Center – Youth Shop and Meeting Point
(Centro de Informação e Documentação do Funchal – Direção Regional de Juventude) at Rua do Canadá, Cave A (near the Church of Nazaré). Open from Monday to Friday 9 am to 8 pm and Saturdays 9 am to 12.30 pm. This documentation and information center is for youth.

Madeira's Regional Archieves
(Arquivo Regional da Madeira) is located at Caminho dos Álamos 35. The archive is open from Monday to Friday from 9.30 am to 8 pm.

Madeira's Parliament Library
(Biblioteca da Assembleia Legislativa da Madeira) is located on the promenade, address Avenida do Mar e das Comunidades Madeirenses. Open from Monday to Friday 9.00 am to 12 am and again from 2 pm to 5.30 pm.

OTHER PUBLIC LIBRARIES IN FUNCHAL:

Biblioteca/Centro de Documentação do Museu Quinta das Cruzes, address Calçada do Pico 1. This library specializes in decorative arts.

Biblioteca Municipal Calouste Gulbenkian, is located in Avenida Arriaga, at the same address as the City Theatre (Teatro Municipal Baltazar Dias). Open from Monday to Friday 9 am to 12.30 pm and again from 2 pm to 7 pm.

English Church Library, Rua da Quebra Costas 18. Open on Tuesdays and Fridays from 10.30 am to 12.30 pm, Saturdays at 11–12 am and Sundays at 10–11 am.

Foreign Culture's Library (Biblioteca de Culturas Estrangeiras) is located in the Quinta Magnolia park, address Rua do Dr. Pita. Library is supported by local foreign embassies and the books are, as a general rule, donated. Books are in several languages. Here you can also donate your read books that you do not wish to take back home. Open from Monday to Friday 9 am to 5.30 pm.

Library and Documentation Center of Art (Biblioteca e Centro de Documentação do Museu de Arte Contemporânea), modern art museum's library, on Rua do Portao de São Tiago. Open from Monday to Saturday at 10 am to 12.30 pm and again from 2 pm to 5.30 pm. This institution has a small library where they have newspapers, catalogues, books, postcards, newspaper clippings etc. related to contemporary art.

Multimedia and Arts Education Library (Centro de Investigação e Documentação, Gabinete Coordenador de Educação Artistica) Regional Education Department, at Travessa do Nogueira 11. Open from Monday to Friday 9 am to 12.30 pm and again from 2 pm to 5.30 pm. This library specializes in education, music, art and multimedia documentation.

Porta 33 – Documentation Center (Centro de Documentação Porta 33 – Porta 33 Associacão Quebra Costas) Contemporary Art Center, at Rua do Quebra Costas 33. Open from Tuesday to Saturday from 4 pm to 8 pm. This non-profit organization maintains an art gallery with collections of contemporary art.

▶ Quinta Magnolia's Library of Foreign Cultures is located in the old mansion.

A peaceful reading moment by the sea

Regional Public Library (Biblioteca Pública Regional), Caminho dos Álamos 35. Open Mondays from 2 pm to 8 pm and from Tuesday to Friday from 9.30 am to 8 pm. Saturdays from 9.30 am to 3 pm.

Study Center and Atlantic History Library (Biblioteca do Centro de Estudos de História do Atlântico), at Rua das Merês 8. Open from Monday to Friday 9 am to 12.30 pm and from 2 pm to 5.45 pm. This library is a scientific research institution of the history of Atlantic Islands.

Teatroteca Fernando Augusto – Biblioteca de Teatro e Artes Performativas do Teatro do Experimental do Funchal, temporarily closed (spring 2015). This library specializes in theatrical and dance art and has approx. 1 500 books loan of Fernando Augusto.

In addition to these mentioned there are libraries in almost every city in Madeira; such as Calheta, Câmara de Lobos, Machico, Ponta do Sol, Ribeira Brava, Santa Cruz, Santana, São Vicente and Porto Santo.

Movies and cinemas

There are two cinemas in Funchal; one in the Madeira shopping center with 7 theatres and the other in the Forum Madeira shopping center with 6 theatres. Out-of-town in Camacha Shopping there is the third cinema with 2 theatres and Porto Santo island has the fourth with 1 theatre. Films are normally changed on Thursdays and

information of the programs you can find from newspapers in Portuguese.

Films are not usually dubbed, they are shown in their original language but sub titled in Portuguese. With the exception of children's movies, which are usually always dubbed. Theatres also have afternoon matinees. Entry fee 6,70 €/person, seniors and students 5,80 € (spring 2015).

The most famous movie filmed in Madeira may be John Huston's Moby Dick (1956), starring Gregory Peck. Other movies filmed in Madeira, most of which are Portuguese, including Os Destinos de Manoel (Raoul Ruiz, 1985), Manoel na Ilha das Maravilhas (Raoul Ruiz, 1985), Tricheurs (Barbet Schroeder, 1984), Ennemis Intimes (António da Cunha Telles (1987), A Corte do Norte (João Botelho, 2008).

Every year in Funchal there are two film festivals; The Funchal International Film Festival in the City Theatre (Teatro Municipal Baltazar Dias) in November and the other in May at Reid's Palace hotel.

Television

In most hotels there are dozens of cable tv channels where you can find programs and series in English, German and French. Movie channels Hollywood and MOV play movies in original languages with sub titles in Portuguese. Portuguese channels include RTP1, RT2 and Madeira's own channel RTP Madeira which broadcasts local news in the morning, afternoon and evening and also weather forecasts in Portuguese. Other channels include SIC and TVI.

Magazines and newspapers

In some hotels they deliver foreign newspapers and printed news releases in a few languages. From news-stands you can buy English, German and French newspapers that can be one day old.

Newspapers in Portuguese are for example Diario de Notícias Madeira and Journal da Madeira. Other Portuguese newspapers are the dailies from continental Portugal.

▶ There are still some old news stand in Madeira.

Theatre and dance

The City Theatre (Teatro Municipal Baltazar Dias) takes its name from the 1500s blind Madeiran poet and playwriter Baltazar Dias. This theatre is the center of the city's cultural life and is located on Avenida Arriaga across the City Park (Jardim Municipal), the beautiful building dates from 1888. In addition, there will be concerts, theatrical works, dance performances and art films. In most cases shows are in Portuguese. See presentations and times either from local newspapers or the theater's lobby.

Cine Teatro Municipal de Santo António is located in Santo António district in address Rua Coolhafal.

There Funchal's experimental theatre group (TEF) performs various theatre gems from it's over 35 years of history. This theatre is thought to be Madeira's best, they also have musical and other performances.

There are theatre performances also outside of Funchal, for example in the Art Center Casa das Mudas, located in Calheta at the address Vale de Amores. In addition, theatre and other cultural and musical performances are also played in different towns' culture centers (Casa da Cultura or Centro Civico).

Dance performances, other shows and cultural happenings can be found depending on time and visitor artists.

The City Theatre café is a popular meeting place.

For example Mariinsky's Bolshoi Ballet visits Madeira once in a while.

Check out also the library of theatre art (Theatroteca Fernando Augusto) which is specialized in theatrical and dance art and has approx. 1 500 books loaned by Fernando Augusto. The address Rua Latino Coelho 54. The library is temporarily closed (spring 2015).

Information about cultural events, theatre and musical performances you can find in Portuguese from local newspapers and in English from hotel receptions, travel agencies and tourist offices. Tourist offices also publish a monthly forthcoming events calendar (Cultural Agenda) about exhibitions, theatres and other events.

An actual central ticket office does not exist on this island, but from the tourist office you can purchase tickets in advance to a number of cultural events. The City Theatre (Teatro Municipal Baltazar Dias) cashier sells tickets for a variety of events and in some hotels they serve their customers by organising tickets for various events. Otherwise tickets can be purchased at the event entrance.

DID YOU KNOW...

You can donate your old read books to Quinta Magnolia's Library of Foreign Cultures. There you can also borrow books in different languages.

A huge Wisteria bordering a wall

▶ **Angel's Trumpet (Angel's Tears) are magnificent.**

Musical performances and concerts

Funchal has a vibrant music concervatoire (Conservatório de Música da Madeira), located at the crossroad of Avenida do Infante and Avenida Luis de Camôes. In addition to music studies there are held student and teacher joint concerts and other concerts with visiting international artists.

Madeira Mandolin orchestra (Orquestra de Bandolins da Madeira), established in 1913 and is one of the oldest European mandolin orchestras. The orchestra consists of young musicians and it has concerts across Europe. In Madeira the orchestra performs in several concert halls but mainly in the English Church on Fridays, at 9 pm. Check times, places and programs either from local newspapers, hotel's reception, street display boards or from tourist offices. Tickets can be purchased from tourist offices, city theatre's cashiers or at the door a few hours before the show.

Madeira Classical Orchestra (Orquestra Clássica da Madeira) performs concerts in several different locations, but chiefly, in Madeira Tecnopolo in Sala Ursa Maior auditorioum. Madeira Classical Orchestra is planning to get it's own concert hall, which has been delayed because of financing. See times, locations and programs either from local newspapers, hotel reception or ask from tourist office.

Organ recitals take place on Mondays at the Colégio church throughout the year. Entry is free. Also in October there are held organ recitals in Funchal's and Ponta da Cruz churches. Check times and locations from local newspapers or ask at the tourist office.

In June there are held international Bach concerts in the Cathedral Sé.

There are lots of other musical performances and concerts every month and almost every day in different churches, concert halls and theatres. Check the times and locations from local newspapers or ask at the tourist office.

Concert halls and places where there will be different musical performances and concerts are:

In Funchal:
▶ City Theatre (Teatro Municipal Baltazar Dias)
▶ Madeira Tecnopolo in University area
▶ Teatro Municipal de Santo António
▶ The Casino's Concert Hall
▶ The English Church (Holy Trinity Church)
▶ City Hall (Câmara Municipal)

Especially in summer and at Christmastime, music and theatre performances are also held in parks and streets of Funchal.

Outside of Funchal:
▶ Casa das Mudas Art Center, Calheta
▶ Casa da Cultura da Câmara de Lobos, Câmara de Lobos
▶ Quinta do Revoredo Centro Civico, Santa Cruz

Also musical and other cultural events and performances are held in different towns Cultural Centers (Centro Civico or Casa da Cultura).

You can listen to fado in some fado restaurants in the old city. Many hotels also organise assorted fado nights.

There are a few places where you can listen to jazz:
▶ SCAT The Funchal Jazz Club and Restaurant, Wednesday and Saturdays, Promenade do Lido, at the Lido

▶ House Jazz, Wednesdays and Saturdays, Rua do Aranhas 16 (close to the La Vie shopping center)
▶ In July there is also the Funchal Jazz Festival held in Santa Catarina Park

Live music can be found in the following bars and restaurants:
▶ Hole in One Pub, Estrada Monumental 238 at the Lido, with live music at weekends
▶ Katz Bar at the Lido, international DJ on weekends
▶ Moynihans Irish Pub, Rua Imperatriz Dona Amelia, live music five nights a week
▶ FX Club, Avenida do Mar (behind Municipal Theatre), live music at weekends
▶ Casino's Cobacabana Garden, live music at weekends

You can listen to music in many hotels and some restaurants where they have dinner shows and themed entertainment.

In Avenida Arriaga there are some musicians in front of cafés and restaurants who entertain with their instruments.

Discotheques:
▶ Kool Klub Café (close to Pestana Carlton Hotel)
▶ Chameleon (across to Pestana Carlton Hotel)
▶ Marginal & Jam (opposite harbour terminal)
▶ Vespa (opposite harbour terminal)

Discotheques open usually late (at 11 or 12 pm) and are open till morning.

▶ Francisceas ('Yesterday, Today and Tomorrow') and a Day Lily in harmony

▶ Beautiful Blue Trumpet Vine (Sky Flower)

▶ Funchal in twilight

▶ Brazilian Spyder Flower (Princess Flower, Glory Bush)

▶ Magnificent rose bed

ART, ART EXHIBITIONS AND ART GALLERIES ▶ ▶ ▶ ▶ ▶ ▶

In hotel lobbies and other public places are exhibited the most spectacular works of art and paintings. Also, in some restaurants, shopping malls and at libraries, Funchal's and Porto Santo's airports, and museums have changing and some permanent exhibitions of art. At the Modern Art Museum (Museu de Arte Contemporãnea), Ethnographic Museum (Museu Etnografico da Madeira) and at the Electric Museum (Museu de Electricidades) there are different art exhibitions.

In addition, art exhibitions are also presented in the City Theatre (Teatro Municipal Baltazar Dias), the English Church (Holy Trinity Church) and in different towns Cultur Centers (Centro Civico or Casa da Cultura) and art galleries such as Casa das Mudas in Calheta, Prazeres Art Gallery in Prazeres and John dos Passos Auditorium in Ponta do Sol. Check the opening hours and exhibitions in local newspapers or ask at the tourist office.

In Rua Santa Maria in the old city many old doors and walls are painted with colourful works of art. There are more than 200 of these works of art and the artists are from around the world. In addition, the doors and walls also have some poems on them.

Also slightly different art can be found on the walls of the yacht marina and

DID YOU KNOW...

In Rua Santa Maria in old city many old doors and walls are painted with more than 200 art works.

dock where the crews of visiting boats have left their artistic handwritings and cards.

In addition, art can be found also in a few interesting art museums:

Casa das Mudas Art Center is located in Calheta, address Vale de Amores. One side of the art center is located in the historic 1500s mansion and on the new side is modern architecture. The art center has changing exhibitions of art shows, music and dance performances. Open from Tuesday to Sunday 10 am to 1 pm and again 2 pm to 6 pm. Mondays closed. Country buses no 80, 115, 139 and 142.

Henrique and Francisco Franco Museum (Museu Henrique e Francisco Franco) is located at Rua João Deus 13. This museum, established in 1987, presents the very well known Madeiran artist

Casa das Mudas Art Center has changing art exhibitions.

brothers' paintings, drawings and sculptures from 1800s and 1900s. Francisco Franco's handiwork is the João Gonçalves Zarco's statue on Avenida Arriaga. The museum is open from Monday to Friday 10 am to 12.30 pm and again from 2 pm to 8 pm. Closed at weekends and on public holidays.

Modern Art Museum (Museu de Arte Contemporãnea) is located in old city in the fortress of São Tiago (Fortaleza de São Tiago), at the east end of promenade, at the address Rua do Portão São Tiago. The fortress was completed in 1614 and has operated since 1992 as an art museum and is an attraction in itself. Collections includes mostly Portuguese modern artists works from 1960s to the present day. The museum has changing art exhibitions and a quality restaurant. The museum is open from Monday to Saturday 10 am to 12.30 pm and again from 2 pm to 5.30 pm. Closed on Sundays and on public holidays.

Sacred Art Museum (Museu de Arte Sacra) is located in the town square at Rua do Bispo 21, in an old palace which was previously the premises of the Bishop of Madeira. The palace was built in the 1500s and it has been a museum since 1955. The collection consists of Flemish paintings and sculptures from the 1500s and 1600s and contains, costumes and jewellery used in religious ceremonies. In front of the museum they have a cafe. The museum is open from Tuesday to Saturday 10 am to 12.30 pm and again from 2.30 pm to 6 pm and on Sundays 10 am to 1 pm. Mondays closed.

Ceramic art and tiles

In Funchal there is ceramic art (azulejos) presented in many locations. This old Portuguese traditional art from the 1600s is represented in churches and on houses with blue and white tiles and also the black-and-white street cobblestones. Many centuries ago in Portugal it was common to decorate churches, public buildings and wealthy people's houses with these ceramic tiles designed by local artists. You can see this kind of art not only in churches but in Avenida Arriaga at The Ritz café (former Toyota dealership), in Regional Government's entrance lobby on Avenida Zarco and the Market place's walls.

Also Funchal's streets are decorated with black and white mosaic and stone ornaments. In some places you can find very beautiful and artistic works.

► **Modern ceramic art in Panoramico Park**

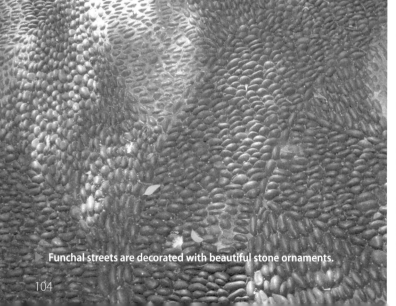

Funchal streets are decorated with beautiful stone ornaments.

104

Traditional ceramic art seen on traditional old houses and walls in churches and palaces

▶ **Santa Maria Street is one of the oldest in Funchal.**

In the old area of Funchal city there are painted colourful works of art and poems on old doors and walls.

EXPERIENCES AND SIGHTS

Levadas pass through breathtaking
landscapes.

Levadas or irrigation channels

Frequently in the north part of island it rains whereas in the south it is mainly dry. For this reason, already in the 1500s, the Portuguese began to build an irrigation system in order to provide water where and when it was needed. Construction of this difficult to access and mountainous land was not easy so construction was carried out by imported slaves from Africa and prisoners from the continent.

Levadas, these original irrigation channels, are designed in such a way that the water flows slowly. They pass through breathtaking landscapes from village to village and were in the past also transport roads for goods and merchandise to these villages. Today levadas do not operate only as irrigation channels and hiking paths but also produce electricity. Previously levadas were privately owned but after the Second World War they were taken under the control of Regional Government management.

One of the highlights of a holiday in Madeira are levadas and there are about 1 500 km on the island. It is recommended that you at least once during your holiday try a levada walk, unless you have a fear of high places. These levadas are all quite different in length, some via easy-to-use paths, others follow very demanding routes. Landscapes also vary and levadas pass through from coast to valleys and follow their way from mountains up to 1800 m height. Next to the levadas are trails which were built only about 50 years ago, the original purpose was for the 'levadeiros', who check the conditions of the levadas and trails. Only in the late 1990s they discovered the value of these levadas for tourists, thus they trained levada guides and printed guides and maps.

If you want to walk levadas by yourself, buy a good guidebook with maps and select levada that fits your own fitness condition and abilities. Although you perhaps are used to hiking in nature, it is best for first timers to participate in a guided tours where the return transport is also organised. These guided tours are for all ages with small groups organised by many different companies (for example MB Tours). There is always an experienced English speaking guide and sometimes also German or French. Some hotels and travel agencies also organise these guided levada tours.

Ranking of these levadas with degree of difficulty are marked with the numbers 1 to 5 and other times with stars, these ratings are just a hint. Usually an easy route is manageable if your physique is normal. More exacting routes require more experience, agility and fitness. It is a good idea to start with the easiest and according to your skills then progress to more demanding routes. Note that some routes also call for a good balance.

▶ There is a good reason for first timers to participate in guided levada tours.

DID YOU KNOW...

There are lots of programmes and interesting things to do for children and teenagers.

▶ **From Prazeres there are magnificent views out to sea and down to a little village and from there some levadas start.**

Remember before taking a levada walk:

▶ Always walk on marked routes
▶ If not with a guided group buy a good guidebook with maps
▶ Select levadas that suit your fitness and abilities
▶ Never walk alone along levadas!
▶ Check local weather conditions in advance so that there will be no surprises
▶ Read all the warnings and check condition of the route prior to departure, because after a heavy rain levadas may be in poor condition
▶ Wear suitable clothing and bear in mind that weather may change very quickly in Madeira, especially in mountains
▶ Also be prepared for rain, but an umbrella is not recommended as they are unwieldy in the wind and cause a hazard for yourself and other hikers
▶ Definitely good footwear is essential and watch your step, because levadas may be slippery and muddy in some places
▶ If the walk takes a long time, it is worth taking something to drink and eat with you. Take along a small torch and take into account the fact that dusk will come quickly in Madeira
▶ If at any time you feel dizzy, fear high places or have any kind of heart-related diseases, bear in mind that aid can take a long time to come to remote forest areas
▶ Make sure that at the end of your levada walk there is a bus or taxi available to take you back
▶ Keep nature tidy and do not leave litter

Parks and gardens

Here on this Atlantic Floating Garden can be found flowers and interesting plants throughout the year. One of the best attractions in Madeira is rich and versatile vegetation and also magnificent parks and gardens. Private and public parks are overflowing with Hibiscus, Bougainvilleas and Birds of Paradise. In rural areas Agapanthus fill the verges of roads and in the yards of farm houses bloom many different kinds of colourful Rhododendrons. In terraced farms grow bananas, grapes, mangos and passion fruits and avenues are edged with Jacarandas, Oleanders and Rosewoods. Fans of roses are stunned at the Quinta do Arco garden in São Jorge where more than 1700 different roses grow side by side.

In addition to Funchal, these parks and gardens can be found in almost all smaller towns around the island, and many hotels have beautiful gardens and an abundance of flower beds. With churches there are gorgeous parks including mansions and palaces and their gardens most of which you can visit.

Ajuda Park (Jardim Publico da Ajuda) was opened to the public in August 2005. The park is located behind the Forum Madeira shopping center, on Rua do Vale da Ajuda. That park was previously a banana plantation and a small area of banana plants have been left in memory of it. The park also has a Dragon Tree square (Praca dos Dragoeiros) and a playground for children. This park is open to the public.

▶ **Most gardens of mansions can be visited.**

Allotment Gardens (Hortas Municipais). There are several allotment gardens around the city, for example in the Lido on Estrada Monumental, São Martinho etc., where local residents grow vegetables, herbs, bananas etc.

Almirante Reis Park (Jardim do Almirante Reis) is a small green oasis in the center of the city. It is located near the cable car terminal on the promenade. This public park was opened in 2001 and there local men are playing card games etc. Beside the park in the same place as the Santa Maria hotel is now, was previously an old shipyard and in the same location as the current multi-story parking was a football field.

The Bird Park (Jardim dos Louros) is located below the Botanical Garden (Jardim Botanico da Madeira), address Caminho do Meio. The park has many exotic and rare birds from around the world; parrots, canaries, peacocks etc. Entry is with same Botanical Garden ticket. The park is open every day from 9 am to 6 pm. Access either with buses numbers 29, 30, 31, by taxi or by cable car from Monte.

Botanical Garden (Jardim Botânico da Madeira) is located about 3 km from the center, address Caminho do Meio. This garden was established in 1960 and in the park there is this old mansion (Quinta do Bom Sucesso) which belonged once to the Reid's family. In the garden area of 3,5 hectares there are more than 3000

▶ In the Bird Park there are wonderful peacocks and other exotic birds.

▶ In the Botanical Gardens more than 3000 plants grow.

tropical plants from all over the world. Some of them are endemic plants of Madeira and some of the trees are from as far away as the Himalayas. There is also a café and Museum of Natural History (Museu de History Natural). Below the garden there is a Bird Park (Jardim dos Louros) with exotic and rare birds from around the world. With the same ticket you can enter to Bird Park too. The park is open every day from 9 am to 6 pm. Access either with buses numbers 29, 30, 31, by taxi or by cable car from Monte.

Campo da Barca Garden (Jardim do Campo da Barca) a popular small park in the center of the city it is located opposite the main police station and close to the Market place. The park is divided into two parts and in between there is the Rua Conde Carvalhal

street. The southern part of the park was originally established in 1818 and the northern part in 1903. There are beautiful Jacarandas and Frangipanis and a gorgeous Dragon Tree with an enormous round top.

The City Park (Jardim Municipal) was also well known as Queen Amélia's Park (Jardim Dona Amélia) and St. Francis Park (Jardim do São Francisco), because there was Franciscan Monastery in the park. This park is located just in the center of Funchal on Avenida Arriaga, near the main tourist office. The park was established in 1880 and there are plants and trees from Madeira and from around the world. The park also has a café, a pond and auditorium where are held all kinds of cultural events and concerts. The park is open every day and access is free.

▶ Splendour of flowers in City Park

Herb and Medicinal Garden

(Jardim de Plantas Aromaticas) is located at Rua da Mouraria 31A. The street entrance is easy to miss and the garden is located between São Pedro Palace and Frederico das Freitas Museum courtyard. This park was established in 2000 and has concentrated only on aromatic, pharmaceutical and poisonous plants. There you can find for example lavender, laurel, mint, aloe and fennel.

Hospício da Princeza Dona Maria Amélia's Garden is located opposite the Santa Catarina Park. This peaceful garden you can visit when the gates are open. In the center of this garden is a stunning building which is now an old people's home. The adjacent buildings are a kindergarten and a school.

Madeira Magic Theme Park and Garden is located below the Forum Madeira shopping mall, address Rua da Ponta Cruz 25. The park is a mini botanical garden for children and there are flowers and plants from all over the world. There is a themed science center where children can also play. In the same building there is a health club, restaurant and also a tea house. Open from Monday to Friday 10 am to 6 pm and on the weekends at 10 am to 7 pm. Closed on public holidays.

Madeira's Tropical Orchid Garden

(Madeira Tropical Orchid Jardim e Quinta or Madeira Orchidearium) is located 2 km from the city center, address Caminho dos Saltos 8. In addition to glamorous orchids and centuries old trees, there are exotic birds and a large collection of fossils and stones. The garden is open every day from 9.30 am to 5 pm. Closed on Christmas Day. Buses number 15A and 28 or by taxi.

Magnólia Park (Quinta Magnólia) and the mansion is located at Rua Dr. Pita just above the Enotel Quinta do Sol hotel. The mansion (Quinta Magnólia) was previously a British club which was expropriated by the Regional Government in 1980 and currently there is the Library of Foreign Languages. In the park with exotic and tropical trees and plants there is an opportunity for relaxation, sport and leisure. There are tennis courts, running paths and a playground. In spring 2015 the swimming pools were under renovation with no time schedule given for finishing. The park continues under the bridge of Estrada Monumental street where you can walk towards the shoreline and

Pestana Carlton hotel. Free access to park but tennis courts have a small fee. Open every day from 8 am to 8 pm.

Nazaré Park (Mata da Nazaré) was established in 1992 in the center of the city's tenement houses on Avenida dos Estados da América, in Nazaré part of the town. The park was established for relaxation and leisure and an educational garden for students. Bus number 48.

Orchid Garden (Jardim Orquidea) is located close to the Botanical Garden, address Rua Pita da Silva 37. There are tens of thousands of great orchids and other tropical plants from around the world. Also a shop, the coffee shop and a terrace with stunning views over Funchal. Open every day from 9 am to 6 pm. Buses number 29, 30 and 31 and by taxi.

▶ Kaffir Lilies are flourishing in the park.

▶ **There are thousands of beautiful Orchids and Cymbidiums in the orchid gardens.**

Orchid Garden Boa Vista (Jardim Boa Vista) connected to a private mansion it is located uphill, about 2 km from the city center, address Rua Lombo da Boa Vista. The garden is also a market garden where you can buy orchids and other exotic plants and seedlings. Flowers and plants are packed well and will be delivered, if desired, to your hotel. The garden is open Monday to Saturday from 9 am to 5.30 pm. Closed on Sundays and on public holidays. You can get close by bus number 32 and by taxi.

Panoramic Park (Jardim Panoramico) is located west from Funchal center on the promenade (Passeio Publico do Maritimo), between Lido and Ajuda. The park was completed in 2001 and is built on terraced levels like the vegetation on slopes of mountains. There are both endemic and tropical plants and cacti. Great views of the Atlantic, many restaurants and coffee bars. Free access.

Promenade (Passeio Publico do Maritimo) is approx. 4 km long and starts in the center of the hotel area of the Lido and runs all the way to Praia Formosa beach. Along the way are parks, many fantastic plants, the ruins of an old shipyard and astonishing views to the Atlantic and of Cabo Girão. There are also two public swimming areas (Lido and Ponta Gorda) and one private area (Clube Naval), a children's playground, many nice restaurants and coffee shops and

▶ **The brand new 'Square of the People' located at the harbour**

benches to sit on and look at this great scenery. The first part of that park was completed in 1993, the second part in 1999 and the third sequel in 2001. With this promenade you will be able to walk along to Câmara de Lobos. Access is free.

Presidential Palaces Garden (Quinta Vigia) is located just next to Santa Catarina Park on Avenida do Infante. When the gates are open you can enter. In addition to flowers and plants there are also exotic birds, sculptures and stunning views of Funchal port. There is also a small chapel (Capela de Nossa Senhora das Anquistias). The park is usually open from Monday to Friday from 9 am to 5 pm but during official receptions the park is closed.

Quinta das Cruzes Garden and the mansion is located at Calçada do Pico 1. In addition to exotic plants and

orchids you can admire sculptures and there is also a small chapel and a coffee shop and museum which present decorative art and furniture items. The park is open from Tuesday to Sunday from 10 am to 12.30 pm and again from 2 pm to 5.30 pm.

Quinta do Poço Park is located near Imaculado Coração de Maria church, at the crossroads of Caminho dos Saltos and Estrada dos Marmeleiros streets. In 1933 they built a huge reservoir of water for the needs of Funchal city and on top of this water reservoir they built this green space and a park. The park has many trees and other interesting plants. Plants are grown there for the needs of Funchal parks.

Quinta Palmeira Garden (Quinta da Palmeira) is located at Rua Levada de Santa Luzia 31A. In this private garden of the 1700's there are in addition to old trees and plants a beautiful mansion and astonishing views down to Funchal. The park has ceramic and mosaic tile art and also a window which belonged to Columbus's residence. The park is open from Monday to Friday from 9 am to 1 pm. Buses number 25 and 26.

Santa Catarina Park (Parque de Santa Catarina) is located above the port, next to the Presidential Palace on Avenida do Infante. The park is centrally situated and therefore very popular among locals, especially at weekends. A cemetery was situated here in 1837, but over the years between 1939-1944 the cemetery was moved to São Martinho. The park

was repaired and it was completed in 1966. In addition to tropical plants, trees and flowers, there is a pond with fountain, swans and ducks, a children's playground, a small chapel (Capela de Santa Catarina) from the 1400s and a cafe. There are also many sculptures, including Prince Henry the Navigator's statue and Christopher Columbus' statue and a variety of other sculptures. From the park there is a superb view of Funchal, the port, and to the sea. It is open every day from 8 am to 8 pm and there is a free access.

Santa Luzia Park (Jardim de Santa Luzia) is located on the corner of 31 de Janeiro and Rua do Til. Previously there was a sugar and alcohol factory on the site from which there is now only a

▶ **Indian Shots are flourishing in Santa Catarina Park.**

chimney left. The park was opened in 2004 and it is themed in five areas; an amphitheatre garden (Jardim do Anfiteatro), a tropical garden (Jardim Tropical), a water garden (Jardim da Agua), a terrace garden (Jardim do Socalcos) and a laurel garden (Jardim da Laurisilva). There is also a playground for children and a café. The park is free and open to the public.

São Martinho Garden (Jardim de São Martinho) is an attractive garden located opposite the church of São Martinho in the district of the same name. The park was established in 1992, and it is terraced like agriculture on mountain slopes and divided into sections by plant species. The park is definitely worth knowing better because there are many interesting flowers and plants, also brilliant views to the sea. The park is located close to a small city allotment garden. Bus number 48.

▶ Montbretias in São Martinho Garden

Square of the People (Praça do Povo) is the newest park and leisure area in Funchal and was opened in December 2014. Located on the promenade this extension of Avenida do Mar is a multi-use area with large green spaces, benches and rest areas and also nice paths for pedestrians surrounded by flower beds. This area was previously a landfill of material and debris from the storms and floods of February 2010.

Vila Guida's small park is located about 3 km from the center, at the cross roads of Rua do Acciaouli and Estrada Conde Carvalhal. It was built in 1938 in two terraces. The upper level has Crotons and large shady trees and the lower level has flower beds with Roses, Begonias, Indian Shots, Lilies, Hibiscuses, Oleanders etc.

In addition to the above parks and gardens, there are many other stunning mansions and villas in Funchal, where parks and gardens are growing magnificent trees and glamorous plants. These private mansions are, unfortunately, not open to the public, but there are several squares and avenues along with planted blooming Jacarandas, African Tulip Trees, Rosewoods, and gorgeous flower beds, fences and hanging baskets.

There are also attractive parks and gardens outside of Funchal, here are a few of them:

Endemic Garden (Jardim de Plantas Indegenas do São Vicente) in São Vicente, on the north coast of the island. There grows only species that

▶ The parks have rare plants.

are natural to Madeira. Free entry. Buses number 4, 80, 132 and 139.

Blandy's Garden or **Palheiro's Garden** (Jardim da Quinta do Palheiro Ferreiro) is located close to the Palheiro golf course outside of the city, address Estrada da Camacha. This private garden is particularly well-known of its Camellias and Magnolias. In the park there is an aristocratic mansion from the 1800s and also a small chapel. This mansion and garden have been in Blandy's family ownership since 1921 and the mansion is currently held by the manor house hotel as Casa Velha do Palheiro. The garden and the chapel are open to the public from Monday to Friday from 9 am to 5 pm. Closed at weekends. Buses number 36A and 37 or by taxi.

Funchal's Ecological Park (Parque Ecologico do Funchal) is located above the city, close to Monte, address Estrada Regional 103 no 259 in Ribeira das Cales. This 1000 hectares forest park was opened in 1994 and it reaches almost 1800 m to Pico do Areeiro slopes. This park was established to maintain the original nature and plants of Madeira, for leisure of residents and tourists, and also as support to schoolchildren and scouts education of ecology. There are a huge number of rare species of trees and other plants, for example laurel trees, Madeiran Mahogany, Tree Heaters and Madeiran Blueberry etc. There also nests a variety of birds, including a rare Madeiran Petrel. The park has many hiking paths and areas for picnics where you can barbecue and eat your sandwiches. It is open daily from 9 am to 5 pm. Best way to go around the park is by car. Buses numbers 56, 103 and 138.

Emperor's Garden (Jardins do Imperador) and the mansion (Quinta do Monte) is located near Monte, close to Monte's City Park at Caminho do Pico Monte. The Austrian-Hungarian Emperor Charles I lived in the mansion while in exile in Madeira. The mansion is currently in poor condition and there is no entry to it, but it is planned to open a tea house in the near future. The garden is open Monday to Saturday from 9 am to 5 pm. Buses number 20, 21 and 48.

Dragon Tree Park (Draguiro) is located in São Gonçalo at Sitio das Neves, a little outside of Funchal. Madeira's Regional Government has established this park to protect areas where these Dragon Trees grow. These Dragon Trees are original and they naturally grow only in Madeira, the Canary Islands and Cape Verde.

Monte City Park (Parque Municipal do Monte) is located in Monte just below the church. The park's construction began in 1894 and was completed just before the millennium in 1899. The park covers almost the entire center of Monte. Also in this park there are many exotic plants and centuries-

▶ **Dragon Trees and Crotons**

▶ **Monte City Park is definitely worth checking out.**

old trees, in 1897 the marble water fountain was completed, which is devoted to the Virgin Mary. There are also two bronze sculptures, one of which is devoted to the toboggan drivers. The garden is open every day from 9 am to 6 pm and access is free.

Monte Palace Tropical Garden (Jardim Tropical Monte Palace) is located above Funchal in Monte, approx. 5 km from the city center. The palace, built in the 1800s, has been also a hotel (Monte Palace Hotel) and in 1991 this private garden was opened to the public. In the garden there have been planted over 100 000 tropical plants from all over the world, some of the them very rare. There is a separate section for Madeiran species

and a Japanese garden. In addition to rare flowers and plants, there are also ceramic tiles, bricks, sculptures and works of art. Monte Palace Museum (Museu Monte Palace) is also in the premises, entry is included with the same garden ticket. The garden is open every day from 9.30 am to 6 pm. Best way there is cable car, by taxi or buses number 20, 21, 22 and 48.

Queimadas Forest Park (Parque das Queimadas) is located approx. 5 km of the Santana, on the north side of the island. In this park forest trees, bushes and plants are growing side by side. Also close is Casa das Queimadas cottage which is used by the forest guards. An ideal place for hiking and picnics. Country buses number 56, 103 and 138.

Quinta do Santo da Serra mansion and park is located as its name indicates, at the Santo da Serra, which is north-east from Funchal. This large mansion was owned by the Blandy family in the past, but now it is owned by the Regional Government. The garden is full of camellias, aghapantuses and hydrangeas and stunning views to the Machico valley. The garden is open to the public and access is free. Unfortunately there is no entry to the mansion. Country bus number 77.

Quinta Splendida (Jardim Botânico da Quinta Splendida) is located in Caniço and it surrounds the hotel and spa Quinta Splendida. This beautiful park was established in 1990 and has over 1000 plants and flowers. Address Estrada Ponta da Oliveira. Open every day from 9 am to 6 pm.

Ribeiro Frio Forest Park (Ribeiro Frio Floresta) is located in 900 m altitude in Ribeiro Frio, about 17 km outside of Funchal. The park has plenty of endemic plants, some of which are quite rare. There are excellent opportunities for walking and hiking and brilliant landscape views. Country bus number 56.

Rose Garden (Roseiral da Quinta do Arco) is located on the north coast of the island in São Jorge, address Sitio da Lagoa. Here is the biggest rose collection on the island, thousands of roses, some of which are very rare. The Rose Garden is open from April until December every day from 11 am to 6 pm. Country buses number 6, 103 and 138.

▶ Glamorous roses in the Rose Garden

▶ Old mansions have magnificent gardens.

▶ Relaxing walks through the parks

Nature reserves

Madeira's nature is well maintained and since 1982 two-thirds of the island's land area has been dedicated to nature and its protection. These areas are laurel forests, uninhabited islands, preserved areas, part of the sea areas and some animals. Part of these natural preserved areas are completely protected and some of them partially protected. In these natural preserves it is not permitted to take plants or disturb the fauna.

Deserted Islands Natural Preserve,

which covers Ilhéu Chão, Deserta Grande and Bugio islands and they have been protected since 1990, and you cannot visit without the relevant permission. In the beginning they simply wanted to protect the rare monk seals (Monachus Monachus) who lived in the area, but today the protection includes everything living and growing on the island. This nature reserve is divided into two parts so that the southern parts of the island Deserta Grande and Bugio islands are totally prohibited areas where boats cannot even go close to the shoreline. Some access is permitted to Northern parts of the islands but access is limited, some companies have rights to organise guided tours with a limited number of participants. Ilhas Desertas islands are located approx. 16 km south east from Madeira.

Garajau Marine Nature Reserve

(Reserva Natural Parcial do Garajau) is located on the southern coast line just outside of Funchal, in front of Garajau and Caniço coast and extends also 50 meters below sea level. This Natural Preserve was established in 1986 to protect the Madeiran coast and its resources. It is the only exclusive deep ocean Nature Reserve in Portugal and the protection includes all live animals and fish, for example Epinephalus guaza. Guided diving tours are made to this area. Fishing strictly prohibited.

▶ **Ponta de São Lourenço natural preserve is the island's easternmost point.**

▶ From Encumeada you can see the sea to the south as well as north.

Ponta Delgada de São Lourenço Nature Reserve is located on the easternmost point of Madeira in the São Lourenço peninsula. It is an area 9 km long and 2 km wide and includes two small islands, Ilhéu da Cevada and Ilhéu da Ponta Delgada de São Lourenço. The area has been protected since 1982 and there you can find in addition to rare plants, also some nesting birds. In São Lourenço Natural Preserve you are free to hike and walk and there are also places for bird monitoring.

Rocha do Navio Coastal Nature Reserve located in Santana was established in 1997, on the request of the local people, to prevent over-fishing with explosives. The area is located between Ponta de São Jorge and Ponta do Clério and extends also to the land 100 meters above the sea level. There Monk seals can be seen and many rare plants thrive.

Selvagens Islands Natural Preserve consists of Selvagem Grande, Selvagem Pequena, Ilhéu de Fora, Palheiro da Terra and Palheiro do Mar islands. This natural preserve was established in 1971, is one of the oldest nature parks in Portugal. It was established to protect rare nesting birds in the sea area. For these islands visitation without authorization is not permitted. Ilhas Selvagens islands is located approx. 216 km south from Madeira.

DID YOU KNOW...

Garajau Marine Nature Reserve (Reserva Natural Parcial do Garajau) is the only exclusive deep ocean Nature Reserve in Portugal and guided diving tours are done there.

Madeiras flowers, plants and trees

The laurel forest (Laurissilva or Laurisilva) is the original forest in Madeira and covers more than 20 % (22 000 hectares) of the island's area, mainly in the northern parts of the island. In Madeira's laurel forest there lives a great deal of rare organisms and plants. And here this surviving species of tree occurs in nature only in Madeira, the Azores, the Canary Islands and Cape Verde. This laurel forest has been protected since 1999 as one of the Unesco's Natural World Heritage subjects. Rare birds also nest in the forest.

Dragon Trees (Draceana draco) are also an original tree species in Madeira and they grow naturally only on Madeira, the Canary Islands and Cape Verde. Madeira's Regional Government has established a park, where these Dragon Trees grow. Dragon Tree Park (Draguiro) is located in São Gonçalo, address Sitio das Neves, just outside of Funchal.

Madeira's species of trees include also; eucalyptuses, as well as various of acasias and pines, plane trees, casuarina, the kapok tree, jacaranda, African tulip tree, orchid tree, sausage tree, various palm trees and spruces and stink laurel. Rare species, such as cheese-wood, Madeiran mahogany, the Canary Islands juniper and lacy tree-fern can also be found on the island.

> **DID YOU KNOW...**
>
> **Laurel forest (Laurissilva or Laurisilva) covers more than 20% (22 000 hectares) of the island's area.**

▶ **Dragon trees are indigenous to Madeira.**

▶ There are dozens of different species of palm trees.

▶ The African Tulip Tree (Flame of the Forest, Fountain Tree) blossoms almost throughout the year.

▶ Acasias (mimosa) can be found many different species.

There are many fruit trees growing in Madeira, for example bananas, passion fruits, guavas, tamarilho, persimmon (sharon fruit), mangos, papayas, custard apple trees, apples, peaches, pears, avocados, oranges, mandarins, lemons, chestnuts etc. Fennel is an indigenous plant from Madeira.

Big bushes and trees with companion species which grow in Northern Europe inside houses in pots; Tree Heath, Tufted Fig Tree, Indian Rubber Tree, Hibiscus, Poinsettia, Fern Tree, Ceriman, Croton, Orange Trumpet Vine, Camellia, Yucca, Hydrangea etc. Bougainvillea's and Hibiscus are used on beautiful and colourful fences with buxus trees.

Other flowering plants are for example Agapanthus, Bottlebrush, Kaffir Lily, Impatiens, Protea, Passion Flower, Bird of Paradise, Flamingo Flower and the different roses, orchids and azaleas. You can also find for example the rare Madeiran Orchid.

Madeira also cultivates flowers for export. Almost 200 growers produces flowers for sale and they export more than 5 million flowers a year, exports are growing all the time. You can take beautiful cut flowers, plants or corms and seedlings back home as souvenirs. On request the sellers pack them care-fully in boxes for the journey home. Flowers and plants can be purchased from the central market place, market gardens, florist shops and from florists next to the Cathedral Sé.

▶ **King Protea is in bud.**

▶ The Bird of Paradise is Madeira's national flower.

Monthly blossoming flowers and trees

Flowers are Madeira's calling card and they grow in every corner, nook and cranny. In public and private parks, gardens and yards there blossom colourful and beautiful flowers, plants, bushes and trees throughout the whole year.

Throughout the year bloom for example Begonia, Morning Glory, Flamingo Flower, Brazilian Spider Flower (Princess Flower, Glory Bush), Bougainvillea (Paper Flower), Hibiscus (Shoe Plant, Rose of China), Lavender, Cape Leadwort (Plumbago), Bird of Paradise, which is Madeira's national flower also Cape Honeysuckle and Peanut Butter Cassia (Popcorn Bush, Golden Wonder).

In January in blossom you can find the African Daisy (Bears Ear), Calla (Calla Lily, Arum Lily), Camellia (Japan Rose), Climbing Aloe, Daisy Tree, Kapok Tree (Floss Silk Tree), Lady's Slipper (Venus Slipper), Mimosa (Mock Acacia, Wild Tamarind, West Indian Lead Tree), Orange Trumpet Vine (Golden Shower), Orchid Tree (Camel's Foot Tree), Poinsettia, Pride of Madeira, Red Hot Poker Tree (Karat Tree), Swan's Neck Agave (The Maguey Plant, Dragon-Tree Agave) and Sword Aloe.

In February the African Daisy, Calla, Camellia, Cattleya, Climbing Aloe, Daisy Tree, Kapok Tree, Lady's Slipper, Mimosa, Nasturtium, Orange Trumpet Vine, Orchid Tree, Poinsettia, Pride of Madeira, Red Hot Poker Tree, Swan's Neck Agave, Tree Rhododendron

(Flame Tree) and Weeping Bottlebrush (Drooping Bottlebrush).

In March are flowering the Acacia (Black Wattle), African Daisy, Calla, Cattleya, Climbing Aloe, Common Broom, Franciscea ('Yesterday, Today and Tomorrow'), Judas Tree (Tree of Judas), Lady's Slipper, Mimosa, Nasturtium, Orchid Tree, Pride of Madeira, Red Hot Poker Tree, Star Jasmine (Chinese Ivy), Tree Rhododendron and Weeping Bottlebrush.

In April blooms the Acacia, African Daisy, African Tulip Tree (Flame of the Forest, Fountain Tree), Angel's Trumpet (Angel's Tears), Bamboo Orchid (Cane Orchid), Calla, Cattleya, Climbing Aloe, Common Broom, Dew Flower, Flame Tree, Franciscea, Indian Shot, Jacaranda, Judas Tree, King Protea (Cape Artichoke-Flower, Giant Honeypot), Lady's Slipper, Nasturtium, Passion Flower (Granadilla), Red Hot Poker Tree, Star Jasmine, Torch Lily (Red Hot Poker), Weeping Bottlebrush, Weigela and Wisteria.

In May you will find in flower for example the Acacia, African Daisy, African Tulip Tree, Agapanthus (African Lily, Lily of the Nyle), Angel's Trumpet, Bamboo Orchid, Calla, Cattleya, Chrysanthemum (Mandon's Chrysanthemum), Climbing Aloe, Common Broom, Dew Flower, Flame Tree, Franciscea, Greek Acanthos (Bear's Breech), Indian Shot, Jacaranda, Jasmine, Judas Tree, King Protea, Lady's Slipper, Madeiran Orchid, Magnolia (Big Laurel, Bull Bay, Large Flowered Magnolia), Nasturtium, Oleander (Rose Bay), Passion Flower, Pride of Madeira, Red Hot Poker Tree, Rock Orchid, Silk Tree (Pink Siris, Persian Acacia), Snowball Tree (Guelder Rose), Torch Lily, Weeping Bottlebrush and Weigela.

In June the African Tulip Tree, Agapanthus, Angel's Trumpet, Bamboo Orchid, Calla, Cattleya, Chrysanthemum, Common Broom, Dew Flower, Flame Tree, Franciscea, Frangipani (Pagoda Tree), Greek Acanthus, Hydrangea, Indian Shot, King Protea, Madeiran Orchid, Magnolia, Nasturtium, Oleander, Passion Flower, Prickly Pear, Pride of Madeira, Red Hot Poker Tree, Rock Orchid, Silk Tree, Snowball Tree, Torch Lily, Weeping Bottlebrush and Weigela.

▶ **Sweet-Scented Jasmine with sensitive yellow flowers**

▶ Beautiful yellow Allamanda (Golden Trumpet) is flowering from July to November.

In July flowers the African Tulip Tree, Agapanthus, Allamanda (Golden Trumpet), Angel's Trumpet, Bamboo Orchid, Cattleya, Chrysanthemum, Common Broom, Coral Vine (Love's Chain, Mexican Creeper), Dew Flower, Flame Tree, Franciscea, Frangipani, Garden Coral, Ginger Lily (Butterfly Lily), Greek Acanthus, Hydrangea, Indian Shot, Lady's Slipper, Madeiran Orchid, Magnolia, Nasturtium, Oleander, Pampas Grass, Passion Flower, Prickly Pear, Pride of Madeira, Red Hot Poker Tree, Silk Tree, Torch Lily, Weeping Bottlebrush and White-Blooming Sage (Mexican Bush Sage, Scarlet Sage).

In August in flower is the African Tulip Tree, Agapanthus, Allamanda, Angel's Trumpet, Bamboo Orchid, Cattleya, Coral Vine, Dragon Tree, Flame Tree, Frangipani, Garden Coral, Ginger Lily, Hydrangea, Indian Shot, Nasturtium, Oleander, Pampas Grass, Passion Flower, Prickly Pear, Red Hot Poker Tree, Stiverbush, Torch Lily and White-Blooming Sage.

In September the African Tulip Tree, Agapanthus, Allamanda, Angel's Trumpet, Belladonna Lily (Cape Belladonna), Cattleya, Coral Vine, Dragon Tree, Flame Tree, Frangipani, Ginger Lily, Guernsey Lily, Hydrangea, Indian Shot, Kapok Tree, Nasturtium, Pampas Grass, Passion Flower, Podranea (Ricasol Podranea), Prickly Pear, Red Hot Poker Tree, Torch Lily and White-Blooming Sage.

In October blossoms the African Tulip Tree, Allamanda, Belladonna Lily, Cattleya, Coral Vine, Frangipani,

Guernsey Lily, Kapok Tree, Pampas Grass, Poinsettia and Sword Aloe.

In November in flower the Allamanda, Belladonna Lily, Calla, Daisy Tree, Guernsey Lily, Kapok Tree, Oranje Trumpet Vine, Passion Flower, Poinsettia and Sword Aloe.

In December the Calla, Camellia, Daisy Tree, Kapok Tree, Lady's Slipper, Oranje Trumpet Vine, Poinsettia, Swan's Neck Agave and Sword Aloe.

> **DID YOU KNOW...**
>
> Funchal got it's name from the fennel (Portuguese funcho) which grew wild before colonization of the island.

▶ Elegant white Callas (Calla Lily, Arum Lily) in Camacha

▶ Sword Aloes and Common Aloes (Barbados Aloe) grow wild beside roads and slopes.

▶ Cock's Comb Coral Tree's (Crybaby Tree) flowers are like bird's beak

▶ The colourful Coral Tree

Poinsettias are flourishing and grow tall.

▶ Firethorn's berries remains of Rowan-berries.

Water Lilies are blooming in many different colours.

Mansions and palaces

In Madeira there are plenty of great, old manor houses (quintas). Many of these beautiful mansions have been demolished over time, in particular in Funchal, but fortunately many still remain. Most of these remaining manor houses and mansions are from golden years of the sugar cane plantation, i.e. 1500s, 1600s and 1700s. In these mansions lived the aristocrats and wealthy traders. Some of these mansions are still in private ownership and cannot be visited. Luckily there are many mansions which are now hotels or museums etc. in public use and these you can visit and in some of them you can stay overnight. Almost all of these mansions have gorgeous gardens, and some mansions have gardens you can explore even though the mansions themselves are private.

Bishop's Palace (Paço Episcopal) was built in the 1600s. Part of the palace was destroyed in the 1748 earthquake, but was soon rebuilt. The bishops of Madeira lived in the palace till 1910, when it was changed to a school. It remained a school until 1943 and then as the Sacred Art Museum which the building has been since 1955. The palace is located on one side of the City Square (Praça do Municipio) and in front of it is a museum café.

Casa da Calçada was built in 1650s for count Calçada's residence. Some changes and repairs have been made for building in 1700s. Since 1940 it has been the Frederico de Freitas' residence. This Madeiran lawyer, a notary and art lover collected art, furniture and ceramics during three decades, and left this manor house and all his worldly possessions as a legacy for Madeira's Regional Governmet. The building has been the Frederico de Freitas Museum since 1988.

Madeira's Regional Government Palace (Palácio Governo Regional) is located opposite the main post office on Avenida Zarco and the building fills almost the entire city block. This palace was previously used as a hospital, there is a beautiful patio inside the building and fantastic ceramic tiles in the entrance hall.

Quinta da Achada mansion is from the 1700s. This mansion has been also a summer house for bishops' of Funchal and it has a stunning garden. Currently this mansion is the garden hotel, Quinta Jardins do Lago and is located at Rua Dr. João Lemos Gomes, in São Pedro, in Funchal.

Quinta da Bela Vista was built in 1844 and belongs still to the same family. It was converted to a hotel in 1989. Surrounding the building is a beautiful park. Address Caminho Avista Navios 4.

Quinta Boa Vista mansion was built in the 1600s and has been in the Garton family since the 1800s. The mansion is located at Rua Lombo da Boa Vista. The mansion is in private use, but it's orchid garden opens at the same time as the market garden and this garden you can visit. Open from Monday to Saturday from 9 am to 5.30 pm. Closed on Sundays and on public holidays. Bus number 32 or by taxi.

▶ Many of the mansions and palaces can be visited.

▶ Funchal City Hall is located in the old palace.

Quinta da Casa Branca was built in 1700s and has been owned by the Leacock family from the beginning. This great baroque building worked as convalescent home for soldiers during the Second World War and is now a hotel. This mansion has a delightful park. Address Caminho da Casa Branca.

Quinta das Cruzes is a baroque style mansion from the 1500s. In this mansion they also tell that João Gonçalves Zarco and his descendants were residents. Little, if any, is remaining of that original building, because it has been extended and a altered throughout the centuries. It has been a museum of decorative art and architecture (Museu da Quinta das Cruzes) since 1953. It is located at Calçada do Pico 1. This stunning mansion has an exotic garden and an attractive small chapel (Nossa Senhora da Piedade), which was build in 1692. There is also a new modern café building. The museum is open from

▶ Roses are flourishing in the spring and summer.

Tuesday to Sunday from 10 am to 12.30 pm and again from 2 pm to 5.30 pm. Closed on Mondays.

Quinta Lyra was built in the 1800s. This small mansion is currently operating as a private medical center (Clínica de Santa Luzia) and is located at Rua Torrinha 5.

Quinta Magnólia is located in Rua do Dr. Pita, just above the Enotel Quinta do Sol hotel. This mansion was built in the beginning of the 1800s and from the 1930s used as a British Club after which was expropriated by the Regional Government in 1980. Today the mansion is a Library for Foreign Cultures. Surrounding the mansion there is a big park where you can walk and enjoy sport and leisure. There is also a playground for children. Free access.

Quinta Mãe dos Homens was built in the 1700s. It was earlier also known as the Quinta do Visconde. Today part of the mansion is a hotel by the same name and part of it is a private residence. In the park there is a small chapel. Address Travessa Manuel Alexandre.

Quinta da Palmeira is a stunning manor house from the end of the 1600s. It is located at Rua Levada de Santa Luzia 31A. This mansion is in private use but the garden can be visited. Open every day from 10 am to 1 pm. Buses number 25 and 26.

Quinta Perestrello was built in the 1800s. It is located just next to the hotel Pestana Miramar at the junction of Estarada Monumental and Rua Dr. Pita. This mansion is currently operating as a hotel and belongs to the same manor house accommodation chain as the hotel Quinta das Vistas, hotel Quinta do Estreito and Quinta do Monte.

Quinta Reid is located and connected with the Botanical Garden (Jardim Botanico da Madeira) at address Caminho do Meio. This mansion was built in the 1880s and belonged at one time also to the Reid family. It is also known as Quinta do Sucesso and Quinta da Paz. Open to the public every day from 9 am to 6 pm. Buses numbers 29, 30 or 31 and by taxi or cable car from Monte.

Quintinha de São João was built in the 1700s and located at Rua da Levada de São João 4. Earlier within the property was also the Quinta de São João, which has been demolished. The Quintinha currently operates as a hotel. In the hotel's park there is a small chapel (Nossa Senhora da Redenção e Mercês).

São Pedro Palace (Palácio de São Pedro) was built in the 1700s as count Carvalhal's family residence. In the middle of the 1800s there have been changes to the building and at the end of the 1800s it was a hotel and in the other wing there was a school. Funchal city bought the palace in 1929 and at present the building works as the Museum of Natural Science, the City Library and Archive also a small aquarium. Beside the mansion there is a Herb and Medicinal Garden (Jardim de Plantas Aromaticas)

which was established in 2000. Address Rua Mouraria 31.

Quinta Vigia mansion is located next to Santa Catarina Park on Avenida do Infante. This palace was built in the 1800s and there have been overnight stays of several royals including Austrian Empress Elizabeth (Sissi). The mansion is well known also as Quinta das Angústias and Quinta Lambert. Under the Regional Government's ownership the mansion moved in 1979 and was in the beginning Madeira's Conservatorio premises. When the current conservatorio moved into it's place in 1981, Quinta Vigia became the official Presidential Palace (Palácio do Governo Regional) in 1984. The park around the mansion was previously wider and reached as far as the current Casino and Pestana Casino Park hotel area. The mansion cannot be visited, other than on official's events. When the gates are open there is a free access to the park, usually from Monday to Friday from 9 am to 5 pm. There is also a small chapel (Capela de Nossa Senhora das Anquistias) in the park.

STUNNING MANSIONS AND MANOR HOUSES CAN ALSO BE FOUND OUTSIDE OF FUNCHAL:

Quinta Dr. Américo Durão in Santa Cruz, at address Sito da Terça, currently operating as manor house hotel, Estalagem Albatroz.

Quinta do Arco mansion is young, constructed only in the 1920s. In this mansion you can stay overnight in small separate cottages. In the mansion's stunning park is a Rose Garden with almost 20 000 roses. The mansion is located on the north coast of the island, in São Jorge, address Sitio da Lagoa. Rose Garden is open every day from April to December from 11 am to 6 pm.

Quinta da Capela is located in Porto da Cruz and it was built in the 1700s. The building was used from the 1940s to the 1960s as a school and is now Casa de Turismo a rural hotel with five rooms, little chapel and great views to the Atlantic. There are a great deal of levadas in the area.

Quinta do Estreito in Câmara de Lobos is located in the midst of vineyards, address Rua José Joaquim da Costa and operates as a manor house hotel of the same name.

Quinta da Serra was built in the beginning of the 1800s and is located in Jardim da Serra, address Estrada do Chote 4. This mansion has a beautiful park with some rare old trees. The mansion has operated as a manor house hotel since 2003.

Quinta do Monte mansion was well known also for names Quinta Cossart and Quinta Gordon in the 1800s but currently as Quinta Jardins do Imperador. This mansion was completed in the late 1700s and is located near the Monte City Garden, address Caminho do Pico Monte. There lived the Austrian Emperor Charles I and Empress Zita, who were in exile in Madeira with their children. The following year the Emperor died in this palace of bronchitis. In his memory there was built a small

▶ An attractive rural hotel A Quinta Estalagem in Santo da Serra

chapel in the garden in the late 1920s. Around the mansion is this Emperor's Garden (Jardins do Imperador) where grow glamorous roses and other plants. The mansion itself is currently in poor condition and cannot be visited, but there is planned to be a tea house in the future. Garden is open from Monday to Saturday from 9 am to 5 pm. Buses number 20, 21 and 22.

Quinta do Monte is currently functioning in Monte as a manor house hotel, which was previously known as Quinta Henrique Felix. This mansion was built in the mid 1700s and is surrounded by a beautiful garden.

Quinta do Palheiro Ferreiro is the largest mansion outside of Funchal and is very well-known for it's splendid garden (Jardim da Quinta do Palheiro Ferreiro), where are flowering Camellias and Magnolias. It is located at Estrada da Camacha, near the Palheiro golf course. This aristocratic mansion was constructed by count Carvalhal early in the 1800s and it has been in the Blandy family since 1885. Connected to the mansion is a chapel. In the mansion there have been special overnight guests for example Empress Leopoldina, Prince Philip and other royalty. The mansion is currently run as a manor house hotel, Quinta Casa Velha do Palheiro. The garden is open from Monday to Friday from 9 am to 5 pm. Closed at weekends. Buses 36A and 37 or by taxi.

Quintas do Prazer is known currently as Monte Palace. It is located above Funchal in Monte, at approx. 5 km

from the city center. This mansion was originally built in the late 1700s and was opened as a hotel in 1904. The hotel was closed during the Second World War and was used to house evacuated troops. In 1987 a Madeiran businessman José Manuel Rodrigues Berardo bought the mansion and converted it into a foundation museum and a private house and garden. The Mansion is for private use and cannot be visited. The Palace's garden was opened to the public in 1991 and there are now additional rare flowers and plants, you can also see ceramic art, bricks, sculptures and all kind of works of art. The garden is open every day from 9.30 am to 6 pm. Best way for access is either by cable car, taxi or buses number 20, 21, 22 and 48.

Quinta da Rochinha is located in Ponta do Sol and currently operates as a manor house hotel.

Quinta do Santo da Serra is a large mansion which was in the past owned by the Blandy family, but now it is owned by the Regional Government. This mansion is also known as Quinta da Junta. It is located in Santo da Serra, north east of Funchal, it has great views to the Machico valley. The mansion's stunning garden with Camellias and other plants is open to the public and access is free. Unfortunately there is no entry to the mansion. Country bus number 77.

Solar de São Cristovão in Machico is located at the address Sito do Caramanchão. It was built in the late 1600s and is currently used as the cultural center of Machico.

Quinta do Vale is located on the north coast of the island in São Vicente. This mansion was built in the 1700s and is currently operating as a manor house hotel.

Quinta das Vinhas is also known as Quinta do Lombo dos Serrões. This farmhouse was completed in the mid 1600s and is located in Estreito da Calheta, surrounded by vineyards and operates as a rural hotel of the same name.

▶ You can also find beautiful palaces and mansions outside of Funchal.

▶ Cycads are not either palms or ferns.

▶ Elegant Palms (Bungalow Palm, Piccabeen Palm) fruits

Australian Tree-Ferns (Lacy Tree-Fern) grow in Macronesia (Madeira, the Canary Islands and Cape Verde).

145

Churches and chapels

Madeirans are Roman Catholic and very religious, which also shows in the number of churches and in many ecclesiastical public holidays. In Madeira there are lots of beautifully decorative churches (igreja) and chapels (capela). It's worth visiting them even if you are not very religious. Most churches are very old and have stunning art, valuables, wood carvings and the Portuguese characteristic ceramic art (azulejos). Churches are normally open from 8 am to 1 pm,

and again from 3 pm to 5 pm. The smallest churches may not have fixed timetables, so it is worth asking at a nearby café or a neighbour for a key. Services are usually on Sunday mornings at 10 or 11 and weekday mornings at 6 or 7 and in the evening at 5 pm. However, it is advisable to check relevant times from bulletin board outside of the church because the times vary.

Cathedral Sé (Sé do Funchal) is the oldest church in Funchal and it's construction began at the end of the

▶ **Cathedral Sé is one of the oldest buildings in Madeira.**

▶ Colégio Church was built in the mid 1600s.

1400s. This amazing representative of church architecture was completed in 1508 and it is also one of the oldest preserved buildings in Madeira. The church is located just in the center of Funchal, on Rua Dr. António José de Almeida. The architectural style is southern European Gothic with a hint of Moorish mixed in with local effect. There are stunning paintings, lots of gilding and a beautiful cedar ceiling in the church. In June there are held international Bach concerts. In front of the church is Pope John Paul II's statue. He visited the island in 1991.

Colégio Church (Igreja do Colégio), also known as Igreja de São João Evangelista, is located on the City Square (Praça do Municipio) in Funchal center. The church was completed in 1647 and was originally part of a Jesuit monastery and school. It's also beautifully decorated with ceramic tiles and paintings from the 1600s and 1700s. The church is open every day from 5 pm to 6 pm and also when services are held. In this church are held organ concerts on Mondays throughout the year.

Santa Clara Convent (Convento de Santa Clara) is located on Calçada de Santa Clara. It was completed in 1497 and is as its name indicates is still a convent. This beautiful convent church's walls are blended with a stunning 1600s ceramic tiles and there is a beautiful painted wood ceiling. From this Santa Clara convent the nuns fled in 1566 to Nuns Valley when pirates attacked Funchal and killed 250

▶ Beautiful crèches (Belém or Lapinhas) decorate the city at Christmas time.

people. In the Santa Clara convent there is also the grave of Madeira's discoverer João Gonçalves Zarco.

Carmo Church (Igreja do Carmo) is located on Rua do Carmo and was completed in the mid 1600s. This church has beautiful wood carvings, ceramic art, a few interesting Madonna statues from 1600s and 1700s and gold and silver items.

Santo António Church (Igreja de Santo António) is located inside the city limits in part of the city named also Santo António. The church was completed in the late 1600s and was beautifully restored in the 1920s when to one of the towers a clock was added. The black and white roof can be seen from afar.

São Martinho Church (Igreja de São Martinho) is located on the side of São Martinho in the foot hills. The church is a landmark the tower of which can be seen from afar and especially in the evenings. The church is quite young for Madeiran churches because it was completed only in the 1950s.

São Pedro Church (Igreja de São Pedro) is located on Rua do São Pedro. The church was completed in 1596. There have been built expansions and a small chapel was added in the 1600s. It has a beautifully decorated and carved altar and the church is covered with magnificent ceramic tiles.

Socorro Church (Igreja do Socorro) or another name Igreja de Santa Maria Maior was completed originally in the late 1500s, but has since been rebuilt several times. This charming church is decorated with beautiful ceramic tiles and paintings and is located in the old city, at the end of Santa Maria street on Largo do Socorro.

Chapel of Corpo Santo (Capela do Corpo Santo) a small chapel was completed in 1559 and it is also one of the oldest buildings in Funchal. It is located on Largo do Corpo Santo, in the middle of the old city in the restaurant area. This chapel is decorated entirely with the great local artists paintings of the time.

148

Chapel of Nossa Senhora das Angústias (Capela de Nossa Senhora das Angústias) is located on Avenida do Infante, in Presidencial Palace's Park. It was completed in the 1700s and decorated with Baroque paintings and statues of that time. When the park's gates are open you can enter.

Chapel of Santa Catarina (Capela de Santa Catarina) is located in the end of Santa Catarina Park, close to Columbus' statue. Originally a wooden chapel which was completed in 1425, but re-built in stone in the 1400s.

Chapel of Santo António (Capela de Santo António) is from the 1700s. This small chapel is located unnoticeably next to the Parliament Building (Região Autónoma da Madeira Assemblea Legislativa) on Avenida do Mar.

Baptist Church (Igreja Baptista do Funchal) is located at Rua do Doutor Sidónio Pais.

English Church (Igreja Inglesa) also known as Holy Trinity Church was completed in 1822 and from outside it does not look like a church at all. It is located at Rua de Quebra Costas 18 and with the church there is also a small library. Services in English will be held there every day at 9 am and on Sundays at 8 am and 11 am. In church they often hold concerts, bingo evenings etc. Close to the British Church on end of Rua da Carreira street there is also the British Cemetery (Cemiterio Ingles) where all the protestants of the island have been buried. Cemetery is open from Monday to Friday from 10 am to 4.30 pm.

▶ A beautiful chapel from the 1400s in Santa Catarina Park

▶ Monte Church's twin towers are illuminated in the evenings and brightly shine down to the city

Monte Church (Igreja de Nossa Senhora do Monte) is located in Monte, just above Funchal and from there you have great views down to the city. The church was completed in 1800s and inside the church there is Austrian Emperor Charles I's grave. The church is also a destination of pilgrimage on the 15th of August, on which date the local believers crawl on their knees up to the church on more than 70 steps. In the evenings the church's twin towers shine brightly down to the city.

Jehovah Witnesses Church (Igreja Testemunhas Jeová) or Igreja de São José no Funchal, is located at Rua do Cano.

Pentecostal Church (Igreja Evangélica Assembleia de Deus Pentecostal) is located at Rua Cid Cabo Galerias D. João 42.

Presbyterian Church (Igreja Evangélica Presbiteriana do Funchal) also known as the Scottish Church is located next to the City Park on crossroad of Rua Ivens and Rua do Conselheiro, and it was completed in 1861. Services at Sunday mornings in English and in German twice a month on Sunday afternoons. Check the times from the bulletin board.

Catholic masses in English are held on Sundays at 10 am in Chapel of Penha França (Capela Penha da França) on Rua da Imperatriz Dona Amélia.

Evangelic services and bible reading in English are held in Madeira's International Christian Association on Sundays at 11 am at address Rua dos Capelistas 18.

Outside of Funchal in the small villages and towns there are many churches and chapels worth visiting. For example, Ingreja Paroquial in Machico and Capela de Nossa Senhora da Piedade in Caniçal were completed in the 1400s. Capela de Nossa Senhora das Neves in Garajau and Igreja Loreto in Calheta were completed in the 1500s and Capela São Vicente in 1694. Also Capela dos Reis Magos in between Estreito do Calheta and Jardim do Mar is worth time to visit.

An interesting destination is also **Sacred Art Museum** (Museu de Arte Sacra) on Rua do Bispo 21. It is located in the old palace which before was premises of Bishops of Madeira. At the museum there are paintings, sculptures, ecclesiastical dishes and beautifully embroidered clerical clothing. The museum is open from Tuesday to Saturday from 10 am to 12.30 pm and again from 2.30 to 6 pm and on Sundays from 10 am to 1 pm. Closed on Mondays and public holidays.

▶ In churches can be found valuable paintings and different works of art.

Museums

In Funchal there is many interesting museums for those interested in a variety of issues. All these destinations under the title 'museums' are not dust-covered museums, but some of them contain items really worth seeing and interesting collections. Students and pensioners receive discounts for entry fees when they show students or pensioners cards. At many museums children pay either half the price or enter free of charge.

Baden-Powell Museum Center,
National Corps of Scouts (CNE) – Portuguese Catholic Scouting, at Rua do Canadá, Cave A (near the Church of Nazaré). The association was founded in 1923 and is the largest scouting organization in Portugal. Open from Monday to Friday from 2 pm to 7 pm. In Funchal on Rua João Tavira there is a small statue of Lord Baden Powell who founded the scout movement.

CR7 Museum is located on Rua Princesa D. Maria Amélia 10 and it opened its door in December 2013. This museum portrays the life of the Madeiran football player Cristiano Ronaldo. There all his trophies are displayed, photographs of his career, videos and a replica of his wax statue. Open from Monday to Saturday from 10 am to 6 pm.

DID YOU KNOW...

In Madeira there are dozens of beautiful mansions and stunning gardens and parks.

Electricity Museum (Museu de Electricidades Casa da Luz) is located in an electricity company house beside the bus station, at Rua Casa da Luz 2. The museum has old, rare machinery and equipment from a hundred years ago as well as a variety of art exhibitions. The museum is open from Tuesday to Saturday from 10 am to 12.30 pm and again from 2 pm to 6 pm. Closed on Mondays, Sundays and on public holidays.

Embroidery Museum (Nucleo Museologico do Bordado Madeira I.B.T.A.M.) is located in Rua Visconde de Anadia 44. The museum's collections includes embroideries from handkerchiefs to clothing and furniture from the 1800s to today. The museum is open from Monday to Friday from 9.30 am to 6 pm. Closed at weekends and on public holidays.

Frederico de Freitas House and Museum (Casa – Museu Frederico de Freitas) is located at Calçada de Santa Clara 7. In this 1650s mansion (Casa da Calçada) are presented all kind of Madeiran objects and materials related to its history and in addition also Chinese porcelain, ceramics and antique furniture, carpets, paintings and sculptures. There are also displayed rare Portuguese, Persians and Moorish tiles from 1500s to 1900s. The museum is open from Tuesday to Saturday from 10 am to 5.30 pm and on Sundays from 10 am to 12.30 pm. Closed on Mondays and public holidays.

Henrique and Francisco Franco Gallery (Museu Henrique e Francisco

Franco) is located at Rua João Deus 13. The museum was established in 1987 and it presents these well known Madeiran artist brothers paintings, drawings and sculptures from the 1800s and 1900s. Francisco Franco's signature is the João Gonçalves Zarco's statue on Avenida Arriaga. The museum is open from Monday to Friday from 10 am to 6 pm. Closed at weekends and on public holidays.

Funchal City Museum (Museu Municipal do Funchal), the Natural History Museum of Funchal was established in 1929 and is located in São Pedro Palace in address Rua da Mouraria 31. In this baroque style palace, originating from the 1700s, are on display Madeira's flora, animals and minerals, as well as stamps and coins. In the same building there is also a small aquarium, city library and archive. The museum is open from Tuesday to Friday from 10 am to 6 pm. Weekends from 12 am to 6 pm. Closed on Mondays.

Jesuits' College of Funchal is located at Rua dos Ferreiros, beside the Colégio Church. It was founded in the 1569. For more than 400 years of its history it served a number of tenants, from British invaders to the University of Madeira, coming to serve as a military facility and a number of schools. There also are held monthly Coimbra Fado concerts and guided tours. Open Monday to Friday from 11 am to 6 pm, Saturdays from 10 am to 2 pm.

Military Museum (Museu Militar da Madeira) is located at São Lourenço

▶ São Lourenço's Palace has been the premises of governors and military executives.

Palace and Fort on Avenida Zarco. The museum comprises three rooms, where are presented old weapons and uniforms from the early days of the island's history to the present day. São Lourenço's fort was completed in the late 1500s and was for military use and as the premises for governors of the island. Open from Monday to Friday from 10 am to 12.00 am and again from 2 pm to 5 pm. Saturday 10 am till noon. Closed on Sundays and on public holidays. Free access.

Modern Art Museum (Museu de Arte Contemporânea) is located in the old city in the São Tiago Fortress (Fortaleza de São Tiago), on east end of the promenade, in address Rua do Portão de São Tiago. The fortress has been completed in 1614 and has operated as a museum and art gallery since 1992 and is an attraction in itself. Collections include mostly Portuguese contemporary artists from the 1960s to the present day. The museum has also changing art shows and a quality restaurant. The museum is open from Monday to Saturday from 10 am to 12.30 pm and again from 2 pm to 5.30 pm. Closed on Sundays and on public holidays.

Museum of Natural History (Museu de História Natural) is located in the Botanical Garden, at Caminho do Meio. In the museum there are presented valuable collections of Madeiran plants, fish, insects and other animals. The museum is open every day from 9 am to 6 pm. With the same ticket you can also enter the Botanical Garden.

Quinta das Cruzes Museum (Museu da Quinta das Cruzes) is located at Calçada do Pico 1. This baroque style mansion from the 1600s, also known as Quinta Madeirense, introduces how wealthy people once lived. The museum, established in 1953, presents Portuguese furniture, French porcelain, paintings and sculptures from the 1500s to 1800s. In addition there are silver items from Europe and the Far East, tombstones and parts of old buildings. The museum also features an amazing, definitely worth visiting garden, a small chapel and a café. Open from Tuesday to Saturday from 10 am to 12.30 pm and again from 2 pm to 5.30 pm. On Sundays from 10 am to 1 pm. Closed on Mondays and on public holidays.

Sacred Art Museum (Museu de Arte Sacra) is located on the City Square at Rua do Bispo 21, in the palace which previously was the premises of the Bishops of Madeira. The palace was

▶ It is said that in Quinta das Cruzes Zarco family once resided.

built in the 1500s and has been a museum since 1955. There are Flemish paintings and sculptures from the 1500s and 1600s and ecclesiastical ceremony dishes, costumes and jewellery. In front of the museum is a café. The museum is open from Tuesday to Saturday from 10 am to 12.30 pm and again from 2.30 pm to 6 pm and Sundays from 10 am to 1 pm. Closed on Mondays and public holidays.

Sugar Museum (Nucleo Museologico a Cidade do Açúcar) is located at Praça Colombo 5, which was previously the sugar trader João Esmerald's home. The museum presents extensively sugar production from the 1400s; sugar exports and this trade's effects to Madeiran art and culture. The museum is open from Monday to Friday from 10 am to 12.30 pm and again from 2 pm to 6 pm. Closed on weekends and on public holidays.

Toy museum (Museu do Brinquedo da Madeira) is located next to the Market place at Rua Latino Coelho 39. This collection consists of more than 20 000 old toys; dolls, lead toy soldiers, miniature cars, games etc. dating from the 1800s till the present day. There is also a café and the workshop for children. Open from Tuesday to Saturday from 10 am to 8 pm and on Sundays from 10 am to 2 pm. Closed on Mondays.

The Universe of Memories João Carlos Abreu Museum (Universo de Memórias de João Carlos Nunes

▶ **From the terrace of The Universe of Memories João Carlos Abreu Museum are stunning views to the city.**

Abreu) is located across Santa Clara Convent, at Calçada do Pico 2. This other than dusty-covered museum's interesting objects and collections were collected by Madeira's former culture minister Abreu during his numerous travels around the world. It contains books, jewellery, sculptures, paintings, porcelain etc. The museum has also a charming tea house and terrace with stunning views to the city. To the tea house and terrace there is no entry fee but to the museum there is a small fee. The museum is open from Tuesday to Saturday from 10 am to 5 pm. Closed on Mondays, Sundays and on public holidays.

Vicentes Photography Museum

(Museu Photografia Vicentes) is located at Rua da Carreira 43. In that building was the first photographer's studio in Portugal it was set up by Vicentes Gomes da Silva. The photographer's studio was launched already in 1848 and had been active for four generations. It has been a museum since 1982. The collection contains photographs, cameras and negatives from the beginning until 1979. The museum is open from Monday to Friday from 10 am to 12.30 pm and again from 2 pm to 5 pm. At weekends and on public holidays it is closed. You cannot take any handbags, backpacks or shopping bags into the museum, they should be left at the cloakroom! Unfortunately in spring 2015 this museum was temporarily closed.

Mary Jane Wilson Museum (Núcleo Museológico Mary Jane Wilson) is located on Rua do Carmo 59–61. Mary Jane Wilson was an English Franciscan sister, who set up orphanages and schools on Madeira. The museum's collections consists of her personal things, as well as photos etc. Open from Tuesday to Friday from 10 am to 12 am and from 3 pm to 5 pm, Saturdays from 10 am to 1 pm. Closed on Mondays, Sundays and on public holidays. Mary Jane Wilson's Foundation's elderly home is located in a charming mansion in São Gonçalo, east of Funchal.

▶ **Lion's Tails (Lion's Ear) on promenade**

DID YOU KNOW...

In the Universe of Memories João Carlos Abreu Museum (Universo de Memórias de João Carlos Nunes Abreu) are displayed many of interesting objects.

▶ In the Wine Museum you can taste different varieties of Madeira Wine.

Wine Museum and the Wine Institute (Museu do Vinho da Madeira) is located at Rua 5 de Outubro 78, in a beautiful yellow building with a tower, just to the rear of the Justice House. The museum presents the history and the importance of Madeira wine for Madeirans. It also presents the process from cultivation to production and from harvesting to bottling. The museum is open from Monday to Friday from 9.30 am to 12.30 pm and again from 2 pm to 5 pm. Closed at weekends.

Wine Museum (Museu da Madeira Wine Company) is located next to the tourist office on Avenida Arriaga, in a baroque style building where once had been a Franciscan Monastery. It has been in current use from 1834. There Madeira wine has been produced and stocked, there also are located the oldest Madeira wine cellars in Madeira. The museum has a wine tasting bar and a shop, where you can buy Madeira wines of which the oldest bottled are from 1860! In the wine tasting bar there are stunning mural paintings which Max Romer painted in 1922. There are guided tours daily in English, German, French and Portuguese. The museum is open from Monday to Friday from 9.30 am to 6.30 pm and Saturdays from 10 am to 1 pm. Closed on Sundays and on public holidays.

DID YOU KNOW...

Everywhere listed under the title 'museums' are not just dust-covered museums, many of them contains really worthwhile and interesting collections.

Many interesting museums can also be found outside of Funchal. For example:

Car Collection Quinta de São Jorge is located in Santo da Serra, just opposite to the Santo da Serra golf course. This private collection consist of Volvo's from different decades, and all of them are beautifully restored to their new glory. There is also a café, restaurant, riding stables and riding school. Bus number 77.

▶ **Santo da Serra's Volvo collection have cars from different decades.**

Christopher Columbus House, Porto Santo Museum (Casa Museu de Cristóvão Colombo) is located on Porto Santo island, in Vila Baleira at address Rua Cristovão Colombo 12. The museum consists of two buildings which it is believed that Columbus (1451–1504) himself was a resident. The museum presents objects of that time, Columbus' portraits from the 1500s to the 1900s, and maps and essays of the conquers. The museum has a library which consists of different language books about Columbus and all the information you can possible find. Museum is open from Tuesday to Saturday at 10 am to 12.30 pm and again from 2 pm to 7 pm. Sundays from 10 am to 1 pm. Closed on Mondays and on public holidays.

Dr. Horácio Bento de Gouveia Home Museum (Museu Dr. Horácio Bento de Gouveia) is located at Ponta Delgada, at Sitio dos Tercos in Vila de Ponta Delgada. Gouveia was a Madeiran teacher, journalist and writer. His home museum presents old antiques and items associated with his life. The museum is open from Monday to Saturday from 3 pm to 6 pm. Closed on Sundays and on public holidays. Country bus number 6.

Ethnological Museum (Museu Etnografico da Madeira) is located in the old 1600s baroque mansion in Ribeira Brava, address Rua de São Francisco 24. The museum was set up in 1996 and presents all kind of objects, photographs and drawings connected to life and culture in Madeira. The museum is open from Tuesday to Friday from 10 am to 12.30 pm and again from 2 pm to 5.30 pm. Saturday and Sunday from 10 am to 12.30 and again from 1.30 pm to 5.30 pm. Closed on Mondays and on public holidays. Country bus number 7.

Limestone Museum (Núcleo Museológico – Rota da Cal) is located in São Vicente, at the address Sitio dos Lameiros. The museum consists of a 12 hectare area where there is a quarry and old fossils. Guided tours should be reserved in advance. Open every day from 10 am to 6 pm. Country buses number 4, 80, 132 and 139.

Monte Palace Museum (Museu Monte Palace) is located above Funchal in Monte, approx. 5 km from the city center, at the address Caminho do Monte 174. It presents minerals, stones, sculptures and art works from around the world. Around the museum's is an incredible tropical garden which in addition to rare flowers and plants, also displays ceramic tiles, bricks, and more sculptures. Access to the garden is with the same ticket. The museum is open from Monday to Sunday from 9.30 am to 6 pm. Best way there is cable car, by taxi or buses number 20, 21, 22 and 48.

Vineyard and Wine Museum of Arco de São Jorge (Museu da Vinha e do Vinho do Arco de São Jorge) is located as its name indicates, in São Jorge at the address Sitio da Lagoa. It is, at the same time a working vineyard and garden, and presents tools and equipments needed for wine-growing. Open from Tuesday to Saturday from 2 pm to 5.30 pm. At other times must be reserved in advance. Country buses number 6, 103 and 138.

Whale Museum (Museu da Baleia) is located in the small fishing village of Caniçal, at the address Rua da Pedra D'Eira. The museum presents whaling with documentation and photos. Whaling was banned in Madeira in the beginning of 1980s. You will find also information about dolphins and seals and there you can listen to sounds of whales. The museum is open from Tuesday to Sunday from 10 am to 6 pm. Closed on Mondays and on public holidays. Country bus number 113.

▶ Jacarandas are blooming on Avenida do Infante in the spring.

Statues and monuments

In Madeira and in Funchal there is a lot of really interesting statues, monuments and sculptures. They are arranged in market places, squares, parks, along the promenade and in front of churches. All are not listed below, but those interested can look with around and make their discoveries.

Christ Statue (Cristo Rei) is located in Garajau. This statue of Christ with open arms facing the ocean is made by French sculptor Georges Serraz. The statue dates from 1927 and it is a smaller version of Rio de Janeiro's Christ Statue in Brazil.

▶ **Beautiful statues can be found in parks and gardens.**

Christopher Columbus bronze statue is located above the port in the Santa Catarina Park.

Cristiano Ronaldo's statue is the newest in the city and has caused lots of comments in public about its appearance. This bronze statue is 3,4 m high and made by Ricardo Veloza.

The Hanging Angel statue (Anjo Caído) is located on Estrada Monumental just a short distance of Forum Madeira shopping center to the west. This tall statue was made by Ricardo Veloza in 1932 and it is a tribute to all building workers.

João Gonçalves Zarco's, the discoverer of Madeira, this statue is located on Avenida Arriaga just opposite the Banco Portugal. This bronze statue was made by Madeiran artist Francisco Franco in 1927 and it has been in it's present location since 1934. The second Zarco statue is along promenade, close to hotel Pestana Grand.

Leda and Swan statue (Leda e Cisne) is located in the courtyard of the City Hall and was made in the 1800's. This statue was originally in Mercado D. Pedro V market place, which does not exist any more. It was moved to this location in 1941.

Madonna Statue of Peace (Nossa Senhora da Paz) is located in Terreiro da Luta, north of Monte, about 8 km from Funchal center. This massive monument pays tribute to World War I and was set up in 1927. Portugal was alongside the British and French in

▶ Anjo Caído statue is a tribute to building workers

▶ Praça da Autonomia statue is made by Ricardo Veloza.

World War I and Madeira was an important strategic point in the Atlantic. German submarines sank three French warships in Funchal harbour and the chain around the monument is made of the anchor cables of those ships.

Peace and Freedom statue (Paz e Liberdade) is located at the junction of Estrada Monumental and Rua do Dr. Pita. It is made by sculptor Manuela Aranha in 1988 and is a celebration of Madeira's autonomy.

Prince Henry the Navigator's statue is located beside the fountain round-about, just where Avenida do Infante

street starts. It is a copy of a similar statue in the city of Lagos in the Algarve.

Pope John Paul II's statue is located in front of Cathedral Sé. The Holy Father John Paul II visited to Madeira in 1991.

Praça da Autonomia statue is located in the Autonomy Square, next to Electrical House and is made by Ricardo Veloza.

DID YOU KNOW...

In Garajau is the statue of Christ (Cristo Rei) and it is a smaller version of Rio de Janeiro's Christ Statue in Brazil.

Madeira Wine

Wine producing has been vital since time began and Madeira wine is famous and excellent. Jesuit monks started wine growing in Madeira and they owned large cultivate areas and vineyards. The first variety was a Greek Malvasia grape, however, subsequently increased by some thirty other varieties. Madeira's volcanic soil and good climatic conditions are favourable for wine growing. The viticulture is mainly focused in the Câmara de Lobos region, but also elsewhere in the island one finds vineyards. Madeira wines were already exported in the 1400s, first to mainland Portugal and elsewhere in Europe and later to the United States and Japan.

Madeira wine was born by chance when the British seamen reloaded Madeira wine on board and during the journey the sun made the wine boil. Wine did not, however, become polluted but this made it even better. First they believed that the wine

▶ **The longer Madeira wine is kept in oak barrels, the better it will be.**

would have to be shipped to create the correct taste, but in the 1700s containers were developed which produced the same results.

There are four different kind of Madeira wines, which have been named after the variety of the grape. They can be served with almost all types of food and at any time. All Madeira wines, except vintage wines, are blended with vintages of several years, of which the youngest wine determines the year on the side of the bottle. The youngest wines are usually at least three years old, reserve wines and special reserve wines at least 5 to 10 years old. The best of vintage wines are from one and the same year's harvest and they have been stored in oak barrels for at least 20 years. The longer the wine is kept in oak barrels the better it will be. After the bottling vintage wines will be stored two more years before they will be sold.

Vinho Sercial is the driest of Madeira wines, the colour is light gold-yellow and the flavour is light. It is suitable for aperitif also with soups and fish when chilled. *Vinho Verdelho* is semi-dry and a more richer wine than Sercial, the colour is amber and becomes darker when ageing. It should be served in room temperature for aperitif or with soups, cheeses and desserts. *Vinho Boal* is semi-sweet and a rich wine, the colour is amber and sweeter than Verdelho it becomes red-brown when ageing. It should be served at room temperature with cheeses and desserts. *Vinho Malvasia* or Malmsey is a sweet rich wine, the colour is dark mahogany and should be served at

▶ Madeira wines last several years when opened, and should be stored in an upright position.

room temperature with desserts and cakes. Malvasia is also an excellent wine when keeping company with friends or blended with coffee. Madeira wines last several years when opened, and they should be stored in an upright position.

Terrantez is now very rare, as well as Solera. Some of them can still be found at very well equipped stores, even though the manufacture of these Madeira wines has already long been finished.

In Madeira they produce some of their own red, white and rose wines mainly for Madeiran own consumption. House wines offered in restaurants are often Portuguese wines from the continent and in the fanciest restaurants house wines are mostly foreign wines. Wines are classified from dry to sweet and in Portuguese they are: seco (dry), meio seco (semi-dry), meio doce (semi-sweet) and doce (sweet).

If you like wines you should visit the wine museums, vineyards or wine stores and taste different varieties of wines. In many places wines may be tasted free of charge. In September Madeira has many wine and harvest festivals in almost every town and village.

The Wine Museum and the Wine Institute (Museu do Vinho da Madeira) is located at Rua 5 de Outubro 78, in a beautiful yellow building with a tower, just rear the Justice House. The museum presents the history and the importance of Madeira wine for Madeirans. It also presents the process from cultivation to production and from harvesting to bottling. The museum is open from Monday to Friday from 9.30 am to 12.30 pm and again from 2 pm to 5 pm. Closed at weekends.

Wine Museum (Museu da Madeira Wine Company) is located next to tourist office on Avenida Arriaga. The museum has a wine tasting bar and a shop, where you can buy Madeira wines of which the oldest bottled are from 1860! Guided tours daily in English, German, French and Portuguese. Museum is open from Monday to Friday from 9.30 am to 6.30 pm and Saturdays from 10 am to 1 pm. Closed on Sundays and on public holidays.

Henriques & Henriques wine factory and shop in Câmara de Lobos is open from Monday to Friday 9 am to 1 pm and 2.30 pm to 5.30 pm.

Vineyard and Wine Museum of Arco de São Jorge (Museu da Vinha e do Vinho do Arco de São Jorge) is located as its name indicates, in São Jorge at the address Sitio da Lagoa. It is, at the same time a working vineyard and garden, and presents tools and equipments needed in wine-growing. Open from Tuesday to Saturday from 2 pm to 5.30 pm. At other times must be reserved in advance. Country buses number 6, 103 and 138.

DID YOU KNOW...

The best of vintage wines are from one and the same year's harvest and they have been stored in oak barrels at least 20 years.

Wineries and Vineyards

In Madeira they grow several varieties of grape vines and the main farming areas are in Estreito de Camâra de Lobos as well as some in the north coast. In some vineyards you can visit and taste wines and, in some of them you can even stay overnight.

Wineries and Vineyards are for example Vineyard and Wine Museum of Arco de São Jorge (Museu da Vinha e do Vinho do Arco de São Jorge) which is located as its name indicates, in São Jorge at the address Sitio da Lagoa. It is, at the same time a working vineyard and garden, and displays tools and equipment needed in wine-growing. Open from Tuesday to Saturday from 2 pm to 5.30 pm. At other times must be reserved in advance. Country buses number 6, 103 and 138.

The second winery is located in Quinta do Furão in Santana. Quinta do Furão

is both a winery and also a comfortable rural hotel.

In Fajã dos Padres, west of Cabo Girão, is Henriques Winery and Madeira wine factory, where they organize guided tours with wine tasting.

Places where you can stay overnight in manor house hotels surrounded by vineyards: Quinta do Furão in Santana, Quinta das Vinhas in Estreito da Calheta, Quinta do Estreito in Estreito de Câmara de Lobos and Quinta do Arco in São Jorge.

In autumn while wine festivals (Festa das Vindimas) are held in Funchal and Estreito de Câmara de Lobos you may taste wines in different wine cellars, bars and restaurants. Also in September in Porto da Cruz they hold a grape festival (Festa da Uva) where you may taste local wines. In most wine stores you can also taste wines throughout the year.

Hydrangea's beautiful white flowers

Forts and castles

São Lourenço's Palace and Fortress

(Fortaleza e Palácio de São Lourenço), was completed in the late 1500s and it has been changed and renovated in the 1600s and 1700s. This Palace has been the premises of Madeira's governors and still is the military commanders head quarters. The actual garrison is located in the Nazaré part of the city. Mandatory military service ended in 2004 and now Portugal has paid professional army. The São Lourenço Fortress is located in the corner of Rua do Zargo and Avenida do Mar streets and the entrance is from Rua do Zargo to courtyard. The Military Museum's entrance is from the Avenida Arriaga side. Open from Monday to Friday from 10 am to 12.00 am and again from 2 pm to 5 pm. Saturday 10 am till noon. Closed on Sundays, weekends and on public holidays. Free access.

Fortress Nossa Senhora da Conceição

(Fortaleza da Nossa Senhora da Conceição). The building construction began in 1656. Connected to the fortress they built a small chapel in 1682. The fortress, of which now only remains the ruins, is located in the Funchal port, at the start of the Pontinha dock.

Fortress Pico (Fortaleza do Pico) was completed in 1632. It is located on the slopes of Funchal, address Calçada do Pico and from there are stunning views over the city and Funchal bay. Open every day from 9 am to 6 pm. This fortress has never been in military use, but there was a Portuguese Marines radio station. Around the fortress is also a park and children's playground.

Fortress São Filipe (Fortaleza de São Filipe) was built in 1581 to protect Funchal for corsair attacks. There were three fortresses protecting Funchal, fortress São Tiago in the east, fortress Nossa Senhora da Conceição in the west and this fortress São Filipe in the middle, located in between the streams of Santa Luzia and João Gomes. From this fortress there are only fragments of the south-west wall

Fortress Pico has never been in military use.

left which was reconstructed to a higher level because of the Santa Luzia streams draining system.

Fortress São Tiago (Fortaleza de São Tiago) is located in the old city on Largo do Corpo Santo. This fortress was completed in 1614 and was extended in the mid 1850s. The fortress is now Modern Art Museum. In the courtyard is also a quality restaurant. The museum is open from Monday to Saturday 10 am to 12.30 pm and again from 2 pm to 5.30 pm. Closed on Sundays and on public holidays.

Fort Ribeira Brava (Forte da Ribeira Brava) is located as its name indicates, in Ribeira Brava. This is from the 1700s a small fortress that has been also a prison and now it is a tourist office.

Fort São João Batista (Forte de São João Batista) in Porto Moniz, was originally built in 1730 to protect the city from pirates. Now the ruins of that fort have been rebuilt again and today it is the location of Madeira's aquarium. Address Rua do Castelo, Porto Moniz.

In the center of Machico, at the shoreline, is also a fortress which is from the 1700s. And on the north coast of the island in Faial, is a small fortress (Fortim do Faial) currently privately owned.

Lighthouses (farol)

Madeira's coast line is a very rugged and stony and the lighthouses (farol) are guiding the sailors through the difficult areas. Madeira's lighthouses

▶ **The lighthouse at Ponta do Pargo is one of the highest located lighthouses in the world.**

are owned and operated by the Portuguese Navy (Marinha de Portugal). Nowadays every lighthouse is automated.

There are several lighthouses on every island of Madeira; the uninhabited Selvagens islands has one and Desertas islands have two lighthouses. These lighthouses cannot be visited because berthing in these protected islands without permission is prohibited. Porto Santo has four lighthouses, which can be accessed only by boat.

The main island Madeira has several lighthouses for example; in Funchal port at the end of the breakwater. You can walk towards the lighthouse along the breakwater, but the tower is closed to the public. Madeira's oldest lighthouse is located on the eastern point at São Lourenço peninsula. This lighthouse was completed in 1870, the only access is by boat and it is closed to the public. Most well-known lighthouse is at Ponta do Pargo, at the western point of the island. This lighthouse was built in 1922 and it is one of the world's highest located lighthouses. Access is prohibited to the tower, but downstairs there is a photo gallery of other lighthouses on Madeira and from its premises there are great views of the Atlantic. In addition, lighthouses are also found in Câmara de Lobos, Ribeira Brava, São Jorge and Caniçal.

▶ The Orange Trumpet Vine (Golden Shower) is framing the doorway.

Other attractions

In addition to museums, parks and mansions there is plenty more to see and do in Funchal.

Madeira Magic Theme Park for children, at Rua da Ponta Cruz 25. This science center offers all kinds of program, including miniature planetarium, three-dimensional films and changing exhibitions. In addition there is a garden where the children can play. In the same building there is also a fitness club, restaurant and tea house. Open from Monday to Friday from 10 am to 6 pm and on weekends from 10 am to 7 pm. Closed on public holidays.

Wartime tunnel is located on the promenade and along it you can walk to Praia Formosa beach. The tunnel was built during the Second World War to defend from German attacks. Temporarily closed in spring 2015.

And other attractions outside of the city:

Casa das Mudas is located in Calheta at Vale de Amores. One part of this art gallery is located in the old mansion, constructed in the 1500s and the new part is a architecturally modern building. The art gallery has changing art shows, music and dance performances. Open from Tuesday to Sunday from 10 am to 1 pm and again from 2 pm to 6 pm. Closed on Mondays. Country buses number 80, 115, 139 and 142.

Living Science Center (Centro de Ciência Viva) is located on the north

▶ Madeira Magic is a science center and theme park for children.

coast of the island in Porto Moniz at the Rotunda do Ilhéu Mole. It is a culture center with lots to see and do for all ages mostly about knowledge and the scientific sectors. It is part of a national science center chain and holds seminars of these fields, as well as various exhibitions. Open from Tuesday to Sunday from 10 am to 9 pm. Closed on Mondays and on public holidays. Country buses number 80 and 139.

Madeira Aquarium (Aquário da Madeira) is located on the north coast of the island in Porto Moniz, in the old fortress (Forte de São João Batista) which was built in 1730. This fortress is located close to Porto Moniz's port. In the aquarium there are 11 water tanks displaying the whole of Madeira's underwater sea life. Open every day from 10 am to 6 pm. Country buses number 80 and 139.

Madeira Theme Park (Temático da Madeira) is located in Santana at Estrada Regional 101, in Fonte da Pedra. This amusement park was opened in 2004 and here the local culture and history are presented using technology and entertainment. There is a presentation of Madeira and the world's creation history interactively using multimedia. In the park there is also a lake, nature parks and hiking trails, a replica of the old Monte train, an ox sledge and all kind of theme park rides. In addition there are restaurants and handicraft stores. The Theme Park is open every day from 10 am to 7 pm. Closed on Christmas Day. Country buses number 103, 132 and 138.

Monte Toboggans (carro de cesto) is an old tradition existing since the 1850s. Beneath the toboggans there are wooden runners which slide on the pavement. This exciting experience starts at the foot of Monte church in a ride controlled by drivers (carreiros). The toboggans run downhill fast on narrow and twisty roads between vehicles. There are always two drivers who wear traditional costumes, white trousers and a shirt with straw hat. In the past these toboggans came all the way down to Funchal but nowadays the route ends to Livramento, just little above the city center. The journey

▶ Monte Toboggans travel fast downhill.

DID YOU KNOW...

Monte Toboggans are an old tradition since the 1850s.

takes 10 minutes and is two kilometers in length. Rides from Monday to Saturday from 9 am to 6 pm. Closed on Sundays and public holidays.

Scenic road runs from Pico do Areeiro to Eira do Serrado. This stunning narrow road is 16 km long and twists around the mountaineous scenery. There are several viewing points to look at the landscapes and take pictures. Access to this road is only on foot or car and the access gates are closed after 5 pm.

Vulcanology Center and the Caves (Grutas e Centro de Vulcanismo) are located in São Vicente, the north coast of the island, address Sitio Pé do Passo. The purpose of this center is to explain all about the geological beginning of the island and the volcanic eruptions using audiovisual and entertaining methods. In connection with the center there is almost a kilometer of caves and tunnels that go approx. 700 meters underground. A beautiful garden with endemic plants of Madeira. Guided tours in Portuguese, English, French and German. Open daily from 10 am to 7 pm. Closed on Christmas Day. Country buses number 4, 80, 132 and 139.

▶ **A hat merchant and a cat in Monte Square**

Cable cars

Cable cars (Teleféricos da Madeira) provide a great alternative transportation instead of bus or taxi and in some places the only access is by cable cars.

Most popular and most well known is the cable car between Funchal and Monte, which has awesome views over the city of Funchal. This cable car was completed in 2001 and carries 800 passengers per hour. The length of the cable is 3718 meters and it takes about 15 minutes. Open every day from 10 am to 6 pm. Closed on Christmas Day. The starting point in Funchal is on Campo Almirante Reis square, on Avenida do Mar and close to bus station and the journey ends to Monte on Largo das Babosas square.

▶ In some places the only access is by cable cars as here at Archadas das Cruz close to Porto Moniz.

Another cable car operates between Monte and the Botanical Garden (Jardim Botanico da Madeira). This cable car route was opened in 2005, it carries 400 passengers per hour and the trip takes about 10 minutes. Open every day from 9.30 am to 5.30 pm. Closed on Christmas Day. With this cable car you can reach the starting points of some levadas, e.g. Tornos, Bom Sucesso and Curral dos Romiros. At the starting point near the Botanical Gardens there is also a bar and a restaurant with stunning views.

In addition cable cars can be found in Achadas da Cruz and Cabo Girão. Achadas da Cruz this cable car close to Porto Moniz is used by local farmers giving access down to their cultivations. The ride down to the cultivations is 450 meters and the views from that cable car are spectacular! Open every day from 10 am to 6 pm.

Rancho's cable car close to Cabo Girão was opened in 2003 access is mainly for local farmers to their cultivations. The cable car runs between Rancho and Cabo Girão. At the bottom it is possible to swim in the sea. Open every day from 9 am to 7 pm. Tourists can also use these cable cars.

DID YOU KNOW...

Cabo Girão is Europe's third highest cliff with vertical height of 580 meters.

Other cities and village attractions

Madeira's best and most popular tourist attraction is nature itself. In addition comes the awesome views, rugged coastline, high altitudes, cozy little villages, many attractive gardens and the ability to enjoy different activities throughout the year.

Achadas da Cruz is a small village close to Porto Moniz. It is an agricultural area where a cable car was built a few years ago so that farmers can get access to their land down at sea level.

Cabo Girão is the third highest vertical cliff in Europe and rises up to 580 meters. The highest cliff is in Norway (604 meters) and the second highest can be found from Ireland (601 meters). Cabo Girão's view point terrace has magnificent views to Funchal, Câmara de Lobos, to the sea and down to the terrace farms. This new view point terrace was completed in 2012 and has a glass floor where you can walk out over the sea. If you go further up on the road, you can find a lonely chapel and a big terrace where you can see over the slopes and the cultivation. In 2003 a cable car was opened between

Fajãs do Cabo Girão and Rancho for farmers to get access down to their cultivations. Tourists can also use the lift. Country bus number 154. Santa Maria boat and catamarans make boat trips below Cabo Girão. From the boat you have a new perspective to the cliff and you can swim from the boat.

Calheta is a sugar town and there are many sugar cane, banana and grapes cultivations in the area. There is also a sugar and rum factory (Engenhos da Calheta), where in March and April you can see how the sugar canes are pressed. From the distilled liquid they prepare local alcohol (aguardente).

▶ Calheta beach's sand is brought from the Sahara.

In the beginning of September Calheta streets will be decorated with flowers and the Festa do Loreto village festival is on. The town has a beautiful church, which was built in 1521. One of the few beaches in Madeira is to be found here in Calheta. The sand has been brought there from the Sahara and here you can swim and dive. In Arco da Calheta above the town is located the Casas das Mudas Art Gallery. Country buses number 80, 115 and 142.

Camacha is a cozy small town about 10 km north-east of Funchal. It is the center of the willow and wicker industry. On the side of the City Square (Largo da Achada) is a Clock Café (Café O Relógio) which received its name from a belfry decorating the building. There is a shop and factory where they sell and make wicker works from baskets to furniture and where you can also see the artisans at their work. In Camacha at the football field the first game of football was played in Portugal in 1875. The Camacha area is a starting and ending point for some levadas. Country buses number 29 and 77.

▶ Camacha is the center of the wicker industry.

▶ **Câmara de Lobos is an idyllic fishing village.**

Câmara de Lobos translates as 'sea wolves (seals) nest'. It is an idyllic fishing village approx. 6 km west of Funchal and one of the earliest settled areas in Madeira. The first houses there were built as early as the 1420s. It is interesting to observe the fishermen working on their boat or playing cards. In Câmara de Lobos they celebrate and have many festivals during the year: at the end of June is the St. Peters Festival (Festa do São Pedro), in the autumn there is the colourful Wine Festival and also the Black Scabbard Fish Festival (Festa do Peixe Espada Preto). The village is surrounded by vineyards and banana cultivation on terraced land. Several levadas begin and end from Câmara de Lobos. Above Câmara de Lobos is Estreito de Câmara de Lobos where they have a weekend market. Country buses number 3, 96, 115, 137 and 154.

Caniçal was previously a lively whaling center, but the factory has been converted to a Whale Museum (Museu de Baleia) because whaling was banned completely in Madeira in 1981. Caniçal still is an important fishing harbour and there you can observe the fishermen with their catch and boats early in the morning. Caniçal also has a deep-water harbour where all the freight from the continent arrives, there is also a free trade area and an industrial park (Zona Franca). Country bus number 113.

Caniço is a charming small town east of Funchal. There is a beautiful church from the 1700s, as well as several old mansions. Caniço de Baixo is located below Caniço and there are in addition to many attractive houses also few hotels, restaurants and a popular beach and bathing site Reis Magos. Every May in Caniço there is an Onion Festival (Festa do Cebola). Country bus number 155.

Curral das Freiras, also known as Nuns Valley, is surrounded by high mountains and is located at the bottom of the valley. The name Nuns Valleys derives its origin from the 1500s when Funchal was attacked by pirates and nuns from the Santa Clara Convent fled there to safety. From the valley there are rugged views up the mountain and from Eira do Serrado's view point breathtaking views down to the valley. You can also walk from Eira do Serrado down to the valley. It takes approx. 2 hours. Curral das Freiras is famous for its chestnut and cherry trees the fruits of which produce a local chestnut liqueur (licor de castanha) or a cherry liqueur (ginja) and also breads. At the beginning of November there will be held the Festival of Chestnut (Festa da Castanha) when you can also taste the chestnut soup. Country bus number 81.

Eira do Serrado viewing point is 1094 meters in altitude above the Curral das Freiras and there is a breathtaking view down to the valley. This Nuns Valley looks very small when viewed from above. You can also walk down to the valley by path and it takes approx. 2 hours. Country bus number 81.

Encumeada viewing point is 1007 meters in altitude, it lies between Ribeira Brava and São Vicente. On a clear days from here there are great views both to the south towards Serra de Aqua valley and to the north towards São Vicente. A few kilometers before Encumeada is Pousada dos Vinháticos, an inn and a restaurant. In the area there is also a short, 2 km long, levada (Levada do Norte) along which you will be able to walk back and forth. Along this levada there are the flowers and a laurel forest. Country bus number 139.

▶ **From Eira do Serrado there are stunning views down to Nuns Valley.**

Faial is located north from Ribeiro Frio, right at the bottom of the Eagle Rock (Penha de Águia). In the area they grow grapes and vegetables. In the town there is a church from the 1700s, a small fortress (Fortim do Faial) currently privately owned and the island's only go-kart track. On a clear day from here you can see Porto Santo island. Country buses number 53 and 78.

Fajã dos Padres is located to the west of Cabo Girão and the village is only accessible by cable car, boat or helicopter. In the area they grow for example mangos, papayas and avocados and there is also a Madeira wine factory with guided tours and wine tasting. Between Fajã dos Padres and Rancho runs the cable car. Country bus number 154.

Garajau means tern and the town has therefore been named after these black-and-white sea-birds. It is also a popular holiday destination, especially among German tourists. In Garajau there is a statue of the Christ (Cristo Rei) from 1927, which is a smaller version of Rio de Janeiro's statue in Brazil. From the viewing point are a stunning views out to sea and to the Funchal bay. From the view point there is a path and cable car down to the sea. In the front of Garajau there is also a Marine Nature Reserve under the sea (Reserva Natural Parcial do Garajau) where guided diving tours are organized. Country buses number 2, 109, 110 and 155.

Jardim do Mar is an idyllic peaceful small village with a cobblestoned alleys it is located to the west of

Funchal. There are many old stone houses with superb gardens, grape vines and flowers. In Jardim do Mar and Paul do Mar the stony beaches have excellent surf waves and the area is popular and well known by surfers the world over. Country buses number 80 and 142.

Machico is a town on which beach João Gonçalves Zarco with his crew were washed ashore in 1419. It is the second largest town in Madeira and is located east of Funchal. There is an old

▶ Machico is the second largest town in Madeira.

church (Igreja Nossa Senhora da Conceição) from the 1400s where Tristão Vaz Teixeira is buried. In front of the church there is a statue of Teixeira. Machico has a fortress dating from the 1700s and a small chapel (Capela dos Milagres) where is held on 8th and 9th of October a festival of the Miracle-Worker (Festa do Senhor do Milagres). There is also a small sandy beach where you can swim, and attractive little streets and alleyways along which to wander. The last week of August is held a Holy Sacrament Festival (Festa di Cantissimo Sacramento). Express bus or country bus number 20, 23, 53, 78, 113 and 156.

Madalena do Mar is a little village located between Ribeira Brava and Calheta. The area is an important banana cultivation area and on its stony beach there are good surf waves. One of the attractions in the village is a Santa Catarina church from the 1457. Country bus number 80 and 142.

Monte is a small town about 550 meters above Funchal. In Monte there is a beautiful church (Igreja do Monte), which holds, on the 15th of August each year, a big Pilgrim Festival (Festa da Nossa Senhora do Monte). Originally the church was built in the 1700s but it was destroyed in the 1748 earthquake being rebuilt in 1818. In Monte there are also three stunning gardens and on the side of Monte Square there is an old railway station which is a relic of a time when a train ran between Monte and Funchal. This train service started in 1893, but was closed following a disastrous accident in 1932. Monte is also the starting and ending point of many levadas. The best way to get to Monte is by cable car which leaves from Funchal old town, by taxi or buses number 20 and 21, as well as on a bus number 48 from Lido area. Traditionally you should return from Monte by Toboggan. These start at the foot of Monte Church and end at Livramento, just a short way above the city center.

Paúl da Serra is a great plain area at an altitude of 1400 meters in the western part of Madeira. On clear days there are fantastic views down valleys and to the sea. In this area it rains frequently and the water is collected in large reservoirs for the needs of the local people. This area is also very important as an electric power producer and there are lots of wind-energy turbine stations. To Paúl da Serra there is no local bus transport.

Paúl do Mar is an attractive small village where there was no access before the 1960s, except by boat.

Paúl do Mar's stony beach has very good surf waves. From here there is one levada up to Prazeres. Country buses number 80 and 142.

Pico do Areeiro is the third highest peak (1818 m) on the island. From there are spectacular views all around and on cloudy days the clouds can be about half a kilometre below the peak. From Pico do Areeiro you can admire the spectacular sunrises and sunsets. In the area there is also the Pousada do Pico do Arieiro Inn. Between Pico do Areeiro and Pico Ruivo is a 6 km long levada. This levada is spectacular, but if you are afraid of heights, this levada walk is not recommended. Because of some landslides this levada was temporarily closed in the spring 2015.

Pico dos Barcelos is a hill on the west side of Funchal, it has an altitude of 355 meters above sea level. There is an outlook where you have stunning views to the Santo António part of town as well as to Funchal and up to the mountains and the banana and grape cultivations. Buses number 9 and 12. Also the double decker sightseeing buses have a stop there.

Pico Ruivo is the highest peak (1861 m) in Madeira and from there you have a stunning views to the mountains and when clear also to Porto Santo island. The summit is accessible only by foot and the hike takes about 2 hours. Between Pico Ruivo and Pico do Areeiro is a 6 km long levada. This levada is extreme, so if you are afraid of heights, this walk is not recommended. Because of recent landslides this levada was temporarily closed in the spring of 2015.

Ponta Delgada is a small charming village on the north coast of the island. There is a beautiful chapel from the 1500s. The first Sunday of September they hold a Festival of Jesus Christ and the Holy Sacrament (Festa do Senhor Bom Jesus e Santo Sacramento). In addition there is Dr. Horacio Gouveia's museum. Country bus number 6.

Ponta de São Lourenço is the easternmost point of the island. This windy and barren area is a 9 km long and 2 km wide nature reserve which includes two little islands; Ilhéu da Cevada da Metade and Ilhéu da Ponta de São Lourenço.

In Pico dos Barcelos there are many souvenir shops.

You can also hike in the park and there are magnificent views of the Atlantic. On the island at the tip of the cape is a lighthouse. Country bus number 113.

Ponta do Pargo is the westernmost point in Madeira. On the projecting rock about 300 meters above the sea level is a lighthouse (farol) which was built in 1922. There is no access to the tower of the lighthouse for the public, but downstairs there is a photography gallery of the island's other light-houses and from the front of the lighthouse there are sensational views of the Atlantic. Next to the lighthouse there is planned to be the third golf course in Madeira. Nearby is also a popular tea house from which terrace there are great views to the sea. Country buses number 80 and 142.

Ponta do Sol is a small idyllic coastal town west from Ribeira Brava. The name means place in the sun. There is a beautiful church from the 1500s and many beautiful alleys to stroll along. There is also the opportunity to dive and surf in the area. In Ponta do Sol there is the John dos Passos Community Center and library. John dos Passos was a well known American author who's grandparents once lived in Ponta do Sol. Country bus number 4.

Portela is a viewing point which is located at 670 meters altitude on the north coast of the island. There you have great views to the Atlantic, the mountains, and down to Porto da Cruz. On clear days you can also see Porto Santo island. Several levadas pass through the area of which the

longest is one through Caniçal to São Lourenço peninsula.

Porto da Cruz is located on the north coast and was previously an important port. The Eagle Rock (Penga de Aguia) on the side of the town is 580 meters high and shadows the town. In the area they still grow sugar canes from which they squeeze local alcohol (aguardente). The factory operates only for a few weeks in April. There are also vineyards in the area and in autumn they hold a Wine Festival. Country buses number 53, 56 and 78.

Porto Moniz is located on the north coast of Madeira and is famous for its

▶ **Porto Moniz is famous for its natural shaped swimming pools.**

natural shaped swimming pools. Porto Moniz was once the main port on the north coast. Fishing and wine-growing are the main income in addition to tourism. Along the old road from São Vicente to Porto Moniz there are several waterfalls. From a point above the town are spendid views down to the town and to the sea. There are several restaurants and souvenir shops in Porto Moniz and there is also located Madeira Aquarium and Living Science Center. They hold an agricultural show in August. In Ribeira de Janela, next to Porto Moniz, can be found the second camping ground in Madeira and which is monitored by the Regional Government. Country buses number 80 and 139.

Porto Santo is the second inhabited islands in the Madeira archipelago. Information about Porto Santo you can find in a separate section at the end of this book.

Prainha the brownish black volcanic sand beach is located on the road along the way from Caniçal to São Lourenço peninsula. It is the only natural sandy beach in Madeira, and particularly in summer weekends it is overflowing with bathers. Country bus number 113.

Rabaçal is a popular local picnic destination. It is located on the small road close to Paúl da Serra. From there begin some popular levadas of which

DID YOU KNOW...

Ponta do Pargo lighthouse is one of the highest situated in the world.

one is easy, about 30 min. circle to Risco waterfalls and the other a more strenuous 3 hour levada walk which twists around the 25 waterfalls (25 Fontes) area.

Ribeira Brava means wild river. It is located west of Funchal and there you will find the port, a square, a few beautiful churches from the 1400s, an Ethnographic Museum (Museu Etnografico da Madeira) and a big sports center outside the town on the road going to São Vicente. In Ribeira Brava they hold a Holy St. Peter Festival (Festa de São Pedro) in June and in October there is an Orchestra Competition (Encontro Regional de Bandas). There are several pleasant cafés and restaurants by the sea and in the adjoining streets. Country bus number 7.

Ribeira de Janela means view to a river. It is located a few kilometers from Porto Moniz towards São Vicente. The area is mostly agricultural, in Ribeira de Janela there is located Porto Moniz's camping ground and along the old road to São Vicente there are several waterfalls.

Ribeiro Frio means cold river. River waters are guided down the valley to reservoirs where they breed trout. In Ribeiro Frio there is a forest park and a miniature botanical garden which are well worth a visit. In the area there is also a small attractive chapel and popular Faisca restaurant. From the area begins and end some interesting levadas of which the shorter one, about 2 km and 45 min. runs to a fantastic Balcões (balcony,) viewing point. The second route is one of the

Idyllic Santa Cruz is located close to the airport.

most popular, about 10 km and approx. 3 hours and runs to the Portela viewing point. Country buses number 103 and 138.

Santa Cruz means the holy cross. This charming small town is located just beside the airport and perhaps that is why it is often unnoticed. This town is definitely worth a visit and from there it is fun to watch the aeroplanes arriving and departing at the end of the runway. Many attractive cafés and restaurants are located at the seaside, with parks, promenade, and a beautiful church from 1479, which is designed by the same architect as the Cathedral Sé in Funchal. Just outside of the city center is located the Water Park (Aquaparque de Santa Cruz). Country buses number 20, 23, 53, 78, 113 and 156.

Richness of colours in Santa Cruz

185

Santana is famous for its small straw roofed A-shaped traditional houses. In these two storey white plastered houses (palheiro) with a red door, red & blue shutters and a straw roof. The town itself is located on the north coast, in the midst of cultivated land, where grow apple, pear, anona and cherry trees and also the laurel forest. Santana means St. Anna (Santa Ana) and there are stunning views to the sea. In Santana they hold a Folk Festival (48 horas a Bailar, Festival de Folclore) in the beginning of July, there is also the Theme Park (Parque Tematico) and from here start and end a number of interesting levadas. Country bus number 56.

Santo da Serra is located north east of Funchal. This area has been previously popular for the wealthy and there are still many beautiful mansions and parks, for example Quinta da Santo da Serra, which is open to the public. They hold every Sunday a farmers' market. Here is also the second golf course of the island, which has great views down to Machico, Caniçal, the São Lourenço peninsula and the Desertas islands. The golf club, shop and cafe are open to non members so you can visit even you do not play golf. Country bus number 77.

São Vicente is located on the north coast. This small charming town is surrounded by country side. There is a beautiful church from the 1600s, several cafés and restaurants, and above the town is a special 14 meters high belfry (Torre de Fatima). In São Vicente there is a little chapel from 1600s which was built from rock quarried from a local quarry. Nearby is the Volcanic Center and the Caves (Grutas e Centro do Vulcanismo). Country buses number 6 and 139.

▶ Santana is famous for its small staw roofed traditional houses.

▶ In Santo da Serra there is a farmers' market every Sunday.

▶ **Unforgettable landscapes and striking views**

DID YOU KNOW...

Churches in Madeira are very old and contain many paintings, valuables and wood carvings.

HANDICRAFTS ▶ ▶ ▶ ▶ ▶ ▶ ▶

Embroideries

Madeiran embroideries (bordados) and lace-making are world famous. This great art of embroidery began in the 1850s in Madeira when the wine trader's daughter Elizabeth (Bella) Phelps wanted to help Madeiran people struggling with poverty and a cholera epidemic by setting up a company in which they could create a small income.

In the beginning the needleworks were made by hundreds of poor country women from whose hands these embroideries spread all over for the use of society women in Victorian England. The embroideries are made on linen, silk, cotton and the other fabrics and which vary depending on the fabric and the purpose it will be used for. Nowadays the patterns are pressed on to the fabrics in the factory and then the fabrics will be sent to be embroidered by people in the villages, because the work is carried out at people's homes. The finished work will then be sent back to the factories to Machico and Funchal where they are washed, ironed and packed. The standards and quality of works are monitored carefully by the Madeira Embroidery Institute (IBTAM – Instituto do Bordado, Tapeçaria e Artesanato da Madeira). This institute was founded in 1991 and each inspected product has a IBTAM hologram tag as a guarantee of its authenticity.

▶ **Sunsets are magnificent in Madeira.**

Even today this embroidery industry employs thousands and thousands of Madeiran women and men. It is an artwork which disappears little by little and loses its market to cheap imported, machine made copies. The majority of exports go to the USA and Europe. There are several embroidery factories in Funchal which you can visit and see demonstrations in several embroidery shops. They decorate and design these embroideries mainly on tablecloths and napkins, but also sheets, skirts, tops and blouses, handkerchiefs and wedding dresses. These items are expensive, because a standard tablecloth can take up to two years to finish. Compared to all the work it takes, prices are low.

It is also definitely worth visiting the Embroidery Museum (Nucleo Museologico do Bordado Madeira I.B.T.A.M.) which is located at Rua Visconde de Anadia 44. The museum's collections includes embroideries from handkerchiefs to clothing and also furniture from the 1800s to today. The museum is open from Monday to Friday from 9.30 am to 6 pm. Closed at weekends and on public holidays.

DID YOU KNOW...

The embroideries are made on linen, silk, cotton and the other fabrics and vary depending on the fabric and the purpose it will be used for.

▶ **The moon over the city**

Wickerwork

When Madeiran women do their needlework, knitting and crocheting, men create their own art from willow. These wickerwork's are another important export article, which employ local men and women in their homes.

In Madeira's moist climate willow grows well, so sufficient material can be found and grown easily. Early in the year the osier are collected, boiled and then scrubbed. Bundles are then delivered to the workers in villages who conjure everything possible out of them, from furniture to baskets and into many household items. When working with willow the artisans use their hands and feet and sometimes their teeth too. These wickerwork's are beautifully handicrafted and do not cost very much. Also this wickerwork craft is handed down from generation to generation and children learn the skill from their parents.

These wickerwork's are exported mainly to Europe and America. If you like to buy one of the larger pieces, companies can arrange delivery of them to your home address.

▶ Handicrafts employs locals at their homes.

▶ They do all kind of works from willow, from baskets to furniture and household items.

Camacha is a cosy small town about 10 km north-east of Funchal. It is the center of the willow and wicker industry. On the side of the City Square (Largo da Achada) is a Clock Café (Café O Relógio) which received its name from a belfry decorating the building. There is a shop and factory where they sell and make wicker works from baskets to furniture and where you can also see the artisans at their work. In Camacha at the football field the first game of football was played in Portugal in 1875. The Camacha area is a starting and ending point for some levadas. Country buses

number 29 and 77. Also in Funchal there are several stores selling wickerworks.

The handicrafts of the men and women are one of the main export items along with the Madeira wine, and one of the main sources of revenue of the island.

Leather works

Along with needleworks and wickerwork also different kinds of leather works make popular souvenirs. In Madeira there are good selections of ladies handbags and shoes for men and women, they are of high quality and at affordable prices. Try also Madeiran boots (boas de vilão), which are made of sheep skin. Shoe and bag stores are found in the center of Funchal and in the alleys of the old city.

Ceramic and clay

Beautiful and colourful ceramic and clay dishes are mainly from continental Portugal.

Knitting

Cardigans, poncho's, hats and gloves, which are sold in souvenir shops and in different tourist locations, are mainly from continental Portugal. Fun wool hats with ear pads which are often worn particularly by the local country men are called barreto.

HAPPENINGS, FESTIVALS AND OTHER EVENTS ▶ ▶ ▶ ▶

In Madeira there is a great deal of fun and festivals to offer. Events and things to do throughout the year, because almost every weekend somewhere on the island are held village festivals, different shows and presentations, culture happenings, exhibitions, concerts etc. Madeirans do not need many reasons to organize parties and festivals.

The main festivals for Madeirans and tourists are, of course, Carnival, Flower Festival, Wine Festival, Christmas and probably the most spectacular main events is New Years Eve (Fim de Ano) and the accompanying firework display.

Carnival

One of the main events is Carnival (Carnaval da Madeira), which takes place every year from the Friday before Shrovetide and continues for

DID YOU KNOW...

In Madeira there is a great deal of fun and events to offer throughout the year. Almost every weekend somewhere are held village festivals, culture events, exhibitions and concerts etc.

five days until Shrove Tuesday. Samba rhythms and carnival parades fill up all Funchal center and the celebration goes on through the night on the streets till morning and in hotels, restaurants, bars and pubs. The carnival parade starts from the roundabout at the harbour and it moves slowly along Avenida do Mar to Praça da Autonomia where finally the event ending party is held and the best costumes are rewarded.

There are several carnival parades: on the Friday morning is the children's parade and on Saturday evening at 9 pm begins the fantastic and colourful main parade (Cortejo Alegórico), for which thousands of people sacrifice many working hours in order to have it to look great. Before Saturday's main parade there is approx. 10 min. of fireworks. Funchals streets will be full of colourful lights, parade cars are decorated with flowers and performers wear the most imaginative costumes. The third parade and, at the same time, the ending parade of the carnival is Slapsticks Parade (Cortejo Trapalhão) which starts on Shrove Tuesday at 4 pm and the route is the same as the main parade. It's a lot of fun complete with extremely funny costume on parade where everyone is welcome to participate, including tourists. Shrove Tuesday is a public holiday in Madeira and the following day, on Ash Wednesday starts 40 days of fasting.

► Carnival is one of the most anticipated events on Madeira.

▶ The Flower Festival is the highlight of glorious spring.

Flower Festival

Flower Festival (Festa da Flor) is really a very colourful event and it is usually held two weeks after the Easter. The Flower Festival starts already on Thursday, when they assemble flower carpets on Avenida Arriaga. On Saturday morning at 10 is the childrens parade where hundreds of beautifully costumed children pass through the City Square (Praça do Municipio) and built there a Wall of Hope with colourful flowers. On Sunday at 4 pm festival will continue with a huge flower parade which participating vehicles are decorated with different and colourful flowers and every participant in the parade are wearing beautifully decorated flower costumes. The festival parade starts from Praça da Autonomia and it moves slowly along Avenida do Mar to Praça do Mar at close to the cruise ship terminal. The Flower Festival is also celebrated elsewhere, on streets, shops, churches, hotels, pubs and on the façades of houses, which are decorated with astonishing flower arrangements. In Largo da Restauracão square there will take place a flower exhibition and all around the city are held folk-dance performances, classical music concerts and other entertainments.

Wine Festivals

The Wine Festival, i.e. harvesting of grapes festival (Festa das Vindimas) is a traditional Madeiran festival, it is held in the beginning of September and it takes place in Funchal and in Estreito de Câmara de Lobos where they also organize a grape harvesting parade. The festival starts from Estreito de Câmara de Lobos where they are actually picking the grapes and pressing them. The festival continues in Funchal on Avenida Arriaga and on Largo da Restauracão with different performances. Later on follows the music and folk-dances and of course, wine tasting in the wine cellars, bars and restaurants with traditional types of food.

Christmas

Christmas festivities (Festa Natal) start in the middle of November when they start installing the illuminations and decorations. The lights will be switched on at the beginning of December in the center of Funchal and all the lights on the island and along the streets at the latest on the 8th of December. The illuminations of Madeira is an extravaganza because almost every house, street, alley and tree is decorated with hundreds of thousands of Christmas lights and the actual crescendo of the lighting is in the center of Funchal. At the beginning of December all the cribs (Belém or Lapinhas) are installed on the streets, in churches, hotels, restaurants and in front of the houses. From speakers can be heard Christmas songs, Christmas carols are performed by choirs and on the city streets there are many different music and dance performances and beautiful flower arrangements. These decorations stay till Epiphany.

For information and schedules about Christmas season events and concerts, ask from the tourist offices.

Nine days before Christmas will start morning masses (Missas do Parto) when Madeirans go early in the morning (at 6 or 7 am) to the church to pray for the Virgin Mary. The last mass is on Christmas Eve when there is celebrated the Midnight Mass (Missa do Gallo). The actual Christmas (A Festa) is celebrated with the same traditions as almost every country in Europe. Preparations start with thoroughly tidying the home and preparing all the dishes for Christmas. A Merry Christmas in Portuguese is Feliz Natal.

▶ **Christmas illuminations are unbelievable and almost every house, street and tree are decorated with lights.**

▶ The night before Christmas Eve there is a Market Night lasting until the next morning.

▶ Christmas markets in Avenida Arriaga

Other Christmas season holidays are the Independence Day on 1st of December (Dia da Independencia or Dia do Restauraçao) when Madeirans are celebrating the return of their independence. On 8th of December is the Assumption of the Virgin Mary Day (Nossa Senhora de Conçeiçao) which are celebrated by holding masses in churches and raising the Virgin Mary statues on the main altar in the churches. Both mentioned days are public holidays.

The night before Christmas Eve, i.e. 23rd of December, throughout the night a Market Night takes place all around the Market place. All the farmers around the island are selling their products in every corner of the Market place. Almost the whole of the island's folks are in motion and in the city center has that carnival feeling. Christmas carols are sung in front of the Market place's fish department starting 11 pm. Year by year this tradition of celebrating Christmas Eve becomes more popular, but the festival starts at midnight. On Christmas Day (Natal) it is time to sit down for lunch with the family and eat pork marinated in wine and garlic. Also Boxing Day will be spent with family and friends. Both Christmas Day and Boxing Day are public holidays.

Linked to the Christmas and the New Year celebrations is also the noise of small bombs (bombas) on streets and in alleys. This tradition is dangerous because the explosions can cause permanent damage to your ears. Fortunately, the bombing is reduced year on year.

▶ **Poinsettias and Hibiscuses (Rose of China, Shoe Plant) on the side of the gate.**

DID YOU KNOW...

On New Years Eve Madeirans have a tradition to keep something borrowed, a few coins in their pockets and 12 raisins in their hands with which they forward 12 wishes during the new year evening.

▶ The turn of the year is celebrated with family and friends.

New Year

The New Year (Ano Novo) and the celebration of it is the biggest festival for Madeirans. The remains of the old year (Fim do Ano) and turn of the new year is celebrated with family and friends. Also in hotels, restaurants, pubs and on the streets New Year's approach and celebrating is at it's highest and the turn of the year party continues throughout the night. Locals traditionally keep something borrowed, a few coins in their pockets and 12 raisins in their hands with which they forward 12 wishes during the New Year Evening. New Years Day is a public holiday. Happy New Year is in Portuguese Feliz Ano Novo.

The fireworks in Funchal are unquestionably one of the biggest and most magnificent spectacles in the world and have got into the Guinness Book of Records. This fireworks show lights up the city when from tens of different locations they simultaneously shoot more than 60 000 fireworks in almost 15 minutes; from the slopes, the promenade, vessels and ships in port and moored in the bay. The fireworks are accompanied by the ships sirens and church-bells. Many cruise ships berth in the port just to see the unforgettable fireworks, and some vessels go out into the bay to see the fireworks better from there.

▶ Funchals magnificent fireworks has got into Guinness World Book of Records

Other events during the year

The Epiphany (Dia de Reis or Epifania) will be celebrated on the same date every year, i.e. 6th January, and in Madeira it is a great religious festival celebrating the arrival of the Three Wise Men. It is a family and friends get together with singing and dancing. At the same time the Epiphany officially ends Christmas and the New Year celebrations and after that they bring down all the decorations related to Christmas.

More than week later on 15th of January is celebrated **Dia de Santo Amaro** which in Madeira means a day when all the cupboards are cleared of all food and pastries related to Christmas. This is just one more reason to celebrate with family and friends and eat well. And this is the last day to clear all Christmas decorations away. In Santa Cruz every year is the religious Festa de Santo Amaro village festival to celebrate the ending of Christmas time.

In addition to the above mentioned events, the so-called main events, there are held all kind of different festivals and village happenings which take place in Funchal and in other towns, these decorate the event calendars of both the locals and tourists throughout the year. In addition to the traditional parties, there are general themes such as harvesting etc. Often these festivals begin with religious meaning but continue in the evening with fireworks, dancing, good food and

drinks. The schedules of these events should be checked from daily newspapers or by asking the hotel reception or tourist office, because it is impossible to list all of them.

The Hiking Festival (Festival de Passeios a Pé) days will be spent in January both in Madeira and Porto Santo. During this five days event you can hike along levadas and nature paths with experienced guides. Every day they have four different levadas on offer varying in levels of difficulty and length. Suitable for all ages.

The Orienteering Festival (Festival de Orientação) is also in January. This three-day event will take place in the mountains and it combines competitiveness with leisure. The participants can choose shorter or longer routes depending their own skills.

In February in Santana they hold the **Festa dos Compadres village festival** which at the same time opens the carnival season. In Faial is celebrated **the anona** (Festa da Anona) in the end of February with the tasting of products made of this fruit.

Annually in March on Madeira is held the **Madeira Island Open** (Torneio Madeira Open Golfe) golf tournament which is part of the European Tour Grand Prix and is held at the Santo da Serra golf course.

Easter (Páscoa) happens each year between March and April. Easter as well as the other events will be spent mainly with family and friends and eating well. On Good Friday they traditionally eat fish and on Easter Day a rabbit, ham or lamb and other goodies, depending on family traditions. At Easter time in the Cathedral Sé and in the other towns and villages the churches hold a number of Easter masses in the mornings and one more later at night. The Good Friday and Easter Sunday are public holidays. Happy Easter is Feliz Páscoa in Portuguese.

In April is the **Lemon Festival** (Festa do Limão) in Santana and Sugar Cane Festival (Mostra da Cana-de açucar) in Calheta.

The 25th of April is **Revolution Day**, remembering the Carnation Revolution day in 1974, and is known in Portuguese as Vigésimo quinto abril,

i.e. twenty-fifth April. Day is a public holiday, and is celebrated mainly with political speeches.

The 1st of May is **May Day**, which in Portuguese is Dia do Trabalhador. This day is celebrated mainly with politics and speeches. At this time spring is in full bloom so often local people go out for picnics in the parks, at beaches or to the mountains. Also 1st of May is a public holiday.

Between 1st to 3rd of May days will be celebrated in Funchal with its own **guardian saints festival** as (Festa da Tiago Menor) mainly on Rua Santa Maria and surrounding streets.

The first Sunday in May is **Mothers Day** (Dia das Mães).

▶ Sugar cane is compressed to squeeze out the liquid which is distilled into local alcohol (aquardente).

Also in May is the **Onion Festival** (Festa da Cebola) in Caniço and **the Week of Natural Preserve** (Semana da Conservacão da Natureza) in Funchal.

The **Annual Book Fair** (Feira do Livro) is held on Avenida Arriaga in May. This event takes nine days and there local book-stores and publishers will be on the street with their products. Live music and rewarding reading sessions.

Cathedral Sé Festival (Festas da Sé) is also held in May in the streets surrounding the church. For a week long festival the streets are decorated, bars and restaurants spread out their tables and chairs on the streets offering food, drink, music, and the other pleasures for people.

June is very busy month for organisers, because there are many events to be organized.

At the beginning of June they have a **Medieval Market** (Mercado Quinhentista) in Machico. This celebration is organised by local schools and their students and the city with travel back in time to the 1500s; people are wearing clothing in the spirit of that era, they can taste food and listen to music of that time. Hundreds of different presentations will be held on the streets, in the main church there is a service in Latin and Columbus' Santa Maria ship arrives at the shore and thousands of people will come to watch it.

► **A long Plane Tree alley in Machico**

▶ Flower Festival's flower arrangements are masterpieces.

Also a **Classical Music Festival** (Fins de Semanda Musicais) will take place in the beginning of June and will run for one week. Visiting international artists and students from local conservatory present classical music in the Cathedral, City Theatre and in other public buildings. This event is part of Atlantic Festival and it has been organised more than 30 times.

The 10th of July is **Portuguese Independence Day** (Dia Nacional), which is a public holiday. The day is political with speeches etc. For Madeirans a more important day for celebration is the Day of Madeira's Autonomy, i.e. 1st of July, when Madeira became self-governing.

The Atlantic Festival (Festival do Atlântico) continues throughout the month of June and it is organized by

Madeira's Tourism and Culture Office. The festival is divided into three sections: Classical Music Festival where the music is performed in churches, the City Theatre, São Lourenço Palace and Casa das Mudas Art Center. An international Fireworks Competition takes place every Saturday in June and the winner of this competition will organize a New Years fireworks. For the third event there are held different kinds of street performances all around the city.

At the beginning of June in Funchal there is **The Parade of the Saints** (Marchas populares) for St Antonio. The procession starts from Largo de São Pedro at 9 am and flows through the streets of Rua das Pretas, Rua da Carreira and Rua de São João. Alongside the procession there will be dancing and singing and afterwards eating and celebrating.

In mid June there will be held in Jardim da Serra and in Câmara de Lobos **the Cherry Festival** (Festa da Cereja). This cherry harvest event consists of a procession where participants wear traditional costumes and carry cherries in baskets. The procession reflects how farmers were walking on foot to Funchal to sell their cherries.

On two weekends in the end of June in Funchal will take place **The Altar Festival** (Festa de São João dos Altares). This festival will be held on the streets of Figueira Preta, Travessa dos Reis and in Largo do Carmo square and everybody can participate. One after the other are beautifully decorated altars made from flowers, also bonfires on the streets, folk-dance, singing, fireworks, good food and drink.

At the end of June in Ribeira dos Boieiros in Camacha will be held **the Annual Sheep Shearing Festival** (Festa das Tosquias) where the women shear sheep as a show in the daytime and in the evening people get together on the streets to celebrate. Kiosks with products made of wool are for sale and, of course, food and drink.

Tour de Madeira by classic sport cars (Volta a Madeira em Automóveis Clássicos) will take place at the end of June. This four-day competition is open to vehicles which meet FIA and FIVA's international rules, i.e. they must be fully original and functional. Vehicles need not, however, be racing cars. This competition has been organized more than 20 times and there are about 60 historic cars participating, some of which are really rare.

There is an amazing collection of restored historic cars in Madeira.

▶ The special looking Popcorn Bush (Peanut Butter Cassia, Golden Wonder) is blooming almost year around.

At the end of June in Câmara de Lobos is held **the Black Scabbard Fish Festival** (Festa do Peixe Espada Preto) which is dedicated to one of the main meal courses in Madeira, espada. This event brings to light the importance of the fishing industry to Câmara de Lobos and in general to this island. With gastronomic tasting, entertainment, music, folk-dance and, finally, fireworks.

Also at the end of June in Ribeira Brava and Câmara de Lobos is held **the St Peter's Festival** (Festa de São Pedro) which lasts through the night until morning. The streets along which the procession walks is decorated with flowers. Food booths, local music and fun, folk-dances and fireworks at midnight. From Funchal they organize boat trips to Ribeira Brava to view the celebrations and fireworks.

In the 1st of July is **Madeira's Day of Autonomy** (Dia da Região Autónoma da Madeira) and they celebrate it around the island. The main event and ceremonies will take place in Funchal, close to the statue of autonomy on Avenida do Mar and in the Cathedral Sé. The day is a public holiday.

In the beginning of July in Santana is held a **Folklore Festival** (48 horas a Bailar, Festival de Folklore), where the island's folk-dance groups dance 48 hours non stop. Festivities, of course, with good food and drink.

The three-day **Funchal Jazz Festival** (Funchal Jazz) will be held at the beginning of July in which also participate international jazz artists. The festival has been organized more than 10 times and the main event is in the Santa Catarina Park. There is more music and all kinds of performances on the surrounding streets, in restaurants and bars.

Also in July will be **the Sea Days** (Semana do Mar) in Porto Moniz which lasts a week and in mid-July is the second largest Agricultural Exhibition (Feira do Gaco) which has taken place since 1955. On show are animals, stewarding and booths selling food and drink.

In mid-July in Madalena do Mar they celebrate **the Banana Festival** (Mostra Regional da Banana) the banana is the most important agricultural product of the island. This festival has taken place more than a dozen times.

Funchal Regatta (Regata do Funchal) is held in mid-July. It starts at noon and this 2,5 km long sailing competition with fishing boats starts at Funchal port and ends at Barreirinha in the old city. The competition has taken place since 2004.

At the end of July you can see in Funchal **the Atlantic World Music Festival** (Raizes do Atlántico Festa), involving the international artists and performers from the branch of world music. The festival has been organized in the City Park (Jardim Municipal) platform from the year 2000, it will last four days and starts daily at 9.30 pm.

▶ **On the shores of the island are also built houses.**

▶ Dwarf Bananas flower is huge.

In the first weekend of August **the Madeira Wine Rally** (Rali Vinho da Madeira) is held. It is the Grand Prix of National series and also at the same time the most important sporting event in Madeira in which some first-class rally drivers participate. Madeirans go out in masses along the special stages to spectate the rally. Some of the roads will then be closed because of the race and those which are not closed, are full of parked vehicles. This two-day rally ends in Funchal center and the celebrations continue on city streets, in restaurants and pubs. In front of the City Theatre (Teatro Municipal Baltazar Dias) are the names of the winners of Madeira Wine Rally on the paving stones, and among them are some famous drivers' names.

On the 15th of August is one of the year's greatest religious festivals in Madeira when they hold a **Pilgrimage Festival** and celebrate the Ascension of the Virgin Mary (Festa da Nossa Senhora do Monte) in Monte. Many of the pilgrims crawl on their knees up to the church more than 70 steps whilst at the same time praying and dancing. In the evening the party continues with dancing, food and fireworks. The day is a public holiday.

On the 21st of August is **Funchal Day** it also is a public holiday. On that day in 1508 Funchal received its town charter. The City is celebrating the day by outdoor concerts, colourful parades and fireworks.

▶ **These rally drivers among others have won the Madeira Wine rally.**

August is a busy month in many respects with festivals and events; in Machico is held a **Food Festival** (Semana Gastronómica) and in São Vicente and Faial an **International Music Festival**. In addition in Santa Cruz in August they hold a **Regatta** (Regata Quebra Mar) where sailing yachts participate and sail from Santa Cruz to Porto Santo and back. Also in August in Camacha is held an **Art Festival** (Festival de Arte Camachense) and a **Canoe Race** (Volta á Madeira em Canoa) around the island.

In September are yet more religious events; a big festival and **religious parade of Jesus Christ and the Holy Sacrament** (Festa do Senhor Bom Jesus e Santo Sacramento) in Ponta Delgada and in Caniçal **Festa da Nossa Senhora da Piedade** a celebration where they carry the Virgin Mary statue in a festive procession.

In addition to many **wine festivals**, in September will also take place many other harvest related festivals, such as **the Grape Festival** (Festa da Uva) in Porto da Cruz, **the Pear Festival** (Festa do Pêro) in Ponta do Pargo and **the Cider Festival** (Mostra da Sidra) in Santo da Serra.

The 5th of October is **Republic Day** (Dia do República) with all the associated political ceremonies. It is a public holiday.

In Ribeira Brava is held an **Orchestra Competition** (Encontro Regional de Bandas) at the beginning of October involving philharmonic orchestras from around the island. In this

happening they cherish Madeira's musical heritage and the competing orchestras perform on the streets and in front of the church. In addition there is a traditional parade and later on the party starts... and continues into the night.

On 8th and 9th of October will be held **Miracle-Workers Festival** (Festa do Senhor do Milagres) in Machico where they respect the salvage of the Jesus statue when local church was destroyed during the floods in the 1803. Thousands of islanders arrive there to spend one of the island's most important religious festivals.

At the end of October in Camacha is **the Apple Festival** (Festa da Macã) which they celebrate by singing, dancing and drinking the cider and apple brandy.

1st of November is **All Saint's Day** (Dia de Todos-os-Santos) when in churches they hold extra masses for that festive day. It is also a public holiday.

On the same day, 1st of November they celebrate **the Chestnut Festival** (Festa da Castanha) in Curral das Freiras (Nuns Valley). This festival starts in the morning and will conclude late at night. There you can taste the liqueurs, home-made cakes and pastries and soups etc. all made of chestnuts.

The Funchal International Film Festival is organized in November when the City Theatre (Teatro Municipal Baltazar Dias) is changed into a movie arena and the best movies in different categories will be rewarded.

On the 11th of November will be held in **São Martinho Festival** (Festa do São Martinho), a village festival with good food, beverages and also music. The event focuses on the surrounding areas of São Martinho church in western part of Funchal.

In addition to the above mentioned events, there will be held in Madeira a wide range of exhibitions, fairs and other events, more detailed information you may check from local newspapers, travel agencies, tourist offices and hotel receptions. Hotels also organise a variety of programs and events in their guests.

National holidays in Madeira when the banks and the shops are closed:

New Year Day, Shrove Tuesday, Good Friday and Easter Sunday, 25.4. Revolution Day, 1.5. May Day, 10.6. A Portuguese Independence Day, 1.7. Madeira's Day of Autonomy, 15.8. The Ascension of the Virgin Mary, 21.8. Funchal Day, 5.10. Republic Day, 1.11. All Saint's Day, 1.12. Independence Day, 8.12. Assumption of the Virgin Mary, 25.12. Christmas Day and Boxing Day.

▶ São Martinho's village festival is a colourful local event.

▶ Ceriman (Monstera, Mexican Bread Fruit, Swiss Cheese Plant) has a special fruit.

FOOD, DRINK AND RESTAURANTS ▶ ▶ ▶ ▶ ▶ ▶ ▶

Foods and drinks

Madeiran food is a mixture of continental Portuguese and the tropical kitchen. Food is simple and good and there is a wide range of meat and fresh fish. One of the most popular is the local barbecued meat on a spit (espetada) spiced with garlic, salt and herbs. The most popular Madeiran fish course is the speciality black scabbard fish (espada), which is served in many different ways. For vegetarians can be found delicious fresh vegetables, salads and soups. In addition to oven-fresh bread (bolo do caco) spread with a lot of garlic butter.

Madeiran starters are, for example, Lapas, consisting of grilled limpets in shells, with a lot of garlic butter and lemon added, this is eaten directly from pan with bread to mop up the juices. Also many delicious soups, which are good and nourishing. Today's soup (sopa do dia) is in most cases a vegetable soup, tomato and onion soup (sopa de tomate e cebola) is often served with a poached egg and a fish soup called caldeirada. Small snacks may be brought to the table unordered and if you eat them, they will be billed, if you leave them untouched, they will not be charged. Same thing often with bread, which is placed at the table without asking.

Meat courses (carne) in addition to the tasty spit roast meat (espetada) are for example, various meat stews and juicy steak on the stone. One of the most popular for locals is wine marinated pork (carne de porco em vinho), which is offered in several village festivals in a bread roll. From the menus you will find also some more familiar dishes such as cutlets, pepper steaks, pork (porco) and lamb (carneiro) cooked in several different ways. Poultry or chicken (frango) is often served with a spicy piripiri-sauce.

Madeirans eat their fish and crayfish fresh, generally caught the same day. In addition to black scabbard fish there is also tuna (atum), which is usually marinated in olive oil, flavoured with garlic, salt and oregano before baking. Cod (bacalhau) is cooked in several ways. It has been said that the Madeiran house wife cooks cod in 365 different ways, one for each day differently. However, cod is not fresh but salted and dried and most of it is imported from Norway or Canada. There are also fresh sardine (sardinhas), mackerel (cavala or carapau), shrimp (camarão or gamba), lobsters (lagosta), calamari (choco or polvo) and clams (concha).

With meat courses French fries (batatas fritas) or rice (arroz) are the usual accompaniment, sometimes also sweet potatoes (batata) and with fish courses often cooked potatoes (batata cozidas) unless you ask for something else. In addition either cooked vegetables (legumes), fried corn cubes (milho frito) or salad. Tomatoes are eaten here greener than we are used to.

For desserts the choice offered is from a selection of different home-made cakes, ice cream (gelado), fruit salad or puddings; for example passion fruit pudding (pudim maracúja), chocolate pudding (musse de chocolate) or creme caramel (pudim flan). For friends of liqueurs there can be found many locally produced liqueurs; for example passion fruit (maracúja), bananas (banana), annona (anona), chestnut (castanha) and cherry (ginja). If you like a stronger spirit you can choose the local alcohol (aquardente), sugar cane rum (aquardente velha), Macieira brandy and, of course, poncha which is made of aquardente flavored with lemon and honey.

Drinks with a meal you can either select Madeira wine, the local red wine (vinho tinto), white wine (vinho branco), rosé wine (vinho rosado) or the so called green wine (vinho verde), which is not green but a semi-sparkling, young wine. Or beer (cerveja), water (água), which can choose with gas (com gas) or without gas (sem gas) or soft drinks (brisa or sumo). There are also available drinks without alcohol (sem alcohol).

With your bill waiters often bring a glass of Madeira wine or local fruit liqueur. These are not charged on your bill but the restaurant offers them as a digestive.

▶ **Vintage wines can be tasted in wine bars and wine museums.**

▶ **Coral is a local beer which is available also without alcohol (sem alcohol).**

▶ **In many restaurants it is possible to eat outdoors year round.**

Restaurants

Restaurants can be found for all tastes and which suit every wallet from fine five-star restaurants (for example Michelin-stared Il Gallo D'Oro in Cliff Bay hotel) to cosy tavernas and fast food restaurants. There are many restaurants in Madeira, you can find Madeiran and Portuguese cuisine, Indian, Italian, Japanese, Chinese, Turkish, Thai and the so-called international cuisine. In many of these restaurants it is possible to eat outdoors year round.

In front of many restaurants the doorman or woman stop and tempt

you with a glass of Madeira wine whilst suggesting you come inside to eat. They are always kind and polite even if you choose this time not to go in. In many restaurants outside of the hotel areas or city center areas they offer a courtesy car service, which means that they pick you up from your hotel to eat in the restaurant and later bring you back to your hotel with no charge.

In some restaurants they charge for everything; bread which they bring into table unordered, different starters, rice, etc. So to prevent unwanted charges, you should always check in advance what is included in the prices and what extra costs may be. In some restaurants they have a 'cover charge' which covers above mentioned starters, bread etc.

Restaurants are generally open from morning till 10 pm or 11 pm. Some restaurants are closed after lunch for a couple of hours, usually between 3 pm to 5 pm. Lunch (almoço) is eaten in general during the period from 12.30 pm to 3 pm and during this period many offices and smaller stores are closed.

Dinner (jantar) is eaten rather late in Madeira, usually at 7 pm to 10 pm. Many restaurants, especially in tourist areas offer food throughout the day. In addition coffee shops and snack bars offer something to eat all day long.

I do not want to make a list of recommended restaurants, because the choice is large, and also businesses come and go. The most popular restaurants, however, remain consistent year after year, so here I have listed a few. As in every country, if a restaurant has many locals eating in it, it usually follows then that there's good food and good value. Most people from Northern Europe are used to eating earlier than Madeirans, so I recommend you to take note of different places when returning from a restaurant, and perhaps go there the next day.

From Funchal's old city there are several attractive restaurants, small bars, fado singing and a cosmopolitan atmosphere. You could perhaps start your dinner at the Jango restaurant at Rua Santa Maria or a small Pizzeria Xarambinha located in Corpo Santo square, just next to a small old chapel. After twilight you might next go and listen to fado or some other music. In Rua Santa Maria there are lots of other cosy restaurants for you to choose from.

Also located in the city centrum is a Armazém do Sal at address Rua da Alfândega, close to the Columbus square. This restaurant is famous for its good food and is in a 200 year old building that once served as a salt warehouse. Located close to the La Vie shopping mall is the attractive House Jazz at Rua do Aranhas 16 which has live music some evenings during the week.

▶ **The high quality 'Armazem do Sal' restaurant which is located in an old salt warehouse.**

► Mamma Mia is a good Italian restaurant with excellent pizzas and pasta dishes.

At the Lido close to the hotel area there are a few restaurants worth a mention. For example popular Mamma Mia restaurant close to the Vidamar hotel, pasta and pizza restaurant Casa Italia on the slope of Rua Gorgulho close to the Eden Mar Shopping Center, as well as Chinese and Thai food at China Town in the Monumental Lido Shopping Center. Close to the places mentioned is the charming Chalet Vicente at Estrada Monumental 238. On the Lido promenade in front of Enotel Lido hotel there is a cozy Brasserie restaurant.

Close to the Forum Shopping mall, accross from the hotel Pestana Grand, at Rua Ponta da Cruz 18A is a restaurant Real Canoa which is worth

of a mention. This restaurant is very popular, there is excellent food and very friendly service. Other restaurants worth mentioning are the Solar da Ajuda who has two restaurants, one in Estrada Monumental 438 close to the hanging angel statue and the other one in Lido at Rua da Casa Branca 102. Also close to the Pico dos Barcelos view point there is a charming Quinta Estacão restaurant which has beautiful view and good food.

Outside the city are also a number of good restaurants which offer courtesy cars to transfer customers from hotels. Among these are A Seta which is located above the city in Livramento. They offer delicious steaks and barbecued spit roast meat (espetada) as well as other local dishes for you to

▶ 'A Seta' is a local restaurant with a great food and live entertainment during your dinner.

enjoy. Vila da Peixe and Vila de Carne restaurants are located in Câmara de Lobos at Rua Dr. João Abel de Freitas and A Central restaurant in Caniço where you can have a huge meat meal. These restaurants will pick you up, take you to the restaurant and drop you off after dinner to your hotel. Out of town in Ribeiro Frio, along the way from Monte to Santana, there is a

well-known restaurant Faísca with Madeiran cuisine.

If you're searching for a really affordable place to eat, many shopping centers and Pingo Doce supermarkets have so called kilo places (Sabores Ao Kg) in which you will be able to collect your choice of food from the counter and pay the price by weight. The food is good and the selection varies on a daily basis.

See also the food vocabulary in Portuguese in a separate section at the end of this book.

DID YOU KNOW...

Popular local dishes are for example espetada (barbecued spit roast meat) and espada (Black Scabbard Fish).

▶ Real Canoa restaurant is very popular and they serve delicious food.

▶ **Number 2 is a very popular sports bar.**

Pubs

Pubs are popular meeting places for locals where they drink beer and other beverages, watch and talk football or other sports. A few examples of popular pubs for tourists are, Hole in One in the Lido on Estrada Monumental and Moynihans Irish Pub close to the Pestana Casino Park hotel. Also popular with locals and tourists is Pub Number 2 which is located opposite the hotel Pestana Carlton.

▶ Hole in One Pub in Lido at Estrada Monumental 238
▶ Pub Number 2 at Rua Favilla 2
▶ Prince Albert Pub at Rua Imperatriz Dona Amelia 86
▶ Moynihans, Rua Imperatriz Dona Amelia 101
▶ The White House Pub, Rua da Casa Branca 62

Wine and drink bars

Almost all hotels have bars and in restaurants they serve drinks and

cocktails, but if you like to show up and have an appetizer or drink in a popular place, you should go to Ritz Café or Café do Theatro at Avenida Arriaga, opposite to City Garden, or behind the corner to Theo's at Avenica Zarco. Or perhaps Santa Maria Bar or Barreirinha Bar Café, both at Rua Santa Maria.

Cafes and tea houses

Cafe culture in Madeira is alive and well, and Madeirans pop into coffee shops several times a day. Cafés and bakeries (pastelaria) are all around the city and from there you can get delicious homemade delicacies among which the most popular is a small pastry (queijados) named 'pastel de nata', made of fresh cheese, eggs and sugar. 'Broas de mel' is corn cake and 'bolo de mel' is a traditional honey cake which previously was only made for Christmas but now is offered throughout the year.

The coffee in Madeira is fresh, dark, strong and good. Each cup is made separately in an espresso machine. Madeirans drink their coffee often standing next to the counter. A large black coffee is a chino (or americano), coffee with milk is a chinesa, a large coffee with milk in a glass is a galão, espresso is a bica and espresso with milk is a garoto. Tea is cha and cocoa is cacau.

From the English heritage there are several tea houses on the island which offer varieties of teas with small refreshments, sandwiches and pastries.

Hotel Reid's Palace serves afternoon tea from 3 pm to 5 pm. In addition to tea houses there are also ice cream parlours and small snack bars where you can get snacks for lunch or a night bite.

▶ **In Ponta do Pargo there is a popular tea house from whose terrace there are amazing views to the sea**

Supermarkets and grocery stores

At local market halls or market places (mercado) you can get fresh fish daily, as well as various exotic fruit, pastries and meat. Hypermarkets, super-markets (super mercado) and some grocery stores are very well supplied and they have separate counters for fruit, bread, meat and fish. In some supermarkets it is not recommended to bring shopping bags or other large items but should be left for storage or in coin operating lockers. Women's handbags are, of course, an exception. Some supermarkets and grocery stores do not accept credit cards with purchases under 20 €.

See also food vocabulary in Portuguese in a separate section at the end of this book.

▶ **Cafés and cake shops are all over the island.**

Night life and live music

Madeira is not really a city with wild night life, but you can find a few discotheques and night clubs; for example Copacabana inside the Casino and in the port there is the Vespa. Usually locals meet at pubs and sport bars, watch football etc. sport on the TV. You can also find wine bars, but restaurants with dance floors you will not find on Madeira. Some large hotels have evening shows, folk-dancing, local artists and fado nights. In some hotels they also have a live orchestra and a small dance floor. You do not have to be a resident at that hotel to enjoy the entertainment. Few of the most well-known dance and show restaurants are the Pestana Casino Park hotel and the Casino itself where they have dinner show on weekends. The hotel Four Views Monumental Lido also has music and dancing most evenings.

The most well-known fado restaurants are Marcelino's and Arsenio's both located in the old city. Marcelino's at Travessa das Torres 22 which opens at 10 pm and is open till 2 am. Arsenio's at Santa Maria 169 and there you can listen to fado during dinner. Outside of the city there is also a popular restaurant A Seta in Livramento where you can listen to fado at a Madeiran evening.

Live music can be found in the following bars and restaurants:
▶ House Jazz, Rua do Aranhas 16 (close to the La Vie Shopping), Wednesdays and Saturdays

▶ **Marcelino's is one of the most popular fado restaurants in the town.**

- ▶ SCAT The Funchal Jazz Club and Restaurant, Wednesday and Saturdays, Promenade do Lido, at the Lido
- ▶ Hole in One Pub, Estrada Monumental 238 at the Lido, with live music on weekends
- ▶ Katz Bar at the Lido, international DJ on weekends
- ▶ Moynihans Irish Pub, Rua Imperatriz Dona Amelia, live music five nights a week
- ▶ Casino's Cobacabana Garden, live music on weekends
- ▶ FX Club, Avenida do Mar (behind Municipal Theatre), live music on weekends
- ▶ Kool Klub Café (close to Pestana Carlton Hotel)
- ▶ Vespa (opposite harbour terminal)
- ▶ Chameleon (across from Pestana Carlton Hotel)
- ▶ Marginal & Jam (opposite harbour terminal)

Casino

At the Casino (Casino da Madeira) where in addition to the one arm bandits, roulette, poker and black Jack there is also a quality dinner show restaurant Bahia, Cobacabana night club, Palm cocktail bar and a small casual dining restaurant Rio. Age limit to the Casino is 18 years. Gambling hall and bar are open from Sunday to Thursday at 3 pm to 3 am and on Friday and on Saturday at 4 pm to 4 am. Restaurant and dinner show from Wednesday to Saturday at 7.30 pm. The show starts at 9 pm and before that dinner is served. You can also go to the restaurant only for the show

▶ **At the Casino you can enjoy quality dinner shows.**

without a dinner. At weekends there is also live music in Cobacabana's Garden. No dress code, but clean, neat and proper attire; no jeans, shorts or sport shoes. Address Avenida do Infante. Reservation recommended, tel. 291 140 424 or 291 140 426.

Smoking

Also in Madeira most restaurants and cafés are adding non smoking areas little by little. Smoking in restaurants and coffee shops is still allowed if there are ashtrays on the tables, but overall the smoking areas have moved outside. Portugal and Madeira along with other EU countries have begun to restrict smoking in working areas, public places etc. or banned it completely.

WELLNESS, HEALTH AND BEAUTY ▶ ▶ ▶ ▶ ▶ ▶ ▶ ▶ ▶ ▶

Madeira is a destination which provides excellent conditions to care for your health. Already in the 1800s people came here to cure respiratory problems and Porto Santo's beach sand contains minerals which is believed to improve rheumatic problems.

In most hotels they have swimming pools, gym, tennis courts, massage parlour, spa and beauty saloon.

In beauty salons (Institutos de Beleza) and spas you can enjoy facials and massage, have a manicure or pedicure or just sit back and enjoy talassoterapia, water massage, relaxing cures or aroma terapia etc.

Hairdressing establishments (cabeleireiro) are a little cheaper than in most European countries. Products, such as hair sprays, mousse etc. will sometimes be invoiced separately.

In salons you often also have the opportunity for a facial, manicure or pedicure. Hotel's hair salons and hair dressers are generally a little more expensive than elsewhere.

Barber (barbeiro) is only for men and 'cabeleireiro unisexo' is a hair salon that cut both mens' and womens' hair. Madeiran barbers and often hair dressers clip your hair in a so called 'all the way', so if you are not vigilant and

careful the result may be a too short hair style.

Gyms (ginácio) and fitness clubs can be found in addition at hotels, but also in the Madeira Magic Theme Park close to Forum Madeira Shopping center, Symmetrix in the Lido area in the Monumental Lido Shopping Center, in connection with Clube Naval's swimming hall in the Nazaré part of city, La Vie Shopping center and in front of Vidamar Hotel on Estrada Monumental in the Lido area.

▶ **From the Lido promenade you can find the ruins of an old shipyard.**

223

LEISURE, TOURS, SPORTS AND OTHER ACTIVITIES ▶ ▶ ▶

Madeira's climate and a flourishing nature allow for all kinds of activities on land and at sea and here you can find something for everyone; gentle walks for nature lovers or extreme sports for daredevils.

By walking exploring the island is most rewarding; you see stunning landscapes, magnificent views from the top of striking mountains and upwards from the bottom of valleys. Also in cities and towns you can walk along promenades, parks and alleys and see beautiful sights and attractions. In Funchal there are two promenades, one on Avenida do Mar in the port and the second one from Lido to Praia Formosa and as far as

Câmara de Lobos. These promenades give you opportunities for a range of activities; walking, jogging, swimming etc.

Most interesting and perhaps unique are **levada walks**. See Levadas and irrigation channels elsewhere in this book. This travel guide does not list individual levadas and routes. If you want to go to a levada by yourself, buy a good guidebook with maps and select a levada that fits your own fitness condition and abilities. For first timers it may be best to participate with a guided tour where the return transport is also organised. These guided tours are for all ages with small groups organised by many different

companies (for example MB Tours). There is always an experienced English speaking guide and sometimes also German or French. Some hotels and travel agencies also organise these guided levada tours. Reservations and inquiries from your hotel, tourist offices, travel agencies and kiosks around the city. In Madeira they hold a five day Hiking Festival in January when you can walk and hike through levadas and nature paths in groups with experienced guides. Every day there are four different levadas varying in levels of difficulty and length.

As well as levadas you can find **nature paths** in Madeira. A few years ago an 8 km long nature path was opened in the valley of the João Gomes river.

Here is a good opportunity to walk and see waterfalls, local flora and fauna. In addition to these walks you can also **hike on the mountains**. There are a few companies organising these hiking trips and you also can do it on your own. However, our advice is never go out alone to the levadas or mountains!

There are a number of companies organising excursions when you can **monitor nature** and rare birds which are nesting only here. These excursions are made on land and on the sea. In addition to bird watching there are also excursions to see flowers and plants of which there are many on the island. Enquiries either from your hotel, tourist office or travel agencies.

Jogging on promenades, parks, or city streets. The disadvantages in Funchal are the steep and narrow pavements and also people wandering at a

▷ In Madeira you have the opportunity for all kinds of activities on land and sea.

different pace. We recommend that you watch your step whilst walking or jogging because the streets are uneven and bumpy and the paving and roots of trees can be sticking up anywhere.

Playing tennis or squash you have an opportunity in some hotels, which have their own courts and rental equipment. These hotel facilities can be used by non residents too and often without advance reservation. Quinta Magnolia park has few tennis courts, which can be rented for a modest charge. These courts are open from 8.30 am to 5 pm, but they do not have rental equipment. As well as Funchal's Tennis Club (Clube de Ténis do Funchal) at Rua Dr. Anexo Pita Barreiros, close to football stadium, you can rent a tennis court and also the necessary equipment.

Well equipped **gyms** (ginácio) and fitness clubs can be found in some large hotels and they are freely used by hotel customers. In addition to hotels there are also a few other gyms on the island, for example in Madeira Magic Theme Park close to Forum Madeira Shopping Center, Symmetrix located in Monumental Lido Shopping Center, in connection with Clube Naval's swimming hall in the Nazaré part of city, La Vie Shopping center and in front of Vidamar Hotel on Estrada Monumental in the Lido area.

Aerobic, Pilates, relaxation etc.
you can exercise in most larger hotels, which have instructed sports personnel. Consult your hotel reception. Also the above mentioned gyms and fitness clubs do offer these instructed exercises. See also section Wellness, health and beauty.

▶ **Tennis can also be played in the Quinta Magnolia Park.**

▶ Rallying is the second national sport after football.

▶ You can spot vintage cars at weekends.

Bowling alleys can be found in the Caniço and Camacha shopping centers. In Camacha there is a four lane and in Caniço a six lane bowling alley.

Dancing can be done in some hotels which have live music and a small dance floor, for example in the Pestana Casino Park and Four Views Monumental Lido. There are no proper dance restaurants in Madeira. During festivals some hotels have ball room dances. In Monumental Lido you can have lessons of line-dancing on Wednesdays at 7.30 pm and on Friday mornings at 11.30 am.

Football fans can spectate on Estádio dos Barreiros Stadium for team Maritimo's football matches at weekends. On weekdays it is possible to watch the teams exercise on the Stadium too. The Stadium is situated on Rua do Dr. Pita. Team Nacional play their matches on Estádio da Madeira which is located above the city in the foothills. Both teams are in a Portugal's

1. division. Team Nacional's games are usually on Saturdays and team Maritimo's on Sundays. Often other teams from the continent visits the island. Tickets can be bought directly from the gates or hotel's receptionists. The famous footballer Cristiano Ronaldo is Madeiran by birth.

Motorsport enthusiasts can spectate at rallies which will be held in spring, summer and autumn in most weekends. Local teams are approx. 50. See dates from local newspapers or motorsport magazines. The Madeira Wine Rally (Rali Vinho da Madeira) will take place in the beginning of August and it is one of the National series rallies. The Madeira Wine Rally begins and ends on Avenida Arriaga in center of Funchal. In front of the City Theatre (Teatro Municipal Baltazar Dias) on the street paving stones are the names of

▶ Jet-skis on Funchal port.

the former winners of Madeira Wine Rally. The second motorsport event is the Tour de Madeira in end of June when many vintage sports cars drive around the island. Old cars can be spotted on streets on weekends, because in Madeira there are a few hundred old vintage cars which are 'aired' on a sunny weekends. You can drive go-carts in Faial where there is the go-cart track (Kartódromo do Faial). Also in the beginning of May they organize a Classic Auto Show in front of the Reid's Palace Hotel and the streets close to it.

Jeep safaris give you an alternative way to experience the island and access places which tour buses or cars cannot reach. Many companies organise these jeep safaris for half or full day trips.

Funchal's narrow, twisty and very steep streets may not fit well on **bicycling** terms. However, you can see cyclists defying the street traffic and the popularity of bicycling and mountain biking is increasing. Bicycling tours are organized and bikes are rented by a few companies, also some shopping centers and

hotels rent bicycles. Every autumn in September or October is held the Tour de Island by bicycles. In this two days international event dozens of cyclists participate.

For nautical sports enthusiasts Madeira coast gives countless of opportunities.

Scuba diving and snorkelling can be done in Madeira around the year because the seawater temperature in summer is 24 °C and in winter 18 °C also the seawater is a bright and clean. In addition to normal scuba diving you can also scuba dive, observe and photograph the underwater life in Garajau's Marine Nature Reserve which extends also 50 meters below sea level. Diving schools are located basically in Funchal and Caniço de Baixo. These diving schools organise courses at all levels and there you can obtain a diving permit and make test dives. They also organise night dives and rent the equipment.

In Madeira there are excellent conditions for **surfing, stand up paddling, wave** and **sail boarding**. Also **kayaking, jetsking** and **water skiing** are worth trying. Beaches are, however, rocky and waves sometimes very strong, so a certain amount of caution is required. Best surfing weather is from September to May and in particular the beaches in Jardim do Mar, Paul do Mar and São Vicente are excellent for these sports.

Whilst on **boat cruises or sailing** you can see Madeira from the same perspective as the first explorers at that time i.e. from the sea. You have the opportunity to rent a sailing boat with crew, but you can also take daily sailing trips with organised tours on coastal waters while enjoying your lunch or make a cruise with catamaran or even with fast rubber dinghies and watch whales and dolphins from a close range.

You can also go back to the time of the explorers by getting on-board the replica of Christopher Columbus ship, Santa Maria de Colombo, and imagine how were sailing and conditions on-board more than 500 years ago. During the journey you can see dolphins, whales, the turtles and rare sea birds. There is possibility to swimming from a boat.

These daily cruises depart from Funchal's luxury yacht marina twice a day in the mornings and afternoons. Except the Santa Maria de Colombo leaves from cruise boat port. Reservations directly from the port at least 30 minutes prior to departure or in advance from hotel receptions, information centers or your travel agency.

Fishing enthusiasts can do fishing trips, big game fishing or try their luck

▶ Its easy to watch dolphins play on catamaran trips.

to catch blue marlin, or different varieties of tuna or shark. These guided tours give lessons for beginners too. Usually the price includes equipments and bait. There are all day or half a day trips and night fishing. Some fishing boats also make excursions to watch the fishermen who are catching black scabbard fish (espada) from deep under the sea. Fishing trips go out from the luxury yacht marina. Reservations directly at the port.

Riding can be done with horses or donkeys. Best places for horse riding are in the Riding Center (Associação Hípica da Madiera) which is located in Quinta Vila Alpires, at Caminho dos Pretos, above Monte. Also in Centro Hipico de São Jorge in Santo da Serra here you can ride and have lessons for beginners and advanced level. Donkey riding (A passo de Burro) can be done in Funchal Ecological Park (Ecológico do Funchal).

Madeira's nature gives a great opportunity and offers good conditions for **extreme sports**. Here you can participate in mountain sports like **trekking, mountain climbing** and **canyoning** throughout the year although the best conditions are in spring and summer, when the water temperature is slightly higher. There are a number of companies organising guided excursions for all these sports for anybody interested, you must be more than 12 years of age and in good physical condition. Trips take about two to six hours. Inquiries from your hotel receptions, tourist offices or travel agencies. In June is held the Madeira International Canyoning Event.

Also for **hang gliding, parachute gliding** and **gliding** there are good opportunities and for advanced pilots Madeira offers many good starting points but few landing places. You can visit the Gliding Center in Calheta, address Sitio da Achada de Santo Antão in Arco da Calheta. More information from your hotel reception, tourist offices or travel agencies. The three-day International Parachute Gliding Meeting is held in April in Madeira.

Madeira has two high-quality **golf courses** and a third in Porto Santo. A fourth course is planned in Ponta do Pargo in the western part of Madeira. Madeira is a paradise for golfers with its spectacular courses' breathtaking scenery. All golf courses have a par 72.

Palheiro Golf is located on a slope above Funchal around the stunning Quinta do Palheiro built in the 1800s. This 18-hole course was designed by Cabell Robinson and was opened in 1993. The length of this course is 6015 m and there are great views down to

▶ For hang gliding and parachute gliding Madeira offers good starting points.

Funchal. Address Rua do Balancal 29, São Gonçalo.

Santo da Serra Golf Club (Glube de Golfe do Santo da Serra) is located in Santo da Serra, about 15 km north-east of Funchal. This 27-hole course was designed by Robert Trent Jones and opened in 1991. The Madeira Island Open PGA European Tour is held every spring at the Santo da Serra Golf course. The lenght of 18-hole course is 6039 m. In bright weather there are breathtaking views down to Machico and São Lourenço peninsula.

Access to these courses either by taxi, rental car or subscribing transport from your hotel or a golf club. Golf clubs restaurants are open to the public.

Porto Santo Golf (Campo de Golfe do Porto Santo) was opened in October 2004 which was designed by Severiano Ballesteros. This 18-hole course is located at Sitio das Marinhas, Apartado 174. From Funchal there is every day a ferry to Porto Santo which leaves Funchal in the morning and returns at the evening. Also three daily flights from Funchal airport.

At Ponta do Pargo the third high standard golf course designed by Nick Faldo is planned. The course should be completed in the near future.

Sport centers are in Água de Pena and Ribeira Brava. Sport center in Água de Pena (Parque Desportivo de Água de Pena, Machico) is located underneath the Madeira airport runway extension. There are several multi purpose fields on which you can practice for example football, handball, basketball, volleyball and also tennis and squash. Address Sitio da Queimada, Água Pena, Machico. Ribeira Brava's Sports Center (Centro Desportivo Ribeira Brava) is located on the road from Ribeira Brava to São Vicente. There you can practice for example football, tennis and kayaking. In addition this sport center has also two playgrounds for children, green spaces and snack bar and underground parking for cars. Address Sitio da Fajã da Tibeira.

If you find any kind of sport boring and you want to do something lighter in your leisure time the English Church (Trinity Church) holds **bingo-nights** every second Thursday of the month at 6.30 pm.

The second casual way to spend your leisure time at the seaside is **ship spotting** at the port. In Funchal port arrive more and more spectacular cruise ships, including Queen Elizabeth, Queen Victoria, Independence of the Seas, Aida, Norwegian Spirit, Mein Schiff and MSC Fantasia. Also luxury yachts and sailing boats come to the port from around the world.

> **DID YOU KNOW...**
>
> Madeira is a paradise for golfers with its spectacular courses and breathtaking landscapes.

From Santo da Serra Golf Club there are magnificent views to São Lourenço peninsula.

SWIMMING, BEACHES AND SWIMMING POOLS ▶ ▶ ▶ ▶

In Funchal there are no sandy beaches and on Madeira there are only a few exceptions; Calheta and Machico have beaches, on both of which sand has been brought in from elsewhere, Prainha volcanic beach in Caniçal is Madeira's only natural sandy beach. Madeira's beaches are stony and because of volcanic nature they are black. However, you can still swim here, because almost all hotels have swimming pools, Funchal has four public swimming-baths and in addition to these there are also natural shaped sea pools and public swimming halls.

Swimming water has set strict quality standards throughout the EU. From the European Commission's annual

▶ **Madeira's beaches are stony.**

232

swimming water report (www.EC.
Europa.eu/environment/water/water-
bathing/report) holiday-makers get
useful information about sea waters.
A blue flag on the beach or port
indicates that water quality, safety,
services and the environment issues
and information standards are met.

Outdoor public swimming-baths

Public swimming-baths are open
every day from 9 am to 6 pm, in
summer time even longer. Both
beaches and public swimming-baths
which have access to the sea, have
flag signs telling the strength of the
waves. When the green flag is on the
pole it is safe to swim in the sea,
when there is a yellow flag showing
swimming is at your own risk and
a red flag means swimming is
prohibited. There is usually a modest
entry fee to public swimming-baths
and often they have a café.

The Lido swimming complex in the
hotel area at the Lido has a large and a
small sea water pools, children's pool,
and the ability to swim in the sea.

▶ **Almost all hotels have excellent swimming pools.**

▶ Outdoor public swimming-baths often have access to swim in the sea.

In addition there is a diving center and a water slide. Temporarily closed in spring 2015.

Complexo Balnear da Barreirinha is located in the old city near the São Tiago fortress. Adults and children's pools also access to the sea. Open only in summer months.

Ponta Gorda public swimming-baths are located on the Lido promenade, below the Forum Madeira Shopping Center. There are pools for adults and children and the possibility to swim in the sea.

Private swimming-bath Clube Naval do Funchal is located on the Lido promenade, below the Forum Madeira Shopping Center. There are two sea water pools and the ability to swim in the sea.

Nature shaped sea pools

There is also a nature shaped sea pool in the Funchal area. For example at the end of the Lido promenade close to Praia Formosa beach, below the Doca dos Cavacas fish restaurant, there is a Complexo Balnear das Doca do Cavacas where there are a few natural shaped sea pools and a pier where you can sun bathe.

In Porto Moniz, outside of Funchal, on the north-west of the island, can be found the most famous natural shaped sea pools on the island. Country buses number 80 and 139.

Indoor swimming-baths

If swimming in seawater is not your thing, you can find a few indoor swimming-baths in Funchal. One is above the old city center, connected with a sports arena and the other the Clube Naval swimming-bath in the Nazaré part of town. The third swimming-bath, Olympic pools, is located in Caminho dos Alamos outside the city center.

Beaches

There are no beaches in Funchal, but at the end of the Lido promenade, about 3 km from Funchal westwards, there is a Praia Formosa's long and rocky beach where you can find a few spots of black sand for swimming.

On the Lido promenade at the Lido there is a small stony Praia do Gorgulho beach which has access to swim in the sea. The second one is in front of São Tiago fortress in Funchal city center where there is a tiny beach for swimming and bathing.

Soon there will be a proper new beach for swimming and bathing in Funchal city when the new cruise ship pier and Square of the People park and leisure area is completed.

DID YOU KNOW...

You can find few real sandy beaches for bathing and swimming in Madeira.

▶ **Nature shaped sea pools**

Praia Formosa beach is located about 3 km from Funchal to the west.

Outside of Funchal beaches can be found for example:

In Caniço there is the small attractive Praia dos Reis Magos beach, Galo Mar's stony beach which has both adult and children pools and the ability to swim in the sea. There is also the Manta Diving Center. Country bus number 103.

In Calheta there is the golden Praia da Calheta beach where the sand has been imported from the Sahara.

In Faial and Garajau you can find stony beaches. Similarly also in Seixal, the north coast, between São Vicente and Porto Moniz. Also in Ponta Delgada close to São Vicente there is a small stony beach as well as two swimming pools.

Prainha's blackish brownish volcanic beach is located on the road leading from Caniçal to São Lourenço peninsula. It is the only natural sandy beach in Madeira and particularly on summer weekends it is crowded. Country bus number 113.

In Santa Cruz there is the Praia das Palmeiras beach which is mainly intended for families with children. The beach is divided into two, swimming pools and stony beach and it is open only on summer months. Also in Santa Cruz there is Roca Mar beach and Water park (Aquaparque de Santa Cruz) which is located at Ribeira da Boaventura. In the Water Park there are several swimming pools, water slides, a black hole and a separate water park for small children. Open every day from mid of March to mid of November.

▶ **Also at Machico beach sand has been brought in from elsewhere.**

237

SHOPPING ▶ ▶ ▶ ▶ ▶ ▶ ▶ ▶ ▶

What to buy from Madeira

Funchal is a very international city and here you can find many top brands (Boss, Gant, Armani, Versace, Gucci, Prada, Dolce & Gabbana etc.), elegant boutiques and modern shopping centers and the assortments they carry are slightly different compared to Northern Europe. Clothes' and shoes' sizes are the same as in most countries in Europe, so are weight and length dimensions in kilograms and meters.

Leather products are high-quality and affordable. In Madeira there is a good variety of ladies bags and shoes for women and men. Brand names may be bit cheaper than on the continent. Also try Madeiran boots (boas de vilão).

Embroideries from handkerchiefs to traditional tablecloths and blouses etc. are good souvenirs from Madeira and they last for the next generation. Embroideries and artefacts are sold all around the city in souvenir shops and factories. It takes hours to make a small handkerchief, not to mention a beautiful big tablecloths, so they are pretty expensive. All genuine embroideries are marked with the IBTAM guarantee.

Other typical artefacts such as wicker products are sold all around the city, but the full range of them are found in the village of Camacha which is the center of the wicker industry. From willow they manufacture products of all shapes and sizes, including baskets, trays, furniture etc. For bigger purchases arrangements can be made for them to be shipped and delivered to your home.

Wine stores that are specialized in Madeira wines are all around the city and connected with wine museums. Madeira's national drink, poncha, you only get it from here on the island, so it is also a good souvenir. It is made from sugar cane alcohol, honey and lemon and it is sold in wine stores and also supermarkets and grocery stores.

▶ **From the Market place you can find exotic fruits, vegetables and fish.**

Madeira also has it's own beer brand, Coral, and soft drinks like Brisa, especially passion fruit (maracuja) which you cannot find anywhere else.

Flowers, such as Orchids, Bird of Paradises, Proteas, Flamingo Flowers etc. florists sell around the city, as well as in the Market place and florists close to the Cathedral Sé. Cut flowers, seedlings and corms of plants can be exported as souvenirs and when requested, they are packed carefully for the trip.

Local music and instruments are sold in souvenir shops and music stores. For example, Madeiran special instrument (brinquinhos) with wooden dolls with regional costumes which have clapping hands and jingle little bells when you move them up and down on a rod.

From fennel and eucalyptus they manufacture tea and sweets. Sugar cane syrup (mel-de-cana) from which they manufacture the popular honey cake (bolo de mel) you may also take this home, and of course the honey cake keeps for a long time. Exotic fruits can also be exported as a souvenir.

In Funchal there are also many antique shops, and collectables, old money and stamp shops for those interested. Many news-stands and stores also sell high quality cigars.

In addition on the island there are many interior design shops where the assortments are little different from those on the continent.

Shopping centers and shopping streets

Madeira Shopping in Santa Quitéria on the slopes above Funchal is the biggest shopping center in Madeira which was opened in 2001. From the balconies you have awesome views out to the sea and to the mountains. This shopping mall has 100 stores and about 20 restaurants and fast food chains, a large Continente supermarket and 7 cinemas. Travelling by bus from Funchal to Madeira Shopping is an extraordinary experience because the bus driver drives like a daredevil on the narrow and twisty city streets! Why not give them a try at least in one direction. Buses number 8 and 16. Open daily from 10 am to 11 pm and on Friday and Saturday open till midnight.

Forum Madeira, the second biggest shopping center which was opened in spring 2005 is located in Ajuda, west from Funchal city center. Forum Madeira has nearly 100 stores, a dozen restaurants and fast food chains, 6 cinemas and a Pingo Doce supermarket downstairs. Open daily from 10 am to 11 pm and on Friday and Saturday until midnight. Buses number 1, 2 and 4 from the city center.

La Vie is a newest and third biggest shopping center, located almost in the center of Funchal city, below Santa Catarina Park and close to the fountain roundabout. It was opened in 2008 and it also includes a five star hotel, condominium apartments, restaurants and fast food chains.

Armazém do Mercado is a new little market center close to Market place. There are two entrances, at address Rua Hospital Velho 28 and Rua Latino Coelho 39. Kiosks, shops, markets, exhibitions, workshops, restaurants etc. Also in the same building is a Toy Museum. Open Monday to Saturday from 10 am to 8 pm and Sunday 10 am to 6 pm.

And here are a few examples of shopping streets in Funchal center: Avenida Arriaga, Avenida Zarco,

Forum Madeira Shopping Center

Rua da Carreira, Rua de João Tavira, Rua da Queimada de Cima, Rua da Queimada de Baixo, Rua dos Ferreiros, Rua Dr Fernão Ornelas etc.

Market places and farmers' markets

The Market place (Mercado dos Lavradores) is located in the center of Funchal at the end of Rua Dr. Fernão Ornelas street in a building which was completed in the early 1940s. They sell upstairs flowers, fruits, vegetables and spices, on the ground floor in addition to the above are also wicker and leather products and downstairs there is a Fish Market (Praça do Peixel). Fish will be available early in the morning and later in the afternoon. On Fridays around the market place local farmers come selling their products. It is better to go earlier in the morning when trade is lively. It is worth tasting exotic fruits when there is the opportunity, but be careful with the prices because they overcharge tourists frequently if

you are not sharp. Also the Fish Market is worth a look, especially for the wild black scabbard fish (espada). There is a terrace café restaurant on the top floor. Open from Monday to Thursday from 7 am to 7 pm, on Fridays from 7 am to 8 pm and Saturdays 7 am to 2 pm. Closed on Sundays and on public holidays.

Local markets usually sell flowers and locally produced eggs, vegetables and fruits and also home-made cakes and food. On the other side of the market are usually fish counters where local fishermen bring their daily catches. Usually local markets are open from Monday to Friday from 8 am to 1 pm. Markets are in Calheta, Câmara de Lobos, Machico, Porto Moniz, Ponta Delgada, Ribeira Brava, Santa Cruz and Santo da Serra.

DID YOU KNOW...
There is a farmers' market every Sunday in Santo da Serra.

▶ **Florists wear the traditional costumes.**

▶ Funchal Market place was completed in the 1940s.

On Sundays there are farmers markets in Ponta Delgada, Porto Moniz's Santa, Santo da Serra and Estreito de Câmara de Lobos, so take time to explore them. In addition to fruits, vegetables and flowers they sell also animals, clothing, shoes, bags etc. in farmers markets. Most popular farmers' market with the best atmosphere is the one in Santo da Serra.

Flea markets and car boot sales

Flea markets will take place every Saturday in the old town near cable car terminal. Open from 8.30 am to 6 pm. Also the last Sunday of every month there is a car boot sale in the Casino's parking lot from 8 am to 6 pm.

▶ Madeira Stork's Bill has beautiful pink flowers.

DID YOU KNOW...

Cut flowers, seedlings and corms of plants can be exported freely in the EU area.

ACTIVITIES FOR CHILDREN AND TEENAGERS ▶ ▶ ▶ ▶ ▶

For children and teenagers you can find lots of programs and interesting things to do in Madeira. They can swim, participate in sports and have adventures in fortresses. For smaller children there are animal parks and playgrounds etc.

There are no real beaches in Madeira, but most hotels have swimming pools. If children do not have separate pools, generally the shallow ends of the swimming pools are for children. In addition there are a few public swimming-baths in Funchal, for example in Lido and Ajuda and a few child-friendly beaches and swimming halls. See Beaches and Swimming pools elsewhere in this book.

Near Santa Cruz close to the airport there is also a Water Park (Aquaparque de Santa Cruz). Here there are several swimming pools, water slides, a black hole and waterfalls. The park is open every day from mid-March to mid-November.

Some hotels have their own tennis courts and at both Quinta Magnolia and the Funchal Tennis Club one can find tennis courts that can be rented for a modest charge. Clube de Ténis do Funchal, address Rua Dr. Pita Anexo Barreiros, near the football stadium and Quinta Magnolia at Rua Dr. Pita.

In child-friendly hotels you can find other stimulative play areas, games and playgrounds for children. Also in Santa Catarina Park, Santa Luzia Park and close to the cable cars there are playgrounds for children. There you can find climbing frames, slides, swings etc. Outside of Funchal in Ribeira Brava there is a sports center (Centro Desportivo Ribeira Brava) where there are two playgrounds for children.

Animals can be seen for example in the Presidential Palace's garden and next to the Botanical Garden (Botanico da Madeira) is a Bird Park (Jardim dos Loiros) where there are lots of colourful birds. In Santo da Serra, outside of Funchal, there is a park where you can find red deer, birds etc. and in Prazeres there is the Quinta

▶ **Funny doggy**

Pedagógica where you can find lamas, emus, pigs, turtles etc. Also in Porto Moniz there is the Madeira Aquarium (Aquário da Madeira), with 11 water tanks showing the whole of Madeira's underwater species.

Fortresses and museums are exciting and interesting attractions for children. For example, São Lourenço's Palace and Fortress (Fortaleza e Palácio de São Lourenço) has also a small Military Museum, Fortaleza do Pico Fortress and São Tiago Fortress are entertaining. Also Fortaleza da Nossa Senhora da Conceição Fortress and São Filipe Fort ruins are interesting.

Museums that children might be interested in, for example Toy museum

▶ Lots of attractions can be found for children of all ages.

▶ **A pleasant sea adventure for children with Santa Maria**

(Museu do Brinquedo da Madeira) which consists a collection of old toys: dolls, lead toy soldiers, miniature cars, games etc. Connected to the Toy Museum there is a children's workshop downstairs. Or the Museum of Natural History (Museu de Historia Natural) and Fuchal City Museum (Museu Municipal do Funchal) where there are collections of Madeiran plants, fish, insects and other animals. In addition there are also the Limestone Museum (Núcleo Museológico – Rota da Cal) in São Vicente and the Whale Museum (Museu da Baleia) in Caniçal.

Madeira Magic Theme Park and Science Center for children with a mini planetarium and three-dimensional films. Also there is the Living Science Center (Centro de Ciéncia Viva) in Porto Moniz where there are interesting things to see and do for all ages on knowledge and scientific sectors.

Madeira Theme Park (Temático da Madeira) in Santana with a lake, nature parks and hiking trails, a replica of the old Monte train, an ox-sledge and all kind of theme park rides. Also in São Vicente is the Vulcanology Center and the Caves (Grutas e Centro de Vulcanismo) which introduces and explains about the volcanic eruptions using audiovisual and entertaining methods.

Several boat cruises depart from Funchal port every day, for example the Santa Maria ship which is a replica of the Christopher Columbus boat. The Santa Maria ship is for families with children an exciting pirate ship and children get a certificate from a pirate captain. Also sailing boats, catamarans and rubber boats where on-board you can see the turtles, dolphins, whales and birds. On some trips you can also swim with the dolphins. It is not always guaranteed that you even see dolphins and whales. In addition you might think about fishing trips with slightly older children.

Cable car rides or Jeep safaris can also be interesting and exciting, or horse-back riding with horses or donkeys. And for children who like hiking guided levada walks might be something, but not for the smallest children.

Football also might be a matter of interest, at least for boys. Madeira's

own teams CS Maritimo play on home ground in Estadio dos Barreiros and Nacional in Estádio da Madeira. Usually matches are at weekends, sometimes on Wednesday. Monday through Friday you may watch teams training in the stadiums.

In addition teenagers can participate in gliding, diving, snorkelling etc.

For teenagers there is also the Information and Documentation Center, Youth Shop and Meeting Point (Centro de Informação e Documentação do Funchal – Direção Regional de Juventude) and Baden-Powell Museum Center and National Corps of Scouts (CNE).

► Exotic birds can be seen in the Presidencial Palace's Park and Bird Park connected to the Botanical Garden.

THEME PARKS, AMUSEMENT PARKS AND WATER PARKS ▶ ▶

Funchal's Ecological Park (Parque Ecologico do Funchal) is located above the city, close to Monte, address Estrada Regional 103 no 259 in Ribeira das Cales. This 1000 hectares Forest Park was opened in 1994 and it reaches to almost 1800 m to the Pico do Areeiro slopes. This park was established to maintain the original nature and plants of Madeira, for the leisure of residents and tourists, and also as support to schoolchildren and scouts education of ecology. There are a huge number of rare species of trees and other plants, for example laurel trees, Madeiran Mahogany, Tree Heaters and Madeiran Blueberry etc. There also nests a variety of birds, including the rare Madeiran Petrel. The park has many hiking paths and areas for picnic where you can barbecue and eat your sandwiches. It is open daily from 9 am to 5 pm. Best way to go around the park is by car. Buses numbers 56, 103 and 138.

Living Science Center (Centro de Ciência Viva) is located on the north coast of the island in Porto Moniz at the Rotunda do Ilhéu Mole. It is a culture center with lots to see and do for all ages mostly about knowledge and the scientific sectors. It is part of a national science center chain and holds seminars of these fields, as well as various exhibitions. Open from Tuesday to Sunday from 10 am to 9 pm. Closed on Mondays and on public holidays. Country buses number 80 and 139.

▶ Beautiful Shade (Ombu, Tree Poke, Umbra Tree) has a huge base.

▶ **Madeiran fishing boats are colourful.**

Madeira Aquarium (Aquário da Madeira) is located on the north coast of the island in Porto Moniz, in the old fortress (Forte de São João Batista) which was built in 1730. This fortress is located close to Porto Moniz's port. In the aquarium there are 11 water tanks displaying the whole of Madeira's underwater sea life. Open every day from 10 am to 6 pm. Country buses number 80 and 139.

Madeira Magic Theme Park and Garden is located below the Forum Madeira shopping mall, address Rua da Ponta Cruz 25. This living science center and theme park offers children all kinds of programs, including a mini planetarium, three-dimensional films, a mini botanical garden where there are flowers and plants from all over the world. There is a themed science center where children can also play. In the same building there is a health club, restaurant and also a tea house. Open from Monday to Friday 10 am to 6 pm and on the weekends at 10 am to 7 pm. Closed on public holidays.

Madeira Theme Park (Temático da Madeira) is located in Santana at Estrada Regional 101, in Fonte da Pedra. This amusement park was opened in 2004

and here the local culture and history are presented using technology and entertainment. There is a presentation of Madeira and the world's creation history interactively using multimedia. In the park there is also a lake, nature parks and hiking trails, a replica of the old Monte train, an ox sledge and all kind of theme park rides. In addition there are restaurants and handicraft stores. The Theme Park is open every day from 10 am to 7 pm. Closed on Christmas Day. Country buses number 103, 132 and 138.

Vulcanology Center and the Caves (Grutas e Centro de Vulcanismo) are located in São Vicente, on the north coast of the island, address Sitio Pé do Passo. The purpose of this center is to explain all about the geological beginning of the island and the volcanic eruptions using audiovisual and entertaining methods. In connection with the center there are almost one kilometre of caves and tunnels that go approx. 700 meters underground. A beautiful garden with endemic plants of Madeira. Guided tours in Portuguese, English, French and German. Open daily from 10 am to 7 pm. Closed on Christmas Day. Country buses number 4, 80, 132 and 139.

Water Park (Aquaparque de Santa Cruz) is located at Ribeira da Boaventura in Santa Cruz, close to the airport. There are several swimming pools, water slides, a black hole, waterfalls and a separate water park for smaller children. The park is open every day from mid of March to mid of November.

CELEBRITIES WHO VISITED
MADEIRA ▶ ▶ ▶ ▶ ▶ ▶ ▶ ▶ ▶

The Austrian-Hungarian Emperor Charles I (1887–1922) was expelled from Austria and he and his family came into exile to Funchal in 1921. He lived in Quinta Gordon (Quinta do Monte) in Monte and died there with bronchitis next year in 1922. His grave is located at Monte Church's crypt and his statue is in front of the same church.

Sir Winston Churchill (1874–1965) was a traveller, writer and statesman. He spent a holiday in Madeira in 1950 with his wife Clementine and daughter Diana, was staying in Reid's Palace Hotel and painted pictures in Câmara de Lobos and in Ribeiro Frio.

Churchill was a prolific writer and his first book was published in 1898.

Christopher Columbus, Cristovão Colombo, (1451–1506) came to Madeira in the late 1470s, lived in Porto Santo, married Bartolomeu Perestrello's daughter Felipa Moniz and fathered a son, Diego. In Perestrello's house in Vila Baleira on Porto Santo is a Columbus museum and a Columbus' statue can be found in Santa Catarina Park's south-east corner in Funchal.

Captain James Cook (1728–1779) was a British explorer and navigator who made detailed maps of unknown

▶ Christopher Columbus' statue is in the Santa Catarina Park.

▶ Sissi's statue is in the garden in front of the Pestana Casino Park.

lands, like the coasts of New Zealand and Australia. He visited Madeira twice, in 1769 on his way to New Zealand and in 1770 on his way to Australia.

Austrian Empress Elizabeth (1837–1898) often visited Madeira. Elizabeth is better known as Sissi, especially because of the famous film where she was played by Romy Schneider. Sissi's statue is in the little garden in front of Pestana Casino Park hotel. The statue was designed by Mestre Lagoa Henriques.

Napoleon Bonaparte (1769–1821) stopped in Funchal port in 1815 when the British naval vessel was taking him to exile to the remote island of St. Helena. Napoleon did not exit the boat, but they brought him Madeira wine.

Pope John Paul II visited the island in 1991. In the memory of the event they put up a statue which is located in front of Cathedral Sé.

George Bernard Shaw (1856–1950) the Irish playwright and author who was given the Nobel prize of Literature in 1925. He stayed in Madeira in 1924–1925.

▶ Hibiscus (Rose of China, Shoe Plant) and Bougainvillea's (Paper Flower) are used on beautiful and colourful fences with buxus trees.

WELL KNOWN MADEIRANS ▶

Perhaps internationally most well-known Madeiran is the footballer **Cristiano Ronaldo**. Cristiano Ronaldo dos Santos Aveiro was born in Funchal on 5.2.1985. Ronaldo is representing a Spanish football team Real Madrid, but is also a team captain of the Portuguese National Team. He is one of the world's fastest top footballer's and has played with Manchester United from which he was purchased by Real Madrid for a record sum of 94 million euros.

▶ Ronaldo's statue has caused lots of comments in public about its appearance.

Also **Fátima Lopes** a fashion designer has created international fame in her own field. She was born in Funhal on 8.3.1965. In 1990 Ms Lopes moved to Lisbon where later she opened her own fashion house. She also has fashion houses in Paris and in Los Angeles and a Model agency in Lisbon.

José Manuel Rodrigues Berardo, Joe Berardo, was born in Funchal on 4.7.1944. This businessman and art collector was few years ago Nr. 677 in Forbes' list of the richest people in the world. Berardo moved to South Africa at age of 19 and made his fortune in gold and diamond mines. He returned to his native Madeira in the end of the 1980s as a rich man and owns currently for example the Monte Palace mansion in Monte which is his private residence. In connection with the mansion is a stunning Jardim Tropical Garden Monte Palace which is open to the public.

Isabel da Silva Andrade, i.e. Nini Andrade Silva is the world famous architect and interior designer. She was born in Funchal on 24.7.1962. She has worked in Lisbon, New York, Paris, South Africa and Denmark, she has had exhibitions in Saudi Arabia, Rome, New Delhi and Miami and her works are presented for example in Berardo's collections, New York galleries and in private collections.

Virgílio Delgado Teixeira i.e. Virgilio Teixeira is a most famous Portuguese

actor who was born in Madeira on 26.10.1917 and died at age of 93 in Funchal on 5.12.2010. This prolific actor played in almost 90 movies from the 1940s, mainly Portuguese and Spanish movies, but also in some Hollywood movies. His last movie was Endless Memories (2010) which was filmed in Madeira.

Henrique (1883–1961) and **Francisco** (1885–1955) **Franco** are well known Madeiran artist brothers, whose paintings, drawings and sculptures can be found in museums and private collections. Francisco Franco's handicraft is João Gonçalves Zarco's statue on Avenida Arriaga.

▶ Adam's Needle (Spanish Dagger, Yucca) blossom is gorgeous.

ROUTE SUGGESTIONS FOR ISLAND TOURS AND SIGHTSEEINGS IN THE CITY

Island tours

A tour throughout the island takes without doubt all day, and then you must drive without stops. But if you want to view only sights and landscapes through the car window, then this is the route in general:

Funchal – Câmara de Lobos – Cabo Girão – Ribeira Brava – Ponta do Sol – Madalena do Mar – Calheta – Jardim do Mar – Paúl do Mar – Fajã da Ovelha – Ponta do Pargo – Achadas da Cruz – Santa – Porto Moniz – Ribeira da Janela – Seixal – São Vicente – Ponta Delgada – Boaventura – Arco de São Jorge – São Jorge – Santana – Faial – Penha de Águia – Porto da Cruz – Portela – Ponta de São Lourenço – Caniçal – Machico – Santa Cruz – Funchal

If you divide the tour over several days then you have time to become more familiar with various destinations and have more detailed sightseeing options. Divided in this way you should reserve the entire day for each of the tours, especially if you stop for the sights and for coffee or lunch etc.

Western island tour:
Funchal – Câmara de Lobos – Cabo Girão – Ribeira Brava – Ponta do Sol – Madalena do Mar – Calheta – Jardim do Mar – Paúl do Mar – Fajã da Ovelha – Ponta do Pargo – Achadas da Cruz – Santa – Porto Moniz – Ribeira da Janela – Seixal – São Vicente – Rosário – Encumeada – Serra de Água – Ribeira Brava – Funchal

Eastern island tour:
Funchal – Caniço – Santa Cruz – Machico – Caniçal – Ponta de São Lourenço – Caniçal – Portela – Porto da Cruz – Penha de Águia – Faial – Santana – São Jorge – Ponta Delgada – São Vicente – Serra de Água – Ribeira Brava – Funchal

Inland tour:
Funchal – Caniço – Camacha – Santo da Serra – Porto da Cruz – Penha de Águia – Ribeiro Frio – Monte – Funchal

For Mountain tour you need also to take time because, for example, to Pico Ruivo you cannot drive but you must walk: Funchal – Monte – Poiso – Pico do Areeiro – Pico Ruivo – Achada do Teixeira – Faial – Ribeiro Frio – Poiso – Monte – Funchal

Sightseeing in the city

An old city tour
you can start from the bus terminal at the promenade: Bus terminal –

Almirante Reis Park – Corpo Santo chapel – São Tiago Fortress – Santa Maria church – Rua Santa Maria with all its alleys – Market place

Cathedral Sé and the surrounding streets:

Sé and the surrounding streets – Columbus square – Rua João Tavira – City Hall – City Square – Colégio church – Wine Museum (Museu do Vinho da Madeira) – Rua dos Netos street up – Calçada Santa Clara street up – Santa Clara Convent – Quinta das Cruzes Museum – The Universe of Memories João Carlos Abreu Museum and tea house – Forte Pico Fortress

Tour in the city center:

Avenida Arriaga street – Wine Museum Madeira Wine Company – City Theatre – São Lourenço Fortress – Rua Carreira street – Port – Guays – Luxury Yacht Marina – The Promenade

Garden and park tours

Hospício da Princeza Dona Maria Amélia Park – Presidential Palace's Park – Santa Catarina Park – The City Park – Herb and Medicinal Garden – Quinta das Cruzes Museum Park

Another trip is to visit the Botanical Garden and the Bird Park connected with it, which are located above the city in east and below the Botanical Garden where the Orchid Garden (Jardim Orquidea) is located.

And definitely worth a visit is also the São Martinho Park in the western part of town and Monte Palace Tropical Garden in Monte.

DID YOU KNOW...

In Camacha at the football field the first game of football was played in Portugal in 1875.

▶ **Florists close to the Cathedral Sé**

20 MOST POPULAR SIGHTS
in Funchal and Madeira
(In random order)

- ▶ Old City
- ▶ Market place
- ▶ Cathedral Sé
- ▶ Fortresses (São Lourenço, São Tiago, Forte Pico)
- ▶ City tour with double decker buses
- ▶ Wine Museums and Madeira wine
- ▶ Parks and Gardens
- ▶ Palaces and Mansions
- ▶ Cable cars
- ▶ Monte Toboggans
- ▶ Island Tours (East and West)
- ▶ Levada walks
- ▶ Boat trips with Santa Maria or catamaran
- ▶ Cabo Girão
- ▶ Fado music listening
- ▶ Architecture and art
- ▶ Promenade from Lido to Praia Formosa and further to Câmara de Lobos
- ▶ Charming cafés and restaurants
- ▶ Scuba diving in the underwater park (Garajau)
- ▶ Porto Santo

▶ **Cabo Girão from the sea**

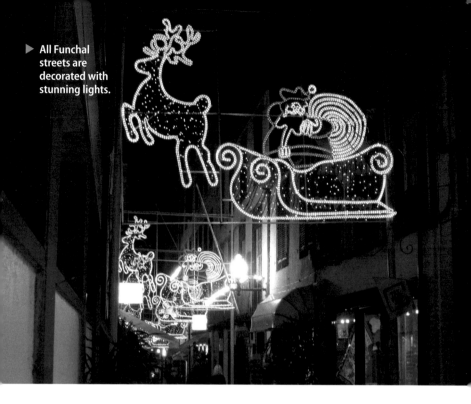

▶ **All Funchal streets are decorated with stunning lights.**

5 MOST POPULAR EVENTS AND FESTIVALS
in Funchal and Madeira

(If the time fits your travel arrangements)

▶ Christmas, Christmas decorations and Christmas lights (November/ December)
▶ New Year fireworks (New Years Eve)
▶ Carnival (February)
▶ Flower Festival (April or May)
▶ Wine Festival (September)

DID YOU KNOW...

The Christmas lights will be switched on at the beginning of December in the center of Funchal and all the lights on the island and along the streets at the latest on the 8th of December.

ENGLISH-PORTUGUESE DICTIONARY ▶ ▶ ▶ ▶ ▶ ▶ ▶ ▶

Here are some useful words and sayings in Portuguese that you may need during your journey. Even if you don't always pronounce the words correctly, Madeirans appreciate you trying.

Introductions and other courtesies

Good morning – Bom Dia (until 12 am)
Good afternoon – Boa tarde (until 7 pm)
Good evening/night – Boa noite
Welcome – Benvindo (Benvinda only if a woman says)
Nice to meet you – É um prazer conhecê-lo (conhecê-la if a woman says)
How are you – Como está
Very good, thank you – Bem obrigado (obrigada if a woman says)
Very well, thank you – Estou muito bem, obrigado (obrigada, if a woman says)
It was nice to meet you – Foi um prazer conhecê-lo (-la if a woman says)
Have a good/pleasant weekend – Bom fim de semana
Till tomorrow – Até amanhã
See you – Até logo
Hello – Olá
Goodbye/farewell – Adeus
Goodbye/Hello – Chiao
Likewise – Igualmente
Thank you – Obrigado (obrigada if a woman says)
Thank you very much – Muito obrigado (obrigada if a woman says)
Please – Faça favor/Por favor
Excuse me – Com licença
I beg your pardon – Desculpe
It does not matter – Não foi Nada/Não faz mal
I am sorry – Sinto muito/Desculpe
No – Não
Yes – Sim

Yes thank you – Sim obrigado (obrigada if a woman says)
No, thank you – Não obrigado (obrigada if a woman says)
It does not matter – De nada
I would like the invoice/Bill, please – A conta, se faz favor (or por favor)
How much – Quanto custa
Good appetite – Bom apetite

Weekdays

Today – Hoje
Tomorrow – Amanhã
Next week – Na próxima semana
This evening – Esta noite
Yesterday – Ontem
Week – Uma semana
Day – Uma dia
Monday – Segunda-feira
Tuesday – Terça-feira
Wednesday – Quarta-feira
Thursday – Quinta-feira
Friday – Sexta-feira
Saturday – Sábado
Sunday – Domingo

Months

Month – Um més
Year – Um ano
January – Janeiro
February – Fevereiro
March – Março
April – Abril
May – Maio
June – Junho
July – Julho
August – Agosto
September – Setembro

October – Outubro
November – Novembro
December – Dezembro
Spring – Primavera
Summer – Verão
Autumn – Outono
Winter – Inverno

Other sayings and useful words

Excuse me, can you help me – Desculpe, pode ajudar-me
Where is... – Onde fica ...
Do you speak English – Fala Inglês
I do not understand – Não compreendo
Talk more slowly, please – Não se importa de falar mais devagar, por favor
Can you show me on the map where am I – Pode mostrar-me no mapa onde estou
How do I get there – Como posso ir lá ter
WC/Toilet – Toalete/Casa de banho
Ladies – Senhoras/Damas
Men – Senhor/homens
Push (door open) – Emburre
Pull (door open) – Puxar
Open (store open) – Aberto
Closed (store closed) – Fechado/Cerrado
Large/Big – Grande
Small – Pequeno
Lot of – Muito
A little – Pouco
Beach/bathing site – Praia
View point – Miradouro
Bus – Autocarro
Bus stop – Paragem
Police – Polícia
Pharmacy – Farmácia

Weather vocabulary

Rain – Chuva
Shower – Aguaceiro de chuva
Drizzle – Chuvisco
Sun – Sol
Sunshine – Calor do sol
Sky – Céu

Cloudy – Nublado
Dry weather/sunny – Dia bonito
Heat – Calor
Hot – Cálido
Cold – Frio
Snow – Neve
Snowing – Nevada
Storm – Tempestade
Wind – Vento
Weak wind – Brisa
Windy – Ventar
South – Sul
North – Norte
East – Este
West – Oeste

Numerals

0 – zero
1 – um
2 – dois/duas
3 – três
4 – quatro
5 – cinco
6 – seis
7 – sete
8 – oito
9 – nove
10 – dez
11 – onze
12 – doze
13 – treze
14 – quatorze
15 – quinze
16 – dezasseis
17 – dezassete
18 – dezoito
19 – dezanove
20 – vinte
21 – vinte e um
30 – trinta
40 – quarenta
50 – cinquenta
60 – sessenta
70 – setenta
80 – oitenta
90 – noventa
100 – cem/cento
101 – cento e um

200 – duzentos
300 – trezentos
400 – quatrocentos
500 – quinhentos
600 – seiscentos
700 – setecentos
800 – oitocentos
900 – novecentos
1000 – mil
2000 – dois mil
10 000 – dez mil
100 000 – cem mil
1 000 000 – um milhão

Food vocabulary

Groceries – Mercaria
Butcher – Talho
Fishmonger – Peixaria
Bakery – Padaria
Pastry shop – Pastelaria
Fish restaurant – Marisqueira

Meat – Carne
Poultry/chicken – Galinha/frango
Turkey – Perú
Lamb – Carneiro
Beef/bull – Boi
Pork – Porco
Liver – Fígado
Beef – Vaca
Calf – Novilha/viteza
Minced meat – Carne picado
Bacon – Touchinho/bacon
Boneless – Não osso
Ham – Fiambre/presunto
Sausage – Salsicha
Spicy sausage – Chouriço

Baked/ripe – Bem cozido/Maduro
Smoked – Fumado
Well done – Bem assado
Medium – Medio
Fried – Frito
Cooked – Cozido
Grilled/barbequed – Grelhado
Raw – Mal passado

Sauce – Molho
Soup – Sopa
Snacks – Petiscos
Cooked potatoes – Batatas cozidas
French potatoes – Batatas fritas
Baked potatoes – Batatas salteadas
Baked corn cubes – Milho frito

Fish – Peixe
Crayfish/sea food – Mariscos
Shrimp – Camarão/gamba
Tuna fish – Atum
Mackerel – Cavala/carapau
Cod – Bacalhau
Salmon – Salmão
Sea bass – Cherne
Scabbard Sword Fish – Espada
Sardine – Sardinha
Octopus – Lula
Boneless – Sem Espinha

Cheese – Queijo
Butter – Manteiga
Margarine – Margarina
Oil – Óleo
Olive oil – Azeite
Milk – Leite
Cream – Nata/creme
Egg – Ovo
Ice cream – Gelado

Salt – Sal
Saltless – Sem sal
Added salt – Com sal
Sugar – Açúcar
Sugar-free – Sem açúcar
Honey – Mel
Spicy – Condimento
Acidic – Acre
Sweet – Dolce

Pepper/paprica – Pimento
Tomato – Tomate
Peas – Ervilha
Cucumber – Pepino
Salad – Salada
Lettuce – Alface
Celery – Aipo
Corn – Milho
Aubergine – Berinjela

Spinach – Espinafres
Radishes – Rabanete
Mushrooms – Cogumelos
Green beans – Feijões verdes
Leek – Alho-porro
Onion – Cebola
Garlic – Alho
Potato – Batata
Carrot – Cenoura
Courgette – Abobrinha
Vegetables – Legumes

Fruit – Fruta
Orange – Laranja
Lemon – Limõe
Apple – Maçã
Banana – Banana
Grapes – Uva
Pear – Pêra
Passion fruit -Maracujá
Pineapple – Abacaxi/ananás
Apricot – Alperce
Peach – Pêssego
Plum – Ameixa
Grape fruit – Toranja
Melon – Melão
Watermelon – Melancia
Figs – Figo

Berry – Baga
Cranberries – Arando
Blueberries – Mirtilo
Strawberry – Morango
Raspberries – Framboesa

Hazel nut – Avelã
Chestnut – Castanha
Peanut – Amendoim
Almond – Amêndoa
Walnut – Noze

Dessert – Sobremesa/dolce
Cookie/biscuit – Biscoito/bolacha
Cake/Tart – Bolo
Pastry/Pie – Empada/pastel
Sweet/candy – Dolce/rebuçado
Bread roll – Molete/pãozinho
Bread – Pão
Dark bread – Pão de cente/pão de prete
Toasted bread – Tosta

Porridge – Papa
Oat meal – Papa de aveia
Flour – Farinha
Wheat flour – Farinha de trigo
Potato flour – Fécula de batatas
Oat – Aveia
Wheat – Trigo
Rye – Centeio
Barley – Cevada
Rice – Arroz
Pasta – Macarrão
Spaghetti – Massa

Water – Água
With gas – Com gás
Without gas – Sem gás
Mineral water – Água mineral
Milk – Leite
Beverage – Sumo
Juice – sumo
Juice extract – Sumo concentrada

Beer – Cerveja
Wine – Vinho
White wine – Vinho branco
Red wine – Vinho tinto
Rose wine – Vinho rosado
Table wine – Vinho de mesa
Sparkling wine – Champanha
Port wine – Vinho do Porto
Spirit – Aguardente

Tea – Cha
Coffee – Café
Black coffee – Chino
Coffee with milk – Chinesa
Big coffee with milk (glass) – Galão
Espresso – Bica
Espresso with milk – Garoto
Espresso with alcohol – Bica pingada
Cocoa – Cacau

PORTO SANTO

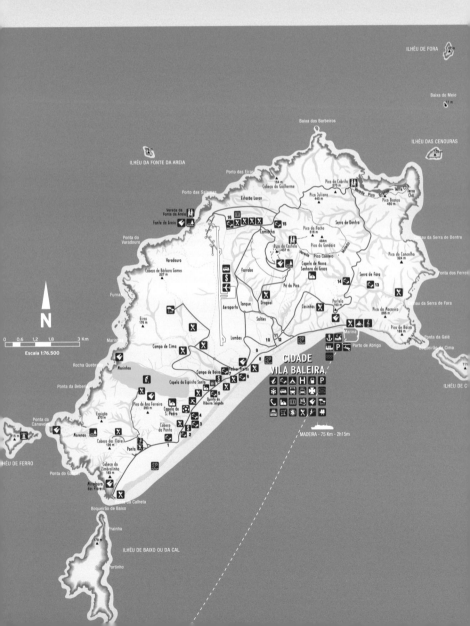

▶ Porto Santo is one of
the 11 municipalities of
Madeira.

CIDADE
VILA BALEIRA

OCEANO ATLÂNTICO

Facts about Porto Santo

Porto Santo means sacred port. It is the second of the inhabited islands in the Madeira archipelago and is located approx. 40 km away from the north east of Madeira island. Porto Santo island can be seen on bright days from the north coast of Madeira. It is also one of the 11 municipalities of Madeira and controlled by the Regional Government.

The island is small, with only 42 km^2, it is 11 km long and 6 km wide. Porto Santo coast includes a few little islands; Ilhéu de Baixo or by another name Ilhéu da Cal, Ilhéu de Cima, Ilhéu de Ferro, Ilhéu da Fonte da Areia, Ilhéu das Cenouras and Ilhéu de Fora. There are approx. 5 000 inhabitants on the island and they mainly live in Vila Baleira which is the capital city. Vila Baleira is a small, idyllic town with whitewashed houses, palms blowing in the wind and many beautiful flowerbeds and plants. Porto Santo has also many nicknames, such as Golden Island, Sunny Island and the Last Paradise in Europe etc.

Madeira's discoverers, João Gonçalves Zarco and Tristão Vaz Teixeira were stranded first on Porto Santo while examining the African coast in 1418 and one year later discovered Madeira island. Zarco's contemporary, Bartolomeu Perestrello, was the first governor of Porto Santo and to his daughter Christopher Columbus got married decades later and they had a son. Perestrello is buried in Nossa

▶ Gorgeous Bougainvillea's (Paper Flower) in the center of Vila Baleira.

DID YOU KNOW...

Small in size, but Porto Santo has a lot of really interesting attractions.

▶ Porto Santo has much lower terrain than Madeira.

Senhora da Piedade church in Vila Baleira.

Porto Santo's economy is essentially based on tourism. And from tourism the main income comes in a few months in July and August, when the holiday makers from the continent fill hotels and restaurants. The island is of course the destination for tourists throughout the year but the main season is in summer. Some also may be interested more in the quieter season when they can calm down and relax in this sunny island surrounded by turquoise waters and whose landscape and scenery just enchants by it's simple beauty.

The climate of the island is dry and comfortable throughout the year. Average temperatures are approximately the same as Madeira, the air

and the water temperature is about 18 to 22ºC. Porto Santo's natural landscape is much more barren, windy and lower than Madeira. The south coast of the island is a golden brown sandy beach and the north coast is harsh, rugged and rough.

They grow a little bit of fruit, grain and vines in the island, but it is not enough for the needs of the inhabitants. Porto Santo has no irrigation channels like Madeira, but water for cultivation comes by collecting rain water and from underground springs. Also drinking water comes from these underground springs.

The highest peak, Pico do Facho, is only 516 meters altitude, and other peaks are Pico da Gandaia (484 m), Pico do Branco (450 m), Pico da Juliana (440 m) and Pico do Castelo (437 m).

▶ **Porto Santo has an almost 10 km long sandy beach.**

Porto Santo has an almost 10 km long golden brownish sandy beach and crystal clear turquoise water. It is both Madeiran and a continental Portuguese popular holiday destination. The sand of the beach has a very high mineral content, including iodine, calcium and magnesium, which has been found to be therapeutic if you are suffering from rheumatism, arthritis, other bone or muscle illnesses, varicose veins, stress or fatigue etc. It has been said that if you dig yourself into the sand for one hour, your illnesses will improve.

Hotels and accommodation

Porto Santo has a few high level hotels, which open in the winter times. You should check in advance because all the hotels are not open between November and April. There is manor house accommodation found in Porto Santo, e.g. Quinta do Serrado in Camacha and also farm and cottage accommodation as well as a campground which is very popular in the summer months.

If you want to spend longer periods of peaceful times on the island, you should ask about apartments and houses for rent from the tourist office in Porto Santo.

Food and restaurants

Porto Santo has also a dozen or so restaurants which offer good fresh fish, crayfish and other Portuguese dishes. In addition there are few bistros and snack bars which will make good lunches and pastries.

DID YOU KNOW...

Sand of the Porto Santo beach has a very high mineral content which has been found to be therapeutic for rheumatism and other illnesses.

Traffic

Porto Santo can be accessed either by ferry or aeroplane. Porto Santo Line's Lobo Marinho (sea wolf) vessel runs on a daily basis from Funchal to Porto Santo. It departs from the port of Funchal at 8 am and returns at 8.30 pm and it takes about 2,5 hours. The ship holds 1153 passengers and on board there is a cinema, restaurant, bar, coffee shop, shops, games room and play area for children. Tickets can be bought in advance either from your travel agent or Porto Santo Line's offices in Funchal center (Avenida do Mar), in Lido (Estrada Monumental 175 C) or from the port. Tel. 291 210 300. Offices are open from Monday to Friday 9 am to 12.30 pm and 2 pm to 6 pm. In addition Lido's office is open at weekends from 9 am to 12.30 pm and 2 pm to 8 pm. From the port to the center of Vila Baleira is about 2 km.

Daily flights from Funchal to Porto Santo. There are a few; morning, afternoon and evening, and it takes about 15 minutes. From Lisbon there are direct flights also to Porto Santo a couple of times a week and it takes about 1,5 hours. Flights are very popular during high season in summer, so it is good to make reservations in advance through a travel agency or TAP Air Portugal office, address Avenida das Comunidades Madeirenses 10 (Avenida do Mar), tel. 291 239 232. Porto Santo airport (Aeroporto do Porto Santo) was opened in 1960 and from there to Vila Baleira it is only a few kilometers. Airport phone number is 291 980 120.

Porto Santo has a well equipped guest marina with a capacity of 165 vessels (max. 15 meters) and there are all the necessary services; water, electricity, showers, laundry, maintenance etc.

▶ **Porto Santo Line's Lobo Marinho vessel runs on a daily basis from Funchal to Porto Santo.**

▶ There is bus transportation from the port to Vila Baleira.

Buses and taxi

There is bus transportation from the port to Vila Baleira center and in the spring 2015 it cost about 1,60 €/person one way. Tickets for the bus must be purchased before boarding from the kiosk. A bus leaves from the center back to port about 45 minutes before the ship departs. Tickets for island tours can be purchased from the bus station kiosk. The tour takes a couple of hours and it cost about 8 €/person.

Taxis are on duty along the way at Avenida Dr. Manuel Gregório Pestana Junior in connection with the bus station. There are also a few car rental companies on the island if you want to go by yourself.

You could go around Porto Santo's every corner in a few days. By taxi or bus the tour takes a few hours, the same with rental car or motorcycle. Traffic is very light and the best transportation is by walking or bicycle which you are also able to rent.

Tourist office

The local tourist office is located in Vila Baleira center at Avenida Dr. Manuel Gregório Pestana Junior and there you can get maps, brochures and information about local events. Tel. 291 985 189.

Useful telephone numbers

In urgent cases, general emergency number is 112, otherwise 291 700 112, which is manned by an English language skilled person.

There is no hospital in Porto Santo, but a health care center (Centro de Saude) can be found at Rua Dr. José Diamantino Lima, tel. 291 980 060. Pharmacy or chemist (farmácia) can be found in Rua João Gonçalves Zarco, tel. 291 982 577 which is open from Monday to Friday from 9 am to 1 pm, and from 3 pm to 7 pm and Saturdays from 9 am to 1 pm.

Telephone booths are few on the island and they require a phone card which you can buy from cafés or the post office.

Other important numbers:
▶ police (polícia) 291 982 423
▶ fire brigade and ambulance (bombeiros, ambulância) 291 982 115
▶ airport (aeroporto) 291 980 120
▶ phone operator (local) 118
▶ phone operator (international) 177

The post office is located on Avenida Henrique Vieira de Castro.

Banks. There are a few and they are open from Monday to Friday from 9.30 am to 3 pm.

City library is located at Dr. Silvestre Nuno Teixeira, just beside the culture and congress center.

▶ **Red Hot Poker's (Torch Lily) blossom reminds us by its name of a torch.**

Sightseeing

For a small island Porto Santo has a lot of really interesting attractions and historic buildings from the 1500s.

Fonte da Areia natural springs name means spring in the sand. The islanders still think that the water in the spring is sacred and that it has therapeutic effects. This spring is located in 2 km west of the village of Camacha.

▶ **Nossa Senhora da Piedade is the main church in Porto Santo.**

Ilhéu de Baixo or Ilhéu da Cal is a rocky little island located on southern tip of the island. There are many quarries and caves. It is separated from Ponta de Calheta by a 400 m wide strait (Boqueirão de Baixo) which you can cross by boat when the sea is calm. There is a plan to built a cable car at some point in the future.

On Ilhéu de Cima island, east of Porto Santo, are limestone caves and a lighthouse completed in 1900.

On Ilhéu do Ferro island, south west side of Porto Santo are also two limestone caves which have their own names. Furna da Chaminé is like a chimney which bubbles smoky sprays when the sea is rough. From another cave Furna-Que-Berra which has a special sound when the waves hit there.

Ethnological Museum (Museu Cardina) is located in the village of Camacha in the northern part of the island. This museum presents old tools, agricultural equipments etc. Open on Wednesdays from 2.30 pm to 6.30 pm

and from Thursday to Saturday from 10.30 am to 12.30 pm and 2.30 pm to 6.30 pm. Closed during holidays.

The City Hall (Câmara Municipal) is located in Vila Baleira center. The original building is from 1500s, but it has been repaired and modernised for today's requirements. Originally the building was used as a prison.

Churches in Porto Santo are a few the Igreja Matriz alias Nossa Senhora da Piedade is the main church. It was initially completed in the 1440s but it was rebuilt in the 1660s. The church is located on the side of City Square (Largo do Pelourinho) in the center of Vila Baleira. Buried there is Bartolomeu Perestrello, the first governor of the island. The second church is Nossa Senhora da Graça, a pilgrim chapel which was built in 1533. This chapel as other churches in Madeira have been destroyed on a number of occasions and been rebuilt again and again. Other churches on the island are Capela do Espirito Santo in Campo de Baixo and Igreja São Pedro on the foothills of Pico Ana Ferreira.

Christopher Columbus' Home Museum (Casa Museu de Cristóvão Colombo) is one of the main attractions and it is located in Vila Baleira at Rua Cristovão Colombo 12. This museum consists of two buildings. In the older one is believed that Columbus (1451- 1504) was a resident. The museum presents the objects of that time, portraits of Columbus from the 1500s to the 1900s, maps and essays of his voyages. The museum also has a library from where you can find every possible piece of information about Columbus in books of different languages. The museum is open from Tuesday to Saturday from 10 am to 12.30 pm and from 2 pm to 5.30 pm and on Sundays from 10 am to 1 pm. Closed on Mondays and public holidays.

Largo do Pelourinho is a square in the center of Vila Baleira. On the side of this square are a few interesting buildings like Nossa Senhora da Piedade church and the City Hall. Close to the square is a small park and below it a children's playground.

Pico do Castelo mountain is 438 m high and from there are views to all of Porto Santo island. On top of this mountain a little fortress was built in the 1500s to protect from pirates attacks. What is left of the fort now is only rusty canons. This place is a popular picnic destination for locals.

Pico do Facho is the highest mountain in Porto Santo, 517 m altitude. The mountain's name comes from a warning fire by which the islanders

▶ Cristopher Columbus' home museum is one of the main attractions of the island.

were warned of pirates attacks. From the mountain there are great views of the island, down to the valleys and to the Nato based airport.

Pico de Ana Ferreira is a 283 m high mountain, formed from irregular columns it is known as piano by the locals. At the top of the mountain is Pedreira view point where you can see Ilhéu da Fora's the little island, Pico do Facho and the Pico do Castelo mountain peaks.

Ponta da Calheta cape is located in the southest corner of the island, approx. 6 km from Vila Baleira. It can be accessed either by taxi or by walking. If walking, on the way you can admire the spectacular landscapes and sandy beach, swim and sun bathe.

Portela view point is located less than 2 km away from Vila Baleira. In addition to windmills and a palm alley there is a view down to the beach, the port and Pico de Baixo mountain and Ilhéu de Cima's little island.

Quintas das Palmeiras is a mini zoo and botanical garden located in Linhares on the center part of the island. There is also a small bird park where most of the birds are free. Open every day from 10 am to 1 pm and 3 pm to 5 pm.

Serra de Dentro and Serra de Fora valleys are located approx. 5 km from Vila Baleira on the east slopes of Pico do Facho. There you can walk, hike and admire the spectacular scenery.

Windmills, the first of which was built in 1794, are a landmark of Porto Santo. These wooden windmills were numerous and traditionally they were used for grinding grain. Today only a few windmills are left.

▶ **The north coast of Porto Santo is rough and rugged.**

▶ **The windmills are a landmark of Porto Santo.**

Of course, in Porto Santo there is a handicraft center (Centro de Artesanato) which is located in Vila Baleira center in the building of the tourist office at Avenida Dr. Manuel Gregório Pestana Júnior. There they sell all the handicrafts made in the Madeira archipelago and also give specimens of the works.

Happenings and other events

Porto Santo has some festivals and other cultural events too about which you can find updated information from the tourist office or travel agencies. For example in January there is held a Hiking Festival (Festival de Passeios a Pé), in June is the São Pedro Festival and Porto Santo Festival Week. In June and July is held the São João Festival, in August Nossa Senhora da Graça Festival, in September Sentissimo Sacramento Festival and almost a week long Columbus Festival. In September is Vindimas Wine Festival and September or October Tour de Porto Santo with bicycles. In autumn is also the Porto Santo Rally which is one of the Madeira Championship Rallies.

Leisure and sports

Porto Santo offers you the opportunity of various sports and leisure. There are no levadas on the island, but there are even more beautiful natural paths, valleys and slopes where walking and hiking is refreshing.

At the seaside it is possible to swim or play beach volley on an almost 10 km long beach, or snorkel or dive in the turquoise waters for example in 2000 the SS Madeirense sank and is now a diving ship wreck. You can also make boat and sailing trips and enjoy the calm and warm seawater or fish in deep sea waters for blue marlin and tuna fish. In addition you can also surf, water ski, wave and sail boarding, kayaking or lease a jet ski.

For extreme sports you could glide or hang glide for which the island offers many good starting and descending places. Horse rides can also be done, because on the island there is a riding center which offers various levels of riding tours in the environs.

You could rent motorcycles or bicycles, because Porto Santo is a relatively flat, or have fun adventure with a Jeep safari.

In the local tennis center you can play tennis and they also rent equipment. You can play golf on the golf course (Campo de Golfe do Porto Santo) which was opened in 2004 and was designed by Severiano Ballesteros. At the address Sitio das Marinhas, Apartado 174.

▶ The new Scenic road twists around the mountaineous scenery.

On the following pages
you will find a few
LOCAL COMPANIES AND
SERVICES ADVERTISING.

More services and businesses
can be found from local phonebook's
yellow pages or from Yellow Pages
web pages: www.pai.pt

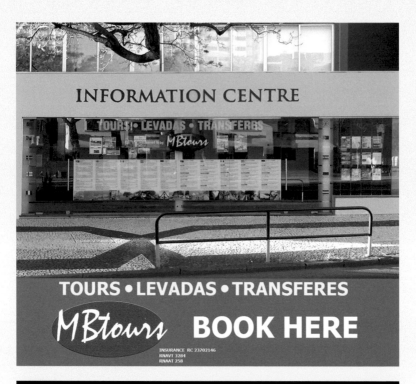

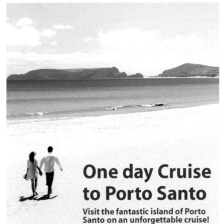

Mamma Mia Restaurant

An affordable sophisticated dining experience from a simple pasta to daily chef's speciality.

Is located adjacent to the Vidamar Resorts Madeira and offers an à la Carte Italian-inspired menu. The perfect place for a romantic dinner for two or a social night with friends.

Special for you:
Please show guide for your free glass of Madeira wine.

Estrada Monumetal 175 -D
9000 - 100 Funchal / t. 291 717 758
www.vidamarresorts.com

Ribeiro Frio – São Roque do Faial
Santana 9230-209
Tel: 2915757634

FAISCA o restaurante que se encontra disposto a proporcionar a melhor comida Tradicional Madeirense.

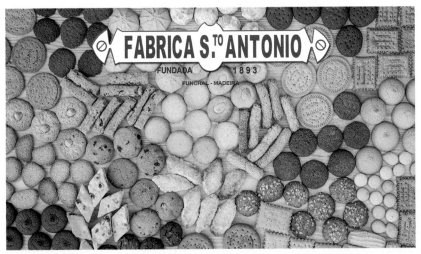

FABRICA S.to ANTONIO
FUNDADA 1893
FUNCHAL - MADEIRA

284

Notes: